Belong

Belonging

Solidarity and Division in Modern Societies

Montserrat Guibernau

polity

First published in 2013 by Polity Press

Polity Press
65 Bridge Street
Cambridge CB2 1UR, UK

Polity Press
350 Main Street
Malden, MA 02148, USA

ISBN-13: 978-0-7456-5506-2
ISBN-13: 978-0-7456-5507-9(pb)

A catalogue record for this book is available from the British Library.

Typeset in 11 on 13pt Sabon by
Servis Filmsetting Ltd, Stockport, Cheshire
Printed in Great Britain by Clays Ltd, St Ives plc

The publisher has used its best endeavours to ensure that the URLs for external websites referred to in this book are correct and active at the time of going to press. However, the publisher has no responsibility for the websites and can make no guarantee that a site will remain live or that the content is or will remain appropriate.

Every effort has been made to trace all copyright holders, but if any have been inadvertently overlooked the publisher will be pleased to include any necessary credits in any subsequent reprint or edition.

For further information on Polity, visit our website: www.politybooks.com

Contents

Acknowledgements

I would like to thank those who have supported me while I have been writing and thinking about this book: Christopher Dandeker, Alain Gagnon, Zig Layton-Henry, François Rocher, Grahame Thompson and Nick Swimm.

As a member of the editorial board of the journal *Nations and Nationalism*, I have greatly appreciated and benefited from debates and conversations with Anthony D. Smith and the other members/friends of the editorial team.

I have also thoroughly enjoyed seminars and debates held at the Cañada Blanch Centre of the European Institute at the London School of Economics. I am especially indebted to Paul Preston for his constant support and advice.

I started this book while being a visiting scholar at the Department of Sociology, University of Cambridge. In particular, I owe a great debt to John B. Thompson for his encouragement and assistance. I am also grateful to Patrick Baert, Christel Lane, David Lehmann and Jackie Scott. My gratitude goes to the College Council at St John's for kindly inviting me to the Fellow's Table at Cambridge, thus providing an opportunity to exchange views and meet fellow-scholars in various disciplines.

At Queen Mary, University of London, I would like to thank my colleagues at the School of Politics and International Relations, in particular Jeremy Jennings, Adam Fagan and Monika Nangia.

I have written this book while holding a Leverhulme Trust Research Fellowship granting me research leave, and I am enormously grateful to the Trust for creating this unique opportunity.

Among those who have contributed to the preparation of this book, I wish to thank Gill Motley, Justin Dyer and Clare Ansell.

This book could not have been written without the constant support of my husband and my parents.

Cambridge, March 2013

Introduction

This book argues that the strength and popularity of belonging seriously undermine arguments pointing to the predominance of individualism as the key feature of modern societies. At present, the tension between solidarity and division reflects the complexities of belonging at a time when social, cultural and ethnic diversity feature prominently.

Identification with a group[1] or community tends to play a major role in the construction of individual identity built by way of inclusion and exclusion and by constant re-negotiation, modification and transformation of shifting boundaries, which, at times, become fuzzy. Individual identities are not clear-cut; rather they are subject to transformations emerging from their intrinsic dynamic nature. Various identities tend to coexist at a time, and their relevance moves and switches according to individual needs, external demands and expectations.

When joining a community, such as the nation or a church, individuals are expected to conform and follow its rules, to be loyal to its principles and aims, and to accept its dogmas and hierarchy so that a sentiment of solidarity can emerge among them. Throughout this process, self-identification with the community's values and objectives becomes paramount.

This book shows that through the process of identification with the group or community, from peer groups and local communities to ethnic groups and nations, the individual's self-identity is gradually replaced by the 'overriding identity' of the collective, which now becomes the key source of the individual's new self-identity. As a result, the individual melts into the group, adopts its values and principles and follows its dictates. The transformation of self-identity under the influence of the newly acquired collective identity encourages the individual to give up a substantial degree of personal freedom in exchange for the security and warmth associated with group membership. In this context the sharing of a collective identity holds a potent emotional content that often becomes instrumental in turning a group into a *political actor* – endowed with varying degrees of power – able to challenge, oppose, transform or endorse the status quo.

Identity is constructed both through belonging and through exclusion – as a choice or as imposed by others – and, in both cases, it involves various degrees of emotional attachment to a range of communities and groups. The innovative character of my argument is that through the process of choosing, belonging is turned into a consequence of free will, which implies a degree of personal commitment absent from assigned forms of membership where individuals are 'expected to' conform to a series of norms, habits and behaviours in the name of tradition.

Here I maintain that membership of a group or community – for example, the nation or a faith – has the ability to offer a vantage point from which human beings are able to transcend their limited existence by sharing some common interests, objectives and characteristic with fellow-members. Belonging by choice entails identification with the group, and this automatically enhances its qualities in the individual's own eyes.

Outline of the book

The book is divided into seven chapters. Chapter 1 focuses upon the construction of identity and its use as a political instrument. It establishes a sharp contrast between traditional and modern societies with reference to the differing degrees of freedom of choice enjoyed by individuals while they are engaged in the construction of their own lives: for instance, the concept of self-identity, as such, was not relevant in traditional societies.

It begins with a theoretical discussion of identity illustrated by the multiple and sometimes contradictory meanings attributed to wearing a burqa or a niqab in the West. In doing so, it highlights processes of reinvention of tradition effected by a radical transformation in the meaning of certain practices, including adherence to a particular dress code. This brings to the fore a detailed analysis of some of the main complexities and contradictions involved in the construction of self-identity which includes the various ways in which conflicting identities both coexist and clash with each other. The chapter analyses the role as well as the fuzzy and fluid nature of boundaries in the construction of identity and it also emphasizes the potential use of identity as a political instrument. It then moves on to discuss the impact of globalization as a transformative force by examining economic insecurity and uncertainty, cultural anxiety and political alienation as the main traits defining individuals in Western liberal democracies.

Chapter 2 appraises the meaning and consequences of belonging by choice as a distinctive feature of modern society. In so doing, it assesses the consequences of belonging and brings to the fore the sentiments of doubt and ambivalence concerning the price to be paid in exchange for being accepted as a member of a particular group or community. Here I analyse the conditions and attributes of belonging and study the processes leading to the construction of collective forms of identity. In particular, I consider the role of symbols in the construction of collective identities. Belonging to the nation entails consciousness of forming a community, sharing a common culture, history, attachment to a particular territory, and having the will to decide upon its political future. The emotional attachment associated with the idea of belonging by choice becomes instrumental in processes of collective identity formation, as well as in processes of political mobilization.

Chapter 3 explores the dual nature of belonging as both enabling and constraining men and women living in modern societies who, up to a point, enjoy freedom of choice. As such, it analyses the meaning of freedom in the work of Immanuel Kant, Erich Fromm, and Michel Foucault. The chapter then focuses on what I define as the 'fiction of original thought': that is, the belief that our ideas and views are unique and original while, in truth, we are just reproducing the views that have been instilled in us by public opinion and the media. This emphasizes that belonging depends upon the willingness to conform to values, norms, dress codes and other conditions imposed by the group that people wish to join. Yet while freedom has enabled the independence and rationality of individuals, it has often left at least some of them with feelings of isolation associated with a sense of anxiety and powerlessness. It is my argument that belonging by choice acts as an antidote to alienation and loneliness. Even so, to escape freedom, people pursue different strategies, ranging from conformity to obedience to a superior power, ideology, faith or community, which, in all cases seems to entail a certain degree of dependence.

Chapter 4 maintains that in modern societies not everybody is entitled to freedom of choice and not everyone is prepared to use his or her freedom. Here I examine the rise of authoritarian politics exemplified by the proliferation and strengthening of new radical right populist parties across Europe and beyond. This trend is also illustrated by the reappearance of various forms of fundamentalism encompassing the market, politics and the resurgence of religious fundamentalism as a force with political aims. The rise of the new radical right, by excluding those considered 'too different', leaves out an important number of people – mainly some immigrants and Muslims. By denying them the right to belong, they are being condemned to the status of 'permanent outsiders'. The ascent of the new radical right raises important issues about tolerance and rights within multicultural liberal democracies. Crucially, it prompts the debate about 'who is' and 'who is not' entitled to belong – a question that has serious economic, political and social consequences associated with it. The chapter offers a fresh analysis of the ideology and political discourse of the new radical right. It also investigates its 'anti-immigrant' position as well as its transnational nature and 'white nativist' programme.

Chapter 5 concentrates on what I refer to as 'the rituals of belonging'. It examines the ability of symbols to embody entities – such as the nation – by endowing them with distinct attributes destined to make them unique. In so doing, symbols bring to the fore their own power as pillars of individual as well as collective forms of identity. Symbols help individuals to make sense of their own lives and they also contribute to define the characteristics, structure and hierarchy of the communities they belong to. To do so efficiently, symbols must retain some ambiguity allowing for a variety of meanings. In turn, ritual communicates authority and hierarchy and, in order to reinforce a sentiment of belonging, it also emphasizes the dependence of the group. The role of ritual in legitimizing political power is illustrated by reference to two examples: the search for new symbols to prompt and consolidate political change brought about by the Arab Spring; and the role of symbolism and ritual aiming to legitimize the dictatorship imposed by General Franco after the Spanish Civil War.

Chapter 6 begins with a question: does loyalty involve a free choice, or is it the outcome of being under pressure? Here I establish a distinction between 'authoritarian' and 'democratic' loyalty. The concept of 'authoritarian loyalty' refers to loyalty as conformity and, as such, it absolves the individual from personal responsibility for actions performed in the service of political superiors. In contrast, 'democratic loyalty' points to a dynamic principle defined by a free devotion to the best interests of the object of loyal attachment. Still a further concept is introduced here, namely 'instrumental loyalty', referring to those cases in which the individual's loyalty is conditional upon whether expected rewards are obtained. This chapter examines the meaning of loyalty as an attitude grounded upon a distinctive emotional commitment and identification. It points out that a shared sentiment of belonging to the nation acts as a potent trigger of loyalty often channelled through nationalism. A certain degree of loyalty is expected from those who belong, but in modern multinational societies we are faced with a paradox: while some individuals who are loyal to the nation are not permitted to belong, others who belong despise their nation and place their loyalty elsewhere.

The discussion of national loyalty in peacetime and wartime leads to the study of opposing reactions prompted by the introduction of loyalty programmes in the USA in the wake of the persecution and conviction of communist sympathizers during the Cold War period. In considering the tensions between freedom and conformity within Western liberal democracies, I raise some fundamental issues brought about by the growing diversity of political and religious ideas, differing definitions of democracy as well as the coexistence of contradictory loyalties within secular multicultural societies.

Chapter 7 studies the – often neglected – role of emotions in selected processes of political mobilization related to nations, nationalism and national identity. It claims that emotions are intrinsic to social and political attachments and focuses upon the emotional appeal of belonging to the nation as one of the most powerful agents of political mobilization. The main argument advanced here is that emotions act as a trigger for political mobilization. This assertion brings to the fore the strong emotional dimension of belonging which involves commitment and identification with the group. It examines the contrast between emotion and the rational imperatives of market capitalism within the framework defined by the tensions and contradictions created by globalization. It also underlines the ambivalent nature of modern political mobilization by introducing a distinction between what I refer to as 'liberating' and 'regressive' social movements. It concludes by identifying some of the emotions that become instrumental in the crystallization of political mobilization and draws attention to the construction of what I call 'healing spaces': that is, public spaces within which certain emotions can be displayed and dealt with within a given community.

To begin with, the book explores the contrasting relevance of identity in modern as opposed to traditional societies. It considers the challenges and contradictions faced by processes of identity construction within the novel context defined by the consequences of globalization, which include economic insecurity and uncertainty, cultural anxiety and political alienation.

1

Identity as a Political Instrument

Conflicting identities

The burqa is a full-body covering leaving just a mesh screen to see through. It is worn by Muslim women over their clothing in Afghanistan and Pakistan's Northwest Frontier province and tribal areas; women remove the garment only when they are at home. While the burqa covers the entire face and body, the niqab or face veil covers the virtual totality of the face and hair down to the shoulders, with the slitted exclusion of the eyes, although it may be worn with a separate eye veil. In turn, the hijab refers to a veil covering everything except the hands and the face.[1]

The burqa is one of many variations of the full-body covering. In Iran, a similar full-body covering is known as the chador. In North Africa, women wear a djellaba or an abaya with a niqab. The result is the same: the full body is cloaked, but the clothing is distinct in each case. While some Muslim women wear them by choice and invoke religious principles and tradition, others use them as a means of protest. However, many women in Afghanistan and parts of Pakistan are compelled to wear the garment following traditional norms or Taliban edicts. The Taliban is a Sunni Muslim[2] movement dominated by people of Pashtun ethnic identity, which controlled Afghanistan from 1996 until 2001.

I am using the following example not in any sense to make a moral judgement but as a tool to examine the intersection of tradition and modernity illustrated by the different meanings attributed to wearing a particular dress in a Western context.

The scene unfolded in Trignac, near Nantes, in the French western Loire-Atlantique region when a woman lawyer took offence at the attire of a fellow-shopper, resulting in an argument during which the pair came to blows before both being arrested. A 26-year-old Muslim convert was walking through the store in Trignac when she overheard the woman lawyer making 'snide remarks about her black burqa'. A police officer close to the case is quoted noting: 'The lawyer said she was not happy seeing a fellow shopper wearing a veil and wanted the ban introduced as soon as possible.'[3]

This incident illustrates the clash of identities and beliefs coexisting within a single society; alternatively it may be viewed as a sign of intolerance and division between different communities. It may be also interpreted as a display of open hostility against Islam, a religion that has already become an integral part of Europe and entered the public sphere, posing some novel questions regarding how to deal with religion in secular multicultural societies.

Above all, this incident points to two main issues: first, the strong emotional component of belonging; and, second, the urge experienced by some people to make a statement about their religious beliefs, or the lack of them, as a fundamental part of their identity. We could even go further and question whether this incident partly reflects the difficulties of the modern nation-state to define and maintain a distinct national identity in the light of rising ethnic and religious diversity within its borders.

Was the woman wearing a burqa considered a 'stranger'? Was she being targeted because, according to this piece of news, she was a 'converted' Muslim – implying that she was probably a French citizen who had decided to abandon the secular nature of French national identity? For this reason, was she regarded as a 'bad or non-loyal French woman'? To what extent does the strong religious statement associated with wearing a burqa question the principles and values of secular France or any other secular society? Is it compatible to be French and Muslim?

Undoubtedly, some French people see the burqa as posing a fundamental challenge to the secular character of the French *République* and as a reminder of the perils of allowing religion to become a powerful force within the nation. France was devastated by the violence of the Wars of Religion (1562–98) fought between French Catholics and Protestants (Huguenots).[4] Religious conflict continued well into the seventeenth and eighteenth centuries and took a dramatic turn during the French Revolution when the so-called De-Christianization of France[5] was effected, paving the way for the less radical *Laïcité* movement. The concept of *laïcité* is based upon respect for freedom of thought and freedom of religion and defends a separation between state and church. In France, *laïcité* involves the rejection of any kind of official recognition of a religion by the state. During the twentieth century this concept evolved to signify equal treatment for all religions. In contrast, secularism refers to the right of people to be free from religious rule and teaching. It also includes the right to freedom from any kind of governmental imposition of religion.[6] As such, secularism has been long associated with modernity, and, most recently, the realization that Islam has entered the public sphere has stirred a fresh debate regarding the public role of religion.

Tensions and concerns associated with the wearing of the niqab in public places have resulted in it being banned in Italy (2010), Belgium (2010), the city of Barcelona (2010), and, most recently, France (October 2011), where special penalties are enforced (one year in prison or €15,000) for anyone who tries to force the burqa upon an unwilling woman or a minor and a fine and/or the obligation to attend a citizenship course. In 2009, Nicolas Sarkozy – then president of France – lent his support to a proposal to ban the wearing of the burqa and the niqab in France.

It is still early to assess the impact and consequences of such measures, however; as shown above, the first example of 'burqa rage' was recorded in France (May 2010) while the process towards the banning of a face-covering veil was being discussed.

In 1802 Thomas Jefferson defended the idea that government is not to interfere with religion. He wrote: 'I contemplate with sovereign reverence that act of the whole American people which declared that their legislature should "make no law respecting an establishment of religion, or prohibiting the free exercise thereof," thus building a wall of separation between Church & State".'[7]

Belonging to church and nation is not always compatible. There are times when the individual is forced to choose, and, for some, the return of religion to the political arena is perceived as a threat to the secular model solidly grounded in the Enlightenment and developed in most modern societies. The tension between church and nation reflects the struggle between two powerful institutions willing to acquire and maintain people's loyalty and define people's identity – in particular, their collective identity; a quality that automatically endows them with political relevance and power.

The role of boundaries

The Taliban regime, which came into power in Afghanistan in 1996, imposed the use of the sky-blue burqa; however, not all Muslim countries follow a similar policy. Saudi Muslim women are required to wear the niqab by law in cities such as Mecca, Medina and Taif, whereas in other cities it remains *de facto* obligatory. In contrast, the niqab is outlawed in Tunisia and the habit of wearing it in Turkey has been losing ground in recent years, at least in cities. As Ernest Gellner points out:

> Contrary to what outsiders generally suppose, the typical Muslim woman in a Muslim city doesn't wear the veil because her grandmother did so, but because her grandmother did not: her grandmother in her village was far too busy in the fields, and she frequented the shrine without a veil, and left the veil to her betters. The granddaughter is celebrating the fact that she has joined her grandmother's betters, rather than her loyalty to her grandmother.[8]

Some Muslim women in Western countries wear the niqab or the burqa as an expression of modesty – a key virtue in Muslim teaching – which is closely related to a sense of belonging to the Muslim community and tied up with patriarchal norms and traditions. However, wearing the niqab or the burqa in this context seems to be less a case of obeying prescribed dress code practices than it is a response to a process of reinvention of tradition related to the willingness to make a statement about cultural, religious and political difference within modern democracies.

In the eyes of a Westerner, finding some common features between busy Mile End Road in the East End of London and elegant Elizabeth Street in Chelsea may be quite striking. In both cases it has become usual to see a woman wearing a niqab or even a burqa – though in Chelsea she may sport designer-label bag and shoes – busy pushing a pram while at the same time holding a child's hand. She always walks a couple of steps behind her husband, who, like their small children, is dressed in Western clothes. This seems to indicate that tradition – if tradition were to justify the wearing of a burqa or niqab – applies primarily to women, since only a small minority of Muslim men in the West appear to adopt traditional clothing themselves.

Regarded from the outside, this distinction highlights what can be interpreted as a very different approach to tradition depending on whether it concerns men's or women's clothing. Such a striking difference is often cited to feed suspicion about gender inequality within Muslim communities. Clothing is important because living and working or studying in a modern city like London, Berlin or Oslo requires a certain degree of mobility – walking, taking the tube, the bus – and certain types of clothing limit movement. Moreover, and crucially, the niqab and burqa act as a physical barrier to the mere identification of the other.

It is unclear whether the obligation of wearing a niqab is to be founded in the Qur'an since different interpretations of its verses result in different practices. Lack of agreement among Qur'an scholars seems to predominate on this matter. For example, some contemporary scholars agree with the practice of wearing the niqab in Muslim countries, but consider that wearing it in the West is harmful and should be avoided. Shaykh Darsh, a prominent UK scholar, provides the following argument:

- Some people believe that niqab is recommended (*sunnah*).
- Everybody believes that inviting people to Islam (*da'wah*) is obligatory (*fardh*).
- The niqab is often a very significant barrier to da'wah in the West where the concept of face covering has never been known.
- If a recommended act is a barrier to an obligatory act, one must not sacrifice the fardh for the sunnah.[9]

When confronted with a woman wearing the niqab or the burqa, many Westerners may react by wondering whether that woman covers her face and body as a personal expression of faith, as a feminist statement or as a sign of oppression. The response to this question is complex and contains important nuances depending on the ways in which women define their identity and their sense of belonging to the Muslim community.

From a Western perspective, often the niqab and the burqa are perceived as a tool of domination employed by husbands and male relatives to control and oppress women. To counter this argument, some Muslim women make a case that it is not them but Western women who are being 'oppressed' by a society that expects them to be 'sexy' all the time no matter what their age or shape. These Muslim women contend that wearing the burqa or the niqab is a liberating experience which sets them free from the continuous gaze of males primarily interested in their bodies.

The various meanings associated with the wearing of the burqa or the niqab exemplify the ways in which modern societies are able to reinterpret an old tradition. Whereas, originally, wearing the burqa or the niqab was associated with religious observance of a Muslim precept, today, in an altogether radical shift, they become tools for political activism when women wear them as a symbol of liberation and protest. For instance, in recent years many Palestinian women, mostly students, have worn white niqabs adorned with green banners with Arabic messages against Israel's actions. Covering one of these demonstrations in 2006, the reporter of the *Boston Globe* wrote: 'With her textured handbag, heavy mascara, and a veil revealing only her eyes, Alaa Awdeh sounds like the ultimate feminist. Women, she believes, should have equal rights in Palestinian society, especially the right to die in the armed struggle against Israel.'[10]

The use of the niqab as a tool to voice political protest stands as a novel reinterpretation of tradition insofar as it goes well beyond expressing a sentiment of modesty, piety or liberation from the gaze of men. Instead of complying with the religious meaning of the niqab within Islam, these Palestinian women are turning it into an instrument to demand political change.

In her most recent work, Nira Yuval-Davis studies alternative contemporary political projects on belonging constructed around the notions of religion, cosmopolitanism and what she defines as 'the feminist ethics of care', employing an analytical intersectional perspective to deconstruct 'simplistic notions of national and ethnic collectivities and their boundaries'.[11] In turn, Judith Squires assesses to what extent the pursuit of gender equality through the use of quotas, policy agencies and gender mainstreaming has contributed to the assimilation of women in male-defined structures. She also considers the future agendas facing gender equality and argues that such initiatives should be framed by appealing to notions of democratic justice.[12]

Of course, it should be noted that wearing the niqab or the burqa in a Muslim country where most women, and in some cases all women, wear it by enforcement, habit or as a sign of status does not carry the same connotations as wearing them in a Western country where its use clearly sets people apart by emphasizing their distinct identity.

The burqa and the niqab produce anonymity for their users, but also generate some uncertainty, uneasiness and even fear among people who cannot identify fellow-citizens. Facial language, including gestures and a range of emotional expressions, disappears and communication is reduced to words with no additional interaction except, in some cases, contact through a specific gaze or voice.

In the West, the controversy over the wearing of the niqab and the burqa combines, on the one hand, concerns about the degree of freedom enjoyed by Muslim women and, on the other, uneasiness about whether their right to wear, in public, a garment covering the full body and making their faces unrecognizable should be acceptable.

The niqab and the burqa set up a barrier between the person wearing it and others by erecting a physical and a symbolic boundary and make a strong statement connecting that particular individual to a section of the Muslim community she belongs to. Furthermore, wearing the niqab or the burqa in a Western society breaks the socially constructed idea of conformity with some patterns which have become 'normal' – commonplace – within that society and which attempt to render interaction predictable. Breaking conformity implies the emergence of a degree of uncertainty regarding expectations.[13]

Wearing the niqab or the burqa prompts an external categorization by others, which generally consists of naming (labelling and often employing stereotypes which do not have to be necessarily detrimental or negative) and generating certain presuppositions concerning religious beliefs, views and behaviour. In the West, it defines its carrier as 'different', critical of mainstream values and ways of life, and willing to emphasize this alienation and dissimilarity.

Expectations can only be tested against interaction, although, prior to that taking place, individuals already adopt specific attitudes based on categorization. This involves making a set of assumptions about a person's views and behaviour according to his or her belonging to a specific group. It also assumes a degree of similarity among group members and presumes that the traits of group membership are, to a significant extent, defining individual identity.

For example, by knowing that X is a Catholic, people may assume that he/she stands against divorce and the use of contraceptives. However, when meeting individual Christians, in some cases this assumption will be confirmed while in others it will prove largely wrong. This raises some questions about the degree of internal diversity and deviance that groups are prepared to tolerate insofar as these are not perceived as threatening to their own ethos, a theme that we will explore later on when discussing freedom and loyalty.

It is only through interaction that the features included in categorization may be challenged, transformed or reinforced. Interaction is the most effective test of ideas and attitudes and it is crucial in the construction of boundaries because it compels individuals to express the values and viewpoints guiding their actions and prompting specific responses from others.

Wearing the niqab is probably not a *sine qua non* attribute for those who wish to belong to more traditional sections of the Muslim community, since its usage varies according to time and place. And as I have already mentioned, wearing the niqab may have multiple meanings for different women. This further illustrates the fluid and permeable nature of boundaries and highlights a certain degree of ambiguity and anomaly, which, according to Richard Jenkins, accounts for the need to map out boundaries and borders with imaginary precision or to dramatize them ritually.[14] It is precisely this ambiguity and anomaly which allows us to understand Thomas Barth's definition of boundaries as 'fluid and permeable' but also as situationally contingent and as a perpetual object of negotiation. As Barth argues, it is the 'ethnic boundary that defines the group, not the cultural stuff that it encloses'.[15]

Traditional versus modern societies

Medieval society conceived the social order as a natural order. The individual was not free; however, he or she was not isolated and experienced feelings of security and belonging within an environment dominated by the family, the church, the absolutist state and nature.

Medieval societies lacked the modern emphasis on individuality and they operated on the basis of lineage, gender, social status and other attributes, all of which were fixed by birth. Roy Baumeister argues that 'only with the emergence of modern societies, and in particular, with the differentiation of the division of labour, did the separate individual become a focus of attention'.[16] Baumeister's analysis recalls that of Durkheim: '[T]he "individual", in a certain sense, did not exist in traditional cultures, and individuality was not prized.'[17]

Thus, while the eighteenth century's rejection of the Christian models of human potentiality and fulfilment led the Romantics into a passionate search for new, secular substitutes, the rejection of the legitimacy of the traditional, stable political and social order led to a troubled recognition of the pervasive conflict between the individual and society.

In the nineteenth century, the prestige of the individual self reached an all-time high that declined in the early twentieth century when 'new social arrangements and events dramatized the relative powerlessness of the individual leading to a devaluation of the self'.[18] However, a process giving special significance to the 'uniqueness' of each individual led to a particular concern about identity, reflecting the individual and collective (group) desire to be 'different'.

The modern individual emerged within the new society created by the advent of capitalism as a mode of production that fundamentally transformed the social, political, economic and psychological spheres. For instance, the concept of 'time' acquired an unprecedented importance; it became relevant, valuable and not to be wasted. In turn, work attained a distinct character; efficiency and productivity were praised. A sense of duty was instilled in individuals, whose own conscience constantly reminded them of their responsibility. Erich Fromm argues that a sense of duty present in religious and secular rationalizations which emerged in the period of the Reformation continues to apply today. In his view, this sense of duty is defined by its hostility towards the self. He refers to 'conscience' as 'a slave driver, put into man by himself', with the aim of tricking him into accepting that the wishes 'he believes to be his own . . . are actually internalizations of external social demands'.[19]

The rise of capitalism eventually involved a transformation of habits, attitudes and values that radically altered society and social relations. The individual was now free from the bonds typical of pre-individualist society – nature, church and the absolutist state – and could enjoy the advantages of independence and rationality. However, while it is true that traditional bonds limited the individual, it is also true that they provided a sense of security, including a sense of belonging to a particular community.

The construction and meaning of identity

The key questions with regard to identity are 'Who am I?' and 'Who are we?' Identity is a definition, an interpretation of the self that establishes what and where the person is in both social and psychological terms. All identities emerge within a system of social relations and representations. As Alberto Melucci observes, all identities require the reciprocal recognition of others: they involve permanence and unity of a subject or of an object through time.[20]

Melucci connects identity with action. In his view, actors must have a perception of belonging, a sense of temporal continuity and a capacity for self-reflection informing a process of constant reaffirmation of one's self-identity and differentiation from others. He argues: '[W]e might define identity as the reflexive capacity for producing consciousness of action (that is, a symbolic representation of it) beyond any specific contents.'[21]

Identities are not fixed, immutable or primordial; rather they have a socio-cultural origin and are subject to transformations prompted by interaction.[22] Similarity and difference are the dynamic principles of identification. Paul Jones and Michał Krzyżanowski point out that 'the tendency to conceive of the complex processes associated with identity formation in a uni-linear way, with identities either "created" or "discovered", overlooks the important question of exactly how identities are constructed frequently through contradictory, dialectical processes'.[23] Identity is never unilateral and depends on the relevance of what Erving Goffman has defined as 'the presentation of the self'.[24] In his view, it is impossible either to ensure its 'correct' reception or interpretation, or to know with certainty how others are to receive or interpret it. There is an internal–external dialectic between self-image and public image: we construct our own self-identify and, at the same time, others construct their image of us according to their own view, to the point that it becomes unavoidable for an individual not to be influenced by his or her own public image as constructed by others.

Individuals lack control concerning the ways in which others are to interpret the public image that they are projecting through their dress code and manners. In spite of that, their own self-identity will be affected by the interpretation of 'others' because one of the components of selfhood includes the way in which others regard ourselves, how they treat us, as well as their expectations. All of this involves a reflexivity whereby individuals react to and become influenced by others' view of themselves. This is a process endowed with the ability to impact upon our thoughts, our self-image and our actions since, ultimately, a sense of self is constructed through interaction; in particular, selfhood is socially constructed by those defined by Harry Stack Sullivan and George Herbert Mead as 'significant others': that is, by those who 'matter'.[25] Mead was a pioneer in acknowledging the significance of 'important others' in the development and maintenance of identity.

Although identity is expected to remain constant through-out the life of a person, this does not mean that it is to remain unchanged. A certain degree of flexibility and transformation remains the norm since identity is constructed via a process of constant self-actualization which requires reacting to life challenges, integrating the outcomes of personal choices, negotiating the content of personal roles and responding to others' expectations. Constructing an identity entails a process of constant self-definition and actualization.

In my view, the defining criteria of identity are continuity over time and differentiation from others. Individuals perceive continuity through a set of experiences that spread out across time and are united by a common meaning. A personal narrative connects all these experiences and presents them as a 'life story'; quite often, individuals introduce some variations when narrating their 'life story' to themselves and when presenting it to others with the aim of enhancing or highlighting coincidence or opposition to the other.

By narrating their life story, individuals seek to project a certain self-image that is bound to be subject to some degree of variation depending upon the individual's aims and the audience being targeted. Telling our 'life story' involves consciously emphasizing certain aspects and events while neglecting, reinterpreting or even deleting others in an attempt to launch a specific self-image. Narrating our life story demands a certain degree of opening up to the other by disclosing some traits, experiences or views considered intimate, and it may even assume sharing some secrets. It also provides the individual with a unique opportunity of redefining and reinterpreting his or her own life and therefore transforming his or her own self-image. Nevertheless, as previously argued, it is impossible to predict the various ways in which the personal 'image' that we are aiming to present will be received, interpreted and defined by others.

Identity refers to the set of attributes that make each person unique, and these attributes are, in turn, the outcome of a complex mesh of exchanges and relationships involving a range of people, situations, values, ideologies and objectives. Individual identity is constructed through interaction and a reflexive interpretation of others' views, attitudes, expectations and demands towards ourselves; however, as indicated earlier, it is only 'significant others' who matter.

Identity is the outcome of a combination of assigned roles and a series of choices, which entails a certain degree of risk resulting from insufficient information about their possible consequences, limited resources to manage their outcomes and the need to choose among a limited range of possibilities. Anthony Giddens writes: 'Modernity confronts the individual with a complex diversity of choices and, because it is non-foundational, at the same time offers little help as to which options should be selected.'[26] It is important to contemplate these choices against a backdrop of constraints limiting the range of 'viable or real' choices available to individuals. Liah Greenfeld encapsulates this point when she writes that 'the advantages of modernity come with a heavy price-tag. The greater is the choice one is given in forming one's destiny, the heavier is the burden of responsibility for making the right choice.

... Life has never been so exciting and so frustrating: we have never been so empowered and so helpless.'[27]

The lack of clear prescriptions on what to choose and how to act, unless a person obeys the principles of a specific doctrine or ideology, adds greater difficulty. Although modern society values freedom and agency as key elements in the active and constant construction and reconstruction of self-identity, not all individuals are prepared to or interested to engage in a dynamic critical and constant process of self-construction. For some, freedom becomes a burden and the possibility of deciding to conform to mainstream patterns offers a source of relief that frees them from the constant pondering and evaluating of the various available options. Identity provides a sense of purpose and meaning in life, it increases self-esteem, it defines who we are as well as how and why we are to behave in normatively specified ways, and, according to Peggy Thoits, it also reduces depression and anxiety.[28]

The consequences of globalization

Economic insecurity and uncertainty in everyday life

The pace of socio-economic change is being accelerated by globalization, and this is making a major impact upon the lives of individuals. Consumption, production, leisure, media, education, travel and politics are all affected by increasing interdependence and speed in communications. But not all individuals have access to the means of globalization: that is, the sophisticated technological tools that have made it possible. In a similar manner, not all are equally affected by its consequences; social class and education tend to fuel a growing divide between those competent to move around and benefit from living in the global age and those on the margins.

The transition from industrial to post-industrial society requires fast-adapting individuals capable of surviving within a dislocated society where moral norms, values, ideologies, traditions and knowledge are constantly challenged and revised. In this context, only a few achieve an elite position while a substantial under-class, having few chances of escaping its situation, grows at the bottom. Inequality is rampant not only between different areas of the world but also within particular societies, and this generates resentment and fragmentation.

While a successful elite benefits from operating in this global flexible market, a growing number of low- and medium-skilled workers are filling the ranks of the unemployed. Among them there is an escalating sense of vulnerability and defeat, often accompanied by an increasing lack of self-esteem. In addition, the perception that immigrants come to their countries to 'steal' their jobs as well as the view, substantiated or not, that asylum seekers and refugees receive greater social benefits than nationals is contributing to a process of increasing resentment towards the state and towards society as a whole. These marginalized workers' own personal insecurity leads them to disregard the generally precarious conditions in which immigrants tend to find themselves and the frequent unwillingness of nationals to take up so-called 'immigrant jobs'. Instead, as will be discussed below, the visibility of certain minorities associated with 'alien' cultures, traditions and ways of life often fosters fear, a lack of trust and open hostility, and, in some cases, it results in xenophobia and racism against those regarded as different.

The rise of the new radical right partly reflects the insecurity and instability brought about by the end of a bipolar division of the world led by the USA and the former USSR; substantial changes concerning the restructuring of the world economy; and a technological revolution which has far-reaching social, cultural and political consequences.

The collapse of communism has irremediably weakened socialism and trade unions together with the traditional values underpinning them. Solidarity and equality have been replaced by competition, individualism and the survival of the fittest. Among the main factors that have created a climate favouring the emergence of the new radical right are: public political distrust of and resentment towards politicians and the political system alike;[29] the proliferation of all sorts of international and transnational institutions, corporations and associations, prompting the transformation of the nation-state's traditional role; and, in Europe, the weakening of the nation-state or, at least, the substantial transformation of its sovereignty associated with European integration – a process that is also contributing to foster anxiety among some citizens ill prepared to take advantage of the opening up of European frontiers and markets. These people feel threatened by prospects of labour mobility and cultural diversity because, in their view, such changes alter their own expectations and restrict their possibilities, creating an environment where they do not feel secure. Fierce competition for jobs, the restructuring of welfare systems and cultural anxiety break the 'imagined' homogeneity, solidarity and sense of community associated with the nation. In addition, the pervasive threat of terrorism since 9/11 is also associated with 'outsiders', people who do not 'belong', even if they are citizens.

The impact of globalization is not restricted to culture and values; it also affects the economic and the political spheres. World trade and the labour market are currently being guided by capitalist principles, resulting, among other things, in the displacement of the manufacturing industry away from traditional industrialized Western societies, where production is more expensive, to Eastern Europe and developing countries, where labour regulations are less strict, wages lower and worker's rights weaker and sometimes non-existent.

Cultural anxiety

A significant number of nations and ethnic groups share a genuine concern about the eventual disappearance of their cultures and languages and feel anxious regarding the worldwide expansion of English. For example, the French are extremely preoccupied about the predominance of English worldwide and, in particular, about the progressive displacement of the use of French within EU institutions as well as the introduction of English expressions into the French language.

Furthermore, increasing numbers of immigrants belonging to cultural, ethnic and religious communities are settling in the West. The substantial influx of refugees and asylum seekers recorded in the last fifteen years or so is contributing to an enhanced perception of diversity in Western Europe and North America, where, in many instances, indigenous cultures are being challenged, rejected and confronted by those of the newcomers. Moreover, some sectors of the indigenous population display a growing mistrust and even hostility towards some of the newcomers' cultures and values, perceived as 'alien' and posing a threat to national cohesion, national culture and a particular 'way of life'. This is illustrated by Hilde Coffé's study of municipal-level support for the radical right party Vlaams Blok in Belgium. She and her coauthors found that the difference in electoral reactions to the presence of different ethnic groups is traced to perceptions of cultural distance and, on the supply side, to the appeals of Vlaams Blok, which typically targets Turkish and Moroccan groups: 'This suggests that it is not so much the presence of foreigners, but rather the fear of the Islamic way of living that leads to extreme right voting.'[30]

Such attitudes are generating heated debates about various models of integration, their success and desirability. They also open up the debate about what should be the basis of a cohesive society and whether this requires the sharing of a common identity grounded upon some cultural, linguistic, religious and civic values among all citizens. Ultimately, it poses questions about the conditions for the coexistence of different identities within a single nation, thus directly addressing a reflection on the limits of toleration within liberal democracies.

According to some theories, there is a link between the revival of the radical right and the *anomie* experienced by some citizens in the West. They argue that 'traditional social structures, especially those based on class and religion, are breaking down. As a result, individuals lose a sense of belonging and are attracted to ethnic nationalism, which according to psychological research increases a sense of self-esteem. For similar reasons, they may be attracted to family and other traditional values.'[31]

The new radical right has managed to capture feelings of insecurity and uncertainty encouraged by a world defined by rapid change, and it has addressed them through a political discourse based on underlining the distinction between those who belong and the 'others'. This has marked the emergence of some kind of ethnic nationalism, cutting across social class cleavages and emphasizing the need to preserve national identity against foreign influences.

Although Western societies are profoundly individualistic, and in some respects as a result of globalization increasingly so, there is a dimension of the individual that can only be satisfied by his or her sense of belonging to a group. This social aspect is generally fulfilled in situations within which individuality is transcended through experiences of feeling in unison with others: that is, by sharing some common interests or objectives which enable individuals to rise above their isolation and feelings of ontological insecurity. National identity has proven capable of playing this role, and the new radical right not only has become fully aware of the relevance of a shared identity but also offers a strong commitment to jealously protecting it against what it perceives as foreign contamination and downgrading.

Political alienation

In the political arena, far-reaching changes at the national, European and global levels have affected people's views of the stature and role of politics and politicians alike, and have added to their sense of powerlessness. In the 1980s, the UK and the USA saw the ascendance of neoconservatism and neoliberalism, which subsequently spread to mainland Europe and to other parts of the world. To some extent as a reaction to this, numerous societies experienced political radicalization, often accompanied by strong anti-system movements beyond the control of traditional conservative parties, a development which, in some instances, has crystallized in the constitution and advancement of radical right-wing populist parties.[32]

At the national level, lack of trust in the political system has weakened the traditional role of the political party as the representative of the interests and concerns of its supporters. A growing number of people regard the political system as alien to their lives and politicians as being primarily concerned with maintaining their own status and privileges. As Colin Hay points out: '[T]he contemporary association of politics with the pursuit of the material self-interest of politicians is . . . oddly antithetical to its very raison d'être.'[33] Yet, for many, '"politics" has become synonymous with notions of duplicity, corruption, dogmatism, inefficiency, undue interference in essentially private matters, and a lack of transparency in decision making'.[34]

Finally, globalization and its consequences have favoured the proliferation of all sorts of international and transnational institutions, corporations and associations with varying degrees of power and competences, which in the eyes of many further undermines the traditional role of the nation-state.

As a result, people are confronted with a radically altered political environment. Many experience the new layers of governance and its impact on the nation-state as a progressive erosion of democracy owing to lack of transparency, corruption and other problems associated with it. This idea, which is often fuelled by certain parts of the media, has resulted in the alienation of significant sectors of the population, who feel disenchanted and who often opt to remain in the margins of institutional politics.

Summary

Traditional societies assigned identity to individuals according to their gender, lineage, status and religion. A distinctive feature of modernity is the unprecedented emphasis it places upon self-identity as the outcome of individual choice, regarded as involving an active reflexive process. The self is in flux and is constructed through interaction. Processes of construction of both self-identity and collective identity are realized through group membership – by inclusion and exclusion, by the setting up of boundaries defined as fluid and permeable (including renegotiation, modification and transformation). The sharing of a collective identity has the potential to turn a group into a *political actor*.

In the West, the use of the burqa (and niqab) exemplifies the intersection between tradition and modernity owing to the different and, sometimes, even radical opposing interpretations of its use, ranging from a symbol of belonging to Islam and an expression of modesty, on the one hand, to a feminist statement and a tool to convey political protest, on the other. The burqa creates a boundary between the person wearing it and the rest. In so doing, it underlines a specific identity founded upon belonging to the Muslim community.

The Trignac incident about the wearing of a burqa in a French supermarket has highlighted the intolerance and division between different communities living within a single society; it has also illustrated a clash of values and different sentiments of belonging coexisting within a Western liberal democracy. However, it is my argument that division can be overcome by a shared sense of solidarity associated with a sentiment of belonging. In the following chapter I examine the meaning of belonging by choice and focus upon the challenges inherent in the construction of collective identity.

2

Belonging by Choice

Belonging and emotion

Modern societies confer unprecedented importance on the individual *per se* and on his or her ability to build a distinct identity, which often involves a reinterpretation of tradition. But how is this personal identity constructed?

The main claim of this book is that self-identity is constructed both through belonging and through exclusion – as a choice or as imposed by others – and that, in both cases, it suggests a strong emotional attachment to a range of communities and groups. The distinctive feature of modern societies is that through the process of choosing, belonging is turned into a consequence of free will, which implies a degree of personal commitment absent from assigned forms of membership where individuals are 'expected to' conform to a series of norms, habits and behaviours in the name of tradition.

In some instances, belonging is the result of assigned membership: for example, most Catholics baptize their children shortly after they are born. Baptism entails welcoming the newborn into the Catholic community of believers through the use of symbolism and ritual. Recently, some parents, though baptized as Catholics themselves, have decided not to baptize their newborn children, arguing that it should be up to them to decide on whether or not to become members of the Catholic Church when they grow up.

Others, usually under the influence of various churches, make a case that children should be baptized only once they have reached the age of reason. To support this view, they contend that Jesus himself was baptized in the river Jordan when he was 30 years of age.

This transformation points to one of the most striking features of our time: the understanding that in modern democratic societies individuals expect to be free to join the groups or communities of their choosing, and that in so doing they engage in the construction of their own self-identity.

Belonging by choice contributes to the empowerment of individuals by allowing them to transcend the assigned membership or role associated with gender, class, lineage and ethnicity. Nonetheless, assigned forms of membership continue to be relevant and they predominate in some parts of the world. For instance, in rural India the caste system remains highly influential in determining life chances, including employment prospects and marriage options. It also involves well-defined economic obligations for the members of a specific caste or sub-caste, and while it presumes a degree of equality within the caste, inter-caste relations are unequal and hierarchical.

Some Western countries – Belgium, Denmark, Liechtenstein,[1] Luxembourg,[2] Monaco, the Netherlands, Norway, Spain, Sweden and the UK – being constitutional monarchies, in which a monarch acts as a head of state within the parameters of a constitution, are based upon the inherited right to rule. Being a king or a queen is the result of assigned membership; although it is possible to opt out, as proved when Edward VIII, King of the UK and the Dominions of the British Commonwealth, and Emperor of India (20 January–11 December 1936), abdicated to marry Wallis Simpson. She was a divorcee, and the Church of England, of which Edward VIII was the head, opposed the remarriage of divorced people if their ex-spouse was still alive.

In contrast, belonging by choice assumes that the individual is, to a certain extent, free to choose among a set of different options. The act of choosing entails a personal decision and a personal commitment to be acknowledged by other members of the group. It fosters a sense of belonging emerging out of the individual's active engagement in the construction of his or her own self-identity to be defined by means of his or her identification with the group.

Members define themselves by invoking the name of the group. While crucially contributing to the construction of self-identity, belonging somehow limits the individual, who, as a result of his or her own choice, is compelled to act in a particular manner and to comply with the group's rules and values. Nevertheless, obedience to the group one has decided to join may be regarded by some as less challenging and painful than the alternative of isolation.

Belonging fosters an emotional attachment; it prompts the expansion of the individual's personality to embrace the attributes of the group, to be loyal and obedient to it. In return, the group offers a 'home', a familiar space – physical, virtual or imagined – where individuals share common interests, values and principles, or a project. Belonging provides them with access to an environment within which they matter.

The group may also be able to offer access to some material and non-material assets, conceived in the broadest possible sense. Material assets may include, among others: admittance to its premises (if it has some); access to information, leisure activities and events, and documents with an instrumental value, such as a passport or a membership card; as well as a range of ventures whose access is restricted to members. Non-material assets are exemplified by the emotional closeness, moral support and solidarity which generally arise among members of a group with a common goal. For instance, the sense of belonging to a nation can somehow be lived through the experience of comradeship arising within the nationalist movement or political party. Other non-material goods comprise opportunities for self-promotion, as well as access to power and resources.

The balance of advantages and disadvantages derived from group membership impacts upon the individual's evaluation of belonging to a specific group as either a rewarding positive experience, or as a limitation only able to offer little incentives. The perceived equilibrium between the rewards and the constraints of belonging plays a key part in the subjective appraisal of group membership. Continuous dissatisfaction and disappointment concerning expectations may lead individuals to search for alternative sources of collective identity able to satisfy their most urgent needs.

Throughout their lives, individuals tend to belong to more than one group, each of which is expected to play a specific role and fulfil a distinct individual necessity. Generally, some features corresponding to various identities coexist and contribute to conform 'individual identity' as a complex combination of loyalties and attachments invoked at different times. Moreover, one of the groups tends to predominate above the others. Paul Jones and Michał Krzyżanowski stress that many different attachments and memberships feed into any emergent belonging, and that sometimes even (seemingly) mutually exclusive belongings coexist within a single identity.[3] They contrast their position with that of Ulf Hedetoft and Mette Hjort, who argue that belonging is conditioned by social and psychological concreteness.[4] Bernard Yack advances a 'more flexible and mundane understanding of community, one that conceives of community as a basic building block of human association, rather than as the negation of the relatively individualistic forms of association developed by modern societies'.[5]

But how free are individuals once they have decided to join a particular community or group? To what extent does belonging impact upon the individual's construction of self-identity? The response to the first question will depend on the type of organization: while some accept free access and exit and exert a more or less limited influence upon the individual's life – for instance, membership of a football club or book group – others demand a longer, perhaps even a life-long, commitment – for example, marriage, being a member of a church or becoming a Mason. There are occasions on which the adoption of a strong group identity – which could be referred to as an '*overriding identity*' – permeates all aspects of the individual's life to the extreme of totally determining and redesigning his or her self-identity. Choice ceases to exist; it was only necessary while the individual was engaged in the process of deciding whether or not to join the group.

In such cases, a new pervasive group identity shapes the individual's values, actions and behaviour and displaces the original emphasis upon individuality, highlighting instead the duties of membership. The name of the group defines the individual's self-identity as a personal project based upon his or her own choice. Self-identity is drastically diminished and becomes a mirror of the collective identity of the group. Henceforth, fellow-members and the group's hierarchy, in particular, are to judge and decide on the individual's life.

Once a strong or influential community or group has accepted the individual as a member, his or her own self-identity melts into the mould of the new 'we' identity. This could be applied, for example, to joining a political community such as a nation or a political party, a secret society or a church. The type of group, its objectives, its power and its location in space and time will crucially contribute to define the group's character, demands and expectations. At that point, the individual's freedom to choose is transformed into the duty to comply, to follow, to obey and to serve. The individual is engaged in a process of self-actualization effected by learning, interiorizing and complying with the rules of the community. Members of a particular party, for example, owe their commitment and support to that party only. They are expected to support the party's interests, to follow its policies and even to contribute financially to its maintenance. Leaving a political party to join another one carries a stigma and is regarded as a controversial move that often questions the integrity of the individual.

After becoming group members, some individuals may not feel fully satisfied with the consequences of belonging: maybe their expectations in terms of material or non-material benefits are not being fulfilled; or they underestimated the personal sacrifices expected from them. They may feel that becoming a group member entails renouncing important aspects of their own life in order to adjust and fit into the group. At this stage, doubt and ambivalence about the value of belonging may emerge.

Giving up freedom, even if this is the outcome of a free choice, is painful, and sometimes individuals may wonder whether all the effort and time devoted to membership tasks is recognized in a way that satisfies them. Ambivalence is founded upon the tension between, on the one hand, the willingness to comply, obey and sacrifice and, on the other, the pressure to renounce certain aspects of life in exchange for the perks of group membership.

Modern individuals are free to choose between a wide range of groups – but not among all existing groups or communities, since many of them set up specific conditions for membership, including a well-defined threshold and a set of barriers to belonging, which only a limited number of people may be able to cross.[6] Although modern individuals enjoy greater freedom than ever before, it would be naïve to believe that our choices are free from constraints, which principally derive from social class, gender, ethnicity and religion.

Belonging and exclusion: a few examples

In what follows I offer a few examples which illustrate the relevance of both belonging and exclusion applied to different environments. I begin by referring to the exclusion of women. It was only in the late twentieth century that some typically English gentlemen's clubs in London were to admit women; for instance, the Reform Club would not start admitting women until 1981. At present, although most clubs are expected to accept women, there are still some which maintain exclusive male-only membership. Access is limited and tends to involve a long and complicated process; membership is exclusive and signals an elite status.

Various criteria are employed to justify inclusion or exclusion. For instance, the Caledonian Club in London welcomes both men and women who are suitably qualified 'by being a Scot or having a close association or empathy with Scotland',[7] while the Yale Club of New York is a private club and membership is restricted to alumni and faculty of Yale University, University of Virginia and Dartmouth College. In turn, Orania is a small whites-only community in the Northern Cape province in South Africa, which has become a preserve for white Afrikaners. Inclusion and exclusion depend upon skin colour. The town was founded with the aim of creating a stronghold for Afrikaans and the Afrikaner identity by keeping their language and culture alive. In December 1990, just a few months after the repeal of apartheid laws and the release of Nelson Mandela from prison, 'about 40 Afrikaner families, headed by Carel Boshoff, the son-in-law of former South African prime minister Hendrik Verwoerd, bought the dilapidated town . . . for around US$ 200,000'.[8]

Finally, in Germany, as soon as they came to power, the Nazis sought the exclusion of Jews. They were denied freedom of movement, work and other basic rights.

Boycotts of Jewish doctors, lawyers and shops began in 1933 and by 1935 Jews were not allowed to join the civil service or the army. The introduction of the Nuremberg laws in 1935 further increased

Jewish marginalization. Jews were banned from marrying non-Jews and their citizenship was removed including their right to vote.[9]

These examples illustrate the importance of both belonging and exclusion, and, in particular, they highlight the fact that, in modern societies, freedom of choice, while being greater than in the past, is not complete. Categories such as gender, ethnicity, religion, nationality, lineage and ancestry, as well as specific conditions connected with the idea of sharing a common interest, faith, view of the world or political objective, to mention just a few, are constantly employed to set up groups and communities. The power of those setting up the norms of inclusion and exclusion determines access, and, in so doing, it impacts upon life-chances and aims.

The conditions of belonging

Belonging implies some type of *reciprocal commitment* between the individual and the group. For instance, citizens identify with 'their' nation, and it is within its boundaries that they enjoy certain rights. In return, the nation demands loyalty, and in extreme circumstances, such as war, citizens are compelled to sacrifice for the sake of the nation.

In a similar manner, the church provides meaning to the life of its believers by offering them a view of the world, a value system with practical responses concerning how to act when faced with life-defining moments, as well as membership of a community re-enacted through ceremonies and rituals. The church accompanies individuals through the most important moments of their life cycle: birth, becoming an adult, marriage, illness and death. In return, churches demand obedience to their norms and doctrines, respect towards their hierarchy and a willingness to sacrifice for their faith. Both church and nation heavily rely on the power of symbols, rituals and ceremonies to foster and strengthen a sense of community among their members.

Belonging involves a certain *familiarity*; it evokes the idea of being and feeling 'at home' – that is, within an environment in which the individual is recognized as 'one of us', he or she 'matters' and has an identity. As a member of the group, the individual entertains certain expectations: for example, to receive support and protection whenever this is needed. In turn, the individual is expected to assist fellow-members and grant them priority over strangers, while the group, as such, demands loyalty and solidarity. Those in positions of power within the group assume the role to caution, judge and punish fellow-members whenever internal laws are violated or remain unfulfilled.

Belonging also often includes the attachment to a distinct landscape – in the case of the nation, this is the *homeland*. The nostalgia of the English emigrant who has not seen the white cliffs of Dover since he left his country; the New Yorker's feeling of being home at the sight of the Statue of Liberty when approaching New York by air or sea; the emotion felt by the Chinese when identifying the Great Wall and following its serpentine shape while approaching Beijing's airport after a long absence – all illustrate the powerful *emotional dimension* attached to the sentiment of belonging. The lyrics of the 1977 hit song 'Mull of Kintyre' by Paul McCartney's band of the time, Wings, capture this attachment with their evocation of 'mist rolling in from the sea' and the expression of a desire 'always to be here'.

Belonging automatically brings about the distinction between *members* and *aliens or strangers*, the distance between those to be trusted and those to be suspicious of, the contrast between familiarity and alienation and the assumption that similar norms and values are shared by those who belong. However, the allowance for a certain degree of transgression is somehow incorporated into belonging; in particular, when the transgressor can be forgiven and brought back into the community because he or she is 'one of us' and belonging is for life. Yet, on other occasions, the transgressor is cast away and no longer identified as a member of the group. While the former is exemplified by the image of the 'prodigal son' who returns home and is forgiven and welcomed by his father; the latter is akin to the citizen forced into exile, having to wander away from his or her own country, abandoning family, friends and being exposed without the protection of the nation.

In some instances, individuality is transcended through the sentiment of belonging emerging out of feeling in unison with others: that is, by sharing some common interests and objectives enabling individuals to rise above isolation. On other occasions, belonging manifests itself as a potent source of pleasure emanating from the atmosphere of trust, complicity and emotional closeness evolving from collective membership. Mike Savage, Gaynor Bagnall and Brian Longhurst have introduced the term 'elective belonging' to refer to a 'way of dealing, at the personal level with people's relative fixity in local routines of work, household relationships, and leisure on the one hand, and the mobility of their cultural imagination on the other'.[10]

Life outside the group is 'hostile', full of dangers and potential enemies. To belong shields us from what we fear and doubt; it also protects us from anxiety by giving us a place in the world. It opens out our life to the emotional warmth of friendship and camaraderie associated with group membership; belonging confers meaning to our life and actions.

Being accepted as a member 'reassures us'; it confirms our value as sound, legitimate human beings since we seek in collective recognition a strengthening of our own self-esteem. However, belonging can also become a source of anxiety and stress whenever the individual feels inadequate, undervalued, misunderstood or ignored within the group. Of course, it might be easier to leave certain types of groups or communities where membership responds to choice, although this is not always the case, than opting out of a group to which belonging is determined by assigned membership. In extreme cases, those who exit might be condemned, persecuted and even killed, and often they are portrayed as traitors.

Numerous examples illustrate how voicing dissatisfaction or opposition to the policies, the rules or the hierarchy of a particular group – such as the state or the church – in some cases has resulted in various forms of punishment. For instance, in Britain during the First World War, a number of pacifists, at the time referred to as conscientious objectors, among them Bertrand Russell, opposed conscription and were punished – some went to prison while others paid a fine. Heresy has been regularly punished within various churches. As early as AD 380, Roman Emperor Theodosius I – who had converted to Christianity after recovering from a serious illness – issued the so-called 'Edict of Thessalonica' establishing Catholic Christianity as the only religion legally tolerated in the empire. He implicitly supported the right of the Catholic Church to persecute heresy; at the time this involved primarily the persecution of Aryanism.

In what follows, I examine the practice of self-identity construction – including the generation of shifting boundaries. I then move on to consider the processes leading to the emergence of collective identity and how this, in turn, is able to foster political mobilization; a topic explored in depth later on in the book.

Collective identity and the power of symbols

It is important to establish a distinction between self-identity and collective identity, between the individual and the collective. While the individual emphasizes difference – that which is unique to him or her – collective identity highlights similarity – those attributes that are shared by members of a group. Richard Jenkins warns us to avoid 'investing collectivities with the kind of substance or agency with which embodiment allows us to endow individuals', since 'the boundedness of a collectivity differs from bodily integrity of an individual'.[11] The transition from 'I' to 'we' emphasizes the political dimension of certain forms of collective identity associated with a sentiment of belonging.

Collective identities are constructed in the dialectic between the two parallel processes of group self-definition (or identification) and categorization. While the group internally constructs the former, the latter responds to its external definition. The two definitions do not tend to coincide; however, they have a proven ability to generate expectations and influence both the behaviour of group members towards outsiders and that of outsiders towards members of a particular group. For instance, the modern state regularly employs some classification procedures, designed by the social sciences, as instruments to control and police its population.[12]

Social identity theory assumes that 'because the personal identity and the social identity are mutually exclusive bases of self-definition, both are unlikely to be operating at the same time'.[13] Social identity is based on membership in a category or group and, as such, it has the ability to provide self-meaning. The individual receives recognition, approval and acceptance but also criticism from other members.

Group members are likely to display different levels of commitment depending on their role. Activation of one identity or various identities depends on prominence, commitment and hierarchy control. Individuals have multiple identities and it is usually the identity with the highest prominence or commitment that guides the individual's behaviour. While multiple identities tend to contribute to greater self-esteem, in some cases competing demands deriving from the multiple roles that an individual is seeking to fulfil may cause anxiety and distress.[14]

Peter Burke and Jan Stets write: '[I]f an identity is not activated, it has no effect, since no identity-verification is taking place and no behaviour is being used to control perceptions relevant to that identity.'[15] It is their argument that group membership requires verification and this depends not on the label concerning what one 'is', but on what one 'does'. Verification is significant as a mechanism to maintain the boundaries of the group.

The continuity of a group is contingent on its ability to maintain the boundary: that is, the distinction between those who belong and are inside the boundary and 'outsiders', 'aliens', 'strangers'. The boundary is generally conceived as porous and subject to transformations and it is not fixed; however, it is presumed that some degree of similarity, encompassing shared values and objectives, acts as a glue among those who belong and are able to recognize each other as members of the same group – be it a nation, a church or a social club. Similarly it often involves following a distinct code of practice, certain traditions and adopting some visible traits in the individual's appearance such as a particular hair style (Buddhist monks), wearing a uniform (army members, police officers, nuns) and displaying some symbols (the Salvation Army badge).

There are what I refer to as *visible* and *invisible* features constituting individual and collective forms of identity. For instance, those belonging to a secret society establish a clear-cut differentiation between the public and the private sphere, the latter being understood as 'restricted to group members'. They avoid the public display of signs that could single them out – although signs and symbols only recognizable by fellow-members may be on display all the time. Symbols also play a crucial role in the private ceremonies and rituals of secret groups and societies such as the Masons. Those belonging to a secret society or a clandestine organization may seek actively to hide their membership; in a similar manner, not all people are keen to display symbols revealing their religious beliefs, since in Western secular societies these are primarily regarded as a trait belonging to the private sphere.

To a large extent, the privacy we encounter in modern secular societies concerning religious beliefs and the display of religious symbols finds its roots in memories of religious persecution across time and space endured by Christians, Jews and Muslims, among many others.

Symbols and rituals are indispensable in the construction of collective identities such as national identity which require a certain degree of similarity among members and difference from outsiders. As Anthony Cohen puts it, a boundary marks the beginning and the end of a community insofar as it encapsulates its identity.[16]

Boundaries are called into being by the exigencies of social interaction. However, not all boundaries and not all components of any boundary are so objectively apparent. They may be thought of, rather, as existing in the minds of their beholders. Boundaries are symbolic in character and imply different meanings for different people. If we consider the boundary as the community's public face, it appears as symbolically simple; however, if we regard it as the object of an internal discourse, then it emerges as symbolically complex. 'The boundary', Cohen argues, 'symbolizes the community to its members in two different ways: it is the sense they have of its perception by people on the other side – the public face and "typical" mode – and it is their sense of the community as refracted through all the complexities of their lives and experiences – the private face and idiosyncratic mode.'[17]

The consciousness of forming a community, such as the nation, is created through the use of symbols and the repetition of rituals that constitute and strengthen the belief in a common identity shared by its members. By bringing about occasions on which they can feel united and by displaying emblems – symbols – that represent its unity, the nation establishes the boundaries that distinguish it from others.

A symbol was originally an object, a sign or a word used for mutual recognition and with an understood meaning that could only be grasped by the initiated. The meaning of a symbol cannot be deduced. Symbols only have value and meaning for those who recognize them; this explains why the sacredness of symbols exists only in the eyes of the believer, or in the eyes of the group member who makes sense of them. Symbols provide a revealing device to distinguish between members and 'outsiders' and heighten people's awareness of, and sensitivity to, their community. The soldier who dies defending the flag symbolizing his nation does so because he identifies the flag with his country, his people and his homeland and not because he reveres a particular coloured piece of cloth.

All communities use symbols as markers. Symbols not only stand for or represent something else, they also allow those who employ them to supply part of their meaning. Hence if we consider a flag as a symbol of a particular country, its meaning cannot be restricted to the relationship flag–country. Rather, it achieves a special significance for every single individual since the flag – as a symbol – has the power to evoke unique personal memories and feelings.

Symbols do not represent 'other things' unambiguously. They express 'other things' in ways which allow their common form to be retained and shared among the members of a group, whilst not imposing upon them the constraints of uniform meanings. An example of the malleability of nationalist symbols is that people holding radically opposed views of the nation can find their own meanings in what nevertheless remain common symbols. The Union Jack – the British flag – for instance, represents the UK; however, it holds different meanings, which include contrasting images of Britain as imagined by its citizens. More than that, the Union Jack surely evokes different memories and views among the English, Scottish, Welsh and Northern Irish regarding Britain's past, present and future, as well as a view on how British culture and identity should be defined in a multicultural environment. Other factors, such as personal experiences of nationhood, political orientation and origin, also impact upon the people's view of the country associated with a versatile symbol such as the national flag.

Something similar applies to believers confronted with the sacred symbols of their faith in that, although they all acknowledge the sacredness of some symbols, they do not perceive, interpret and relate to them in the same way. Their own personal perception is mediated by their particular experiences, circumstances and emotional attachment to their faith. Both the experience of belonging to the nation and that of being a member of a church or religious faith are socially constructed but individually experienced. It is important to emphasize that symbols are effective because they are imprecise. They are, as Cohen states, 'ideal media through which people can speak of a "common" language, behave in apparently similar ways, participate in the "same" rituals . . . without subordinating themselves to a tyranny of orthodoxy. Individuality and commonalty are thus reconcilable.'[18] The nation, by constructing and disseminating a particular image of itself accompanied by a set of symbols with which people can identify, seeks to overcome internal difference. It is by transforming the reality of difference into the appearance or illusion of similarity that people are able to construct a shared sense of community.

If successful, such a process explains the ability of nationalism to cut across social, cultural, ethnic and gender boundaries. Symbols mask difference and highlight commonalty by fostering a sense of belonging among a diverse population. People construct the community in a symbolic manner and turn it into a referent of their identity.

National identity

I define national identity as a collective sentiment based upon the belief of belonging to the same nation and sharing most of the attributes that make it distinct from other nations. National identity is a modern phenomenon of a fluid and dynamic nature. While consciousness of forming a nation may remain constant for long periods of time, the elements upon which such a feeling is based may vary.

Belief in a common culture, history, kinship, language, religion, territory, founding moment and destiny has been invoked, with varying intensity, by peoples claiming to share a particular national identity. At present, national identity is generally attributed to citizens of a nation-state. However, distinct national identities may also be shared among individuals belonging to nations without their own states. These nations[19] – such as Catalonia, Flanders, the Basque Country and Scotland[20] – are currently included within the boundaries of a larger state, yet an important part of their populations does not identify with it.

Among the main strategies generally employed by the state in its pursuit of a single national identity capable of uniting its citizens are the following:

- The construction and dissemination of a certain image of the 'nation', often based upon the dominant nation or ethnic group living within its boundaries and comprising a common history, a shared culture and a demarcated territory.

- The creation and spread of a set of symbols and rituals charged with the mission of reinforcing a sense of community among citizens.

- The advancement of citizenship, involving a well-defined set of civil and legal rights, political rights and duties and socio-economic rights. By conferring rights upon its members, the state facilitates the rise of sentiments of loyalty towards itself. It also establishes a crucial distinction between those included and those excluded from the community of citizens: that is, between those entitled to certain rights and those deprived of them within the boundaries of the state.

- The creation of common enemies. The prosecution of war has proven decisive for the emergence and consolidation of a sense of community among citizens united against an external threat, be it imminent, potential or invented.

- The progressive consolidation of national education and media systems as key instruments in the dissemination of a particular 'image of the nation', with its symbols and rituals, values, principles, traditions and ways of life and common enemies, and, even more importantly, a clear-cut definition of a 'good citizen'.

The construction of national identity responds to a complex process by means of which individuals identify with symbols having the power to unite them and emphasize a sense of community encapsulated in a shared sentiment of belonging. This process involves a continuous flow between individuals and symbols, so that individuals do not merely have to accept already established symbols, but engage in their constant re-creation and reinvention. Intrinsic to this is the attributing of new meaning to traditional symbols in order to understand the changing circumstances affecting the life of the community. Tradition is, then, reinvented and persistently actualized. Yet if, as Ernst Renan argues, the nation is the result of a daily plebiscite, the identification with its symbols also needs to be refreshed constantly to avoid the risk of losing meaning.

According to Ludwig von Bertalanffy, symbols are signs that are freely created, represent some content, and are transmitted by tradition.[21] However, although part of the strength of symbols stems from their capacity to express continuity with the past, they need to be constantly reinterpreted, and even re-created, in order to avoid the danger of becoming stereotyped, decorative or meaningless. Symbols possess an inherent non-static character; they are subject to an evolution that, as Dan Sperber mentions, can take place not only from generation to generation, but also within one generation, because the period of acquisition of symbolism is not limited to a particular chronological age.[22]

If the symbols that represent the nation were to receive a completely fixed, restricted and confined interpretation, they would probably die and become 'empty shells of fragmentary memories'.[23] Nationalism, to retain the vitality of its symbols, must constantly readapt and reinterpret them within fresh contexts. Symbols have their origin in the past, but the power of nationalism lies not only in expressing this by linking symbols with tradition; rather, nationalism engages also in the active re-creation and reinvention of old symbols as well as in the creation of new ones with the aim of maintaining and increasing national cohesion.

As Émile Durkheim argues, societies are likely to create 'gods' during periods of general enthusiasm, and he mentions the French Revolution as a period in which 'things purely laical by nature were transformed by public opinion into sacred things: these were the Fatherland, Liberty and Reason. A religion tended to become established which had its dogmas, symbols, altars and feasts'.[24] However, it would be a mistake to think that elements once elevated to the category of symbols could remain as such forever. The celebration of the bicentennial of the French Revolution in Paris in 1989 was an example of the evolution of symbols once adopted to represent the nation. Symbols have become transmuted to fulfil the task of increasing a sense of community in a radically different society from that of 1789.

On cosmopolitan identity

Various forms of cosmopolitan identity, restricted to a selected elite, have existed since ancient times. In its modern form, cosmopolitan identity is intrinsically bound up with the intensification and expansion of globalization. Previous images of the world were incomplete to the point of neglecting millions of peoples. Limited awareness of other cultures and civilizations resulted in partial accounts of human diversity entirely mediated by the particular experiences and circumscribed knowledge of various peoples who sought to describe the world from their own perspective and cultural parameters.

A cosmopolitan identity is fluid, dynamic, open and a prerogative of a selected elite. Today's cosmopolitans belong to the middle and upper classes, tend to speak English as a mother tongue or as a lingua franca, enjoy sufficient resources to take advantage of the goods and life-styles associated with post-industrial societies, and feel comfortable using the latest gadgets. Acquiring a cosmopolitan identity is a matter of personal choice. In this respect it differs from national identity, which most Westerners have experienced since the moment when they were born and to which they have been socialized within their own specific cultures endowed with their own specific languages. Craig Calhoun argues:

> The new cosmopolitanism is generally antinationalist, seeing nations as part of the fading order of political life divided on lines of states. Its advocates rightly refuse to rely on this tacit nationalism. But as they offer no new account of solidarity save the obligations of each human being to all others, they give little weight to 'belonging', to the notion that social relationships might be as basic as individuals, or that individuals exist only in cultural *milieu* – even if usually in several at the same time.[25]

The eventual materialization of a genuine cosmopolitan identity would involve a militant attitude in favour of human freedom and equality. I am aware of the controversial character of these assertions because cosmopolitan principles[26] – egalitarian individualism, reciprocal recognition and impartial moral reasoning – ought to be defined cross-culturally and they cannot be implemented until a global shared meaning is agreed. I do not think that cosmopolitan identity requires the weakening of national identity; however, it urges a critical attitude towards non-cosmopolitan principles present within national cultures as well as the commitment to change them. This implies neither the renunciation of national identity nor the outright condemnation of a particular culture, but it clearly points to the need to foster cosmopolitan principles. I do not regard cosmopolitanism as a synonym of disengagement with the national; on the contrary, it is founded upon a set of ethical principles able to inform political action with the aim of permeating national and other forms of culture with a cosmopolitan outlook. The quest for a cosmopolitan identity should best be described as the endeavour towards the addition of a moral layer, defined by respect for cosmopolitan principles, to national, ethnic and other cultures.

Belonging to the nation

Symbols are generally employed as key elements in the performance of rituals that hold together the members of the nation at regular intervals. Durkheim's study of religion is particularly relevant when analysing the ways in which national symbolism and ritual operate. We should note that both the nation and the church are long-standing examples of communities able to foster a strong sense of belonging among their members. Nationalism began to gain strength at a time when religion was declining in Europe. As religion, nationalism has its rites, and these are not merely received and performed individually. Rather, as Durkheim stresses, they are what give the group its unity: 'The individuals who compose the group feel themselves bound to each other by the very fact that they have a common faith.'[27] A common faith requires a 'church', and it could be argued that the 'nation' fulfils this role, while intellectuals could be considered as its 'priests'. As beings sharing the same totemic principle, the members of the same nation feel morally bound to one another. But as members of the tribe, the individuals who form the nation need to renew and give strength to the community by periodically reviving their ideals.

Individuals belonging to the same nation – that is, to a community sharing the same culture and history, feeling attached to a particular territory and willing to decide upon their political future[28] – need to create occasions on which all that unites them is emphasized. In these instances individuals forget about themselves, and the sentiment of belonging to the nation occupies a prime position. The collective life of the community stands above that of the individual. Through symbolism and ritual, persons are able to feel an emotion of unusual intensity that springs from their identification with an entity – the nation – which transcends them, and of which they actively feel a part.

In these situations the members of the nation gain strength and resilience, and are able to engage in heroic as well as barbaric actions in order to protect the national interest. As Durkheim points out, because such a member 'is in moral unison with his fellow men, he has more confidence, courage and boldness in action, just as the believer who thinks that he feels the regard of his god turned graciously towards him'.[29]

All groups need symbols and rituals in order to survive, maintain cohesion and reaffirm the collective ideas which they create. Durkheim acknowledged this when he wrote: 'It is by uttering the same cry, pronouncing the same word, or performing the same gesture in regard to some object that they [individuals] become and feel themselves to be in unison.'[30]

Collective identity and political mobilization

The construction of a collective identity has the potential to transform a group into a political actor. If this happens, efforts to strengthen a sense of shared identity and solidarity among group members are likely to grow. At the same time, pressure to comply with the group's position and ethos tends to rise to a level at which loyalty is not only enormously praised and expected but deviance is to be severely punished. One of the greatest challenges innate to the construction of a shared identity concerns the degree of internal freedom and diversity to be tolerated within the group. In some instances, demands for homogeneity among group members may clash with demands for the recognition of internal differences, in particular if democratic principles are to be upheld. Charles Taylor raises the dangers inherent in defining identity as 'sameness' with regard to demands for recognition on behalf of minority groups.[31]

This has become a heated issue in liberal-democratic societies defining themselves as secular but having to respond to and manage cultural and religious diversity within their borders. It openly raises a possible confrontation between the secular views, norms and values dominant in the political community and those defended by cultural and religious minorities living within its territory. This is so because some sections of these religious-cultural minorities are not only extremely critical of the values and principles of modern liberal democracy but are also prepared to undermine them and even to use violence to make their own views prevail. Tolerance versus fundamentalism does not work. Tolerance and fundamentalism are not compatible because often the objective of religious-cultural fundamentalism is the destruction of the secular political community.

In the quest for political aims, sharing a common identity stands as a powerful asset. Nevertheless, only time will reveal whether a shared identity could be mobilized in support of an emancipatory movement or whether, on the contrary, it could be employed as a tool to control, oppress and discriminate. Ultimately this will depend upon the aims to be pursued by the leaders of the movement, the ends to be achieved and the means to be employed.

Numerous examples confirm the strength of collective identity as an instrument for political mobilization. In what follows I concentrate on two cases, both from the second half of the twentieth century: the civic society movement of resistance against Franco's dictatorship in Spain that culminated in the creation of the Assembly of Catalonia; and the African–American civil rights movement in the USA.

Catalonia's civil society against Franco's dictatorship

The fostering of a shared sense of Catalan identity in the struggle against Franco's dictatorship in the 1960s culminated in the constitution of the 1971 Assembly of Catalonia as a civil society movement in favour of the democratization of Spain, amnesty for political prisoners and a Statute of Autonomy for Catalonia, after the derogation of the previous Statute during the Civil War (1936–9).

On 7 November 1971 about three hundred people representing different political, social and professional sectors of Catalonia founded the Assembly of Catalonia,[32] a clandestine organization that soon became the broadest and most important unitary Catalan movement since the Civil War. No similar unitary movement, in view of its scope and its relevance, was created in any other part of Spain. The Assembly, initially founded by the socialists and, in particular, the communists, received economic support from the group led by Jordi Pujol (who would become president of

the Catalan government, 1980–2003), which subsequently joined
it.[33] The MSC (Catalonia's Socialist Movement) and the PSUC
(Catalonia's communist party, or the Unified Socialist Party of
Catalonia) won over the support of significant sectors of the working class and of a high number of Castilian-speaking immigrants.
They all voiced the need to bring together democracy, left-wing
policies and autonomy for Catalonia.

Cultural resistance – that is, the use of all kinds of symbols of
Catalan identity in both the public and the private sphere – evolved
from the performance of isolated risky actions to the achievement
of numerous activities enlisting mass support.[34] Resistance actions
culminated on 11 September 1977 when one million demonstra-
tors demanded a Statute of Autonomy for Catalonia. Franco had
died two years previously and an overwhelming majority had rati-
fied the political reform proposed by Adolfo Suárez, then prime
minister of Spain. The Catalans, through this display of strength,
manifested their outright rejection of a simple administrative
decentralization of the state and demanded political autonomy.

The mobilizing action of the Assembly continued until the first
democratic parliamentary election held on 15 June 1977. The unity
of the democratic front was now replaced by competing 'images'
of Catalonia, including its status within Spain. Jordi Pujol was
elected as president of Catalonia in 1980, he was re-elected and
governed it until 2003, when he decided not to stand for office.
Pujol led the CiU, a liberal-democratic nationalist pro-European
party, and played a key role in building Catalan institutions, language and culture after forty years of repression.

The African–American civil rights movement

The second example refers to the African–American movement
which stood for civil rights while embracing the US flag; its main
objective was to achieve equal rights for all regardless of their race
and ethnicity. The participation of blacks in the First World War
and, above all, in the Second World War revealed a deep incon-
sistency in the American creed: up until then African–Americans
were dying abroad for the preservation of a democracy they did not
enjoy at home. Opposing reactions emerged from the black leadership, some in favour of participation in the war effort, others,

such as Richard Wright, standing strongly against enlistment.[35] At that point, some blacks initiated 'the Double V campaign: victory against the foreign enemy, Japan, and the enemy at home, racial prejudice'.[36]

In the period leading to the 1964 Civil Rights Act, most African–American activists, apart from leaders of the black nationalist movement such as Malcolm X, emphasized their own American identity and embraced the melting-pot model. The black integrationist movement shared common interests with wider American society, and with European-Americans in particular. It advocated the constitution of interracial organizations, non-economic liberalism and cultural assimilation. Black integrationists played a leading role within the black church and enjoyed greater access to external resources; their own integrationist position was, and remains, functional in accessing external support.

But the integrationist stance has not always been welcome among white Americans; rather, until 1964, it was under attack from white supremacist organizations such as the Ku Klux Klan,[37] condemning what they saw as discriminatory practices regarding housing, schools and employment. More recently, African–Americans have denounced the pervasiveness of some hostile institutional barriers in the private and the public sector, plus some remaining institutional and individual forms of racism.[38] The ambivalence between many integrationists and a black nationalist position has been a constant in the black leadership. The black nationalist movement has defended the formation of racially exclusive political organizations and the construction of a self-sufficient black economy and, instead of focusing on their American identity, has emphasized a black and mainly pan-African identity.

Harold Cruse, in his book *The Crisis of the Negro Intellectual*,[39] echoed the blacks' ambivalence between integrationism and nationalism. He referred to it as the 'pendulum thesis' and argued that it is not sufficient to empower individuals, regardless of the ethnic or racial group to which they belong. In his view, cultural group is important, and failure to appreciate this 'is debilitating to the black community because even as individual blacks ascend America's social ladder, blacks as a group remain outcast and denigrated, consistently ranking below whites across any meaningful standard of quality of life and equality of opportunity'.[40]

The African–American movement epitomizes the role of ethnicity in the creation of a collective identity mobilized to foster political change. At the same time, this particular case reveals the divisions existing within the black community, which culminated in the emergence of two major positions exemplified by black integrationism and black nationalism. On this occasion, ethnicity is highly relevant but it does not result in a unified political position, an outcome confirming that ethnicity is insufficient to prompt a shared consciousness of belonging and agenda for political action.

The movement to win civil rights for African–Americans (then called American blacks) reached its high point when US President Lyndon Johnson's administration secured their legal and political rights in 1965. Subsequently, the perception gained ground that legal rights were not enough, but that this in turn led to two tendencies, one arguing that affirmative action must continue, the other that something had to be done to alter the nature of the African–American family and community. The civil rights movement was triumphant in part because it tapped the lode of revolutionary potential within the black community, and in part because it galvanized the support of political allies outside the black community, including white liberals. Furthermore, this movement not only achieved its immediate objectives, but also was the major catalyst for progressive change in the twentieth century. A major milestone in the empowering of the African–American community emanating from the civil rights movement was the election of Barack Obama as 44th president of the USA in 2008.

Summary

Identity is constructed through belonging and exclusion and it invariably entails a strong emotional attachment to the group or community to which one belongs. In modern societies, belonging by choice empowers the individual to construct his or her own self-identity, and it is through the process of choosing that belonging is turned into a consequence of free will, implying a degree of personal commitment absent from assigned membership. However, it would be naïve to believe that our choices are free from constraints emerging from class, gender, ethnicity and religion.

Belonging implies a reciprocal commitment between the individual and the group he or she is to join; it suggests familiarity and, most crucially, it brings about the distinction between members and aliens or strangers.

Belonging acts as a shield from what people fear and doubt; it provides support and it can raise self-esteem, but it may also be a source of anxiety whenever the pleasures or belonging are overtaken by the urge to comply, to obey and to follow the norms of a particular group or community. There is a certain degree of ambivalence founded upon the tension between individuals' freedom to choose and the obedience and conformity that is expected from them once they have become group members. There are occasions on which the adoption of a strong group identity – 'overriding identity' – permeates all aspects of the individual's life to the extreme of totally determining and redesigning his or her self-identity. Choice ceases to exist; it was only necessary while the individual was engaged in the process of deciding whether or not to commit him- or herself to the group. The following chapter points out that belonging by choice on some occasions acts as enabling force, while on others the individual can perceive it as a burden and a limit to individual freedom.

3

Freedom and Constraint

The consolidation of liberal-democratic governments involved a separation of powers and with it a diffusion of authority indispensable for the enjoyment of freedom. Michael Oakeshott's caution should always, however, be borne in mind: 'Arrangements which in their beginnings promoted a dispersion of power often, in the course of time, themselves become over-mighty.'[1]

In what follows I analyse the concept of freedom in Immanuel Kant, Michel Foucault and Erich Fromm. They have carefully examined the nature of freedom within their own societies and provided contrasting arguments in their analysis. In the 1980s, Foucault argued that he was engaged in a kind of critical work having some parallels with that of Kant; an assertion that could be understood as an attempt to transform the Enlightenment beliefs and values from within rather than attempting a total critique. The ultimate objective was a transformation of one's own present in its historical specificity, for the sake of promoting the values of freedom and autonomy.

In 1941, Fromm published the book *The Fear of Freedom* (known in North America as *Escape from Freedom*), in which he claimed that modern man had 'not gained freedom in the positive sense of the realization of his individual self; that is, the expression of his intellectual, emotional and sensuous potentialities'.[2] He believed that to embrace freedom of will was healthy, whereas the use of escape mechanisms was connected to the emergence of psychological tension. He identified conformity, authoritarianism and destructiveness as some of the most common mechanisms employed by individuals seeking to escape freedom.

After studying the contrasting theories of freedom presented by Kant, Foucault and Fromm, the chapter then moves on to consider the tensions between constraint and dependence endured by modern individuals in their quest for freedom. It emphasizes the role of belonging as the most powerful antidote against feelings of alienation and doubt felt by some individuals overwhelmed by what I refer to as 'the burden of freedom'. To avoid freedom some individuals have turned to new forms of dependency; the latter part of this chapter focuses upon submission to a leader, compulsive conformity and addiction.

Immanuel Kant

Kant regards freedom to act as the most fundamental attribute of human beings; the ability to choose is what makes them responsible for their actions and stands as the basis of morality as different from natural law. Kant claims that (external) freedom is a greater good than life itself: 'We are obliged to enter civil society and authorized to compel others also to do so; this is predicated on a prior contingent condition, the unavoidability of social contact' (6:236–7).[3] In the *Metaphysics of Morals*, part two, Kant argues that,

> Prior to the establishment of civil society, any attempt to defend one's property coercively – however well grounded one's claim may be in a 'provisional sense' – constitutes an implicit injury to the fundamental right of others to do 'what seems right and just to them' and not be dependent in this on the arbitrary will of someone else. . . . [As a result] any attempt to realize private right is, as it were, self-cancelling: I cannot defend my property – even property that is duly mine in a 'provisional' sense – without doing violence to the right of others to act as seems just and good to them. But desisting from defending my property is also morally impermissible: I cannot choose not to defend my property (even that acquired only provisionally) without violating another duty – that toward the right of humanity in my own person. (6:240)

In a state of nature, the concept of right is 'unexecutable'; even so, Kant insists that the concept of right 'cannot be given up'. There are two possible avenues to resolve this. One is to flee from contact with others. The other possibility is to join with others, 'if necessary by force, in establishing a civil society in which the violence of the state of nature is replaced by a judge authorized to impute with rightful force' (6:226–7). In Kant's view, unless one is prepared to renounce all concepts of right, one must abandon the state of nature – although this need not be *per force* a state of injustice – in which individuals follow their own judgement. Instead of that, they have to unite and enter a state in which what is to be recognized as 'one's own is lawfully determined and distributed by a sufficient might (which is not one's own but external)' (6:312). It follows that moral norms are imposed by ourselves on ourselves, acting rationally and freely; this is the reason why they are principles or rules, but not natural laws.

Even while we submit to moral norms, we remain free. Submitting to them is the outcome of our decision, and we can also break them, if so we choose, at the price of acting irrationally. The fundamental principle of morality is the law of an autonomous will upon itself: 'This is precisely the formula of the categorical imperative and of the principle of ethics, so that a free will and a will subject to moral laws are one and the same.'[4] Kant attributes having a will and reason to every 'rational being' – women, children and those with no, or insufficient, property are excluded – and understands this as a condition for the idea of freedom under which they act. The presence of a self-governing reason in each person is what moved Kant to assert their equal worth and deserving of equal respect.

When considering agency – that is, the will to act rightly or wrongly, virtuously or viciously – Kant takes into account 'external' factors – physical, chemical, biological, physiological, geographical, ecological – that can prevent or destroy freedom, and also 'internal' psychological factors. Autonomy refers to one's ability to give laws to oneself; its opposite, heteronomy, implies the obedience of laws issued from outside oneself.

Kant defines freedom as the right to do what does not deprive another of his right. External lawful freedom may be defined as the authority not to obey any external laws except those which I have consented to. Kant defines freedom of choice as 'independence from being determined by sensible impulses; this is the negative concept of freedom'. The positive concept of freedom 'is that of the ability of pure reason to be of itself practical', something that can only be attained 'by subjection of the maxim of every action to the condition of its qualifying as universal law'.[5]

The state of nature is not necessarily a state of injustice but a state lacking in justice, since, whenever a conflict of rights emerges, no competent and powerful judge is available to issue a verdict. The state of nature is ruled through force or contract, but 'its acquisition is only provisional so long as it still lacks the sanction of a public law, because it is not determined through any public justice, nor secured through an authority executing this right' (6:312).

In turn, 'Civil society is instituted not only to protect men's life and property but also (and primarily) our freedom from subjection to the arbitrary will of our juridical (and moral) equals' (6:237–8). The primary right is the right to be recognized by others as 'one's own master' (8:295). But only where we encounter some sort of law and order does the concept of right cease to be self-cancelling in practice. According to Kant, the 'civic state' as a 'legal state' should be founded on three a priori principles. These are: the *freedom* of each member of society as a *man*; the *equality* of each member with every other as a *subject*; and the *autonomy* of each member of a commonwealth as a *citizen*. He regards them as the 'only principles according to which a state could be constituted [and be in keeping with] the rational principles of the external law of man'. It is important to note that for Kant 'a patriotic attitude is one which makes the citizens consider themselves authorized to protect the rights of the commonwealth by laws, but not authorized to subject the commonwealth to the absolute discretion [of the head] for its purposes'.[6]

For Kant, the only qualification for being a citizen is being fit to vote, a quality that presupposes the independence of the subject. Kant excludes all those whose 'preservation and existence' does not depend upon themselves but upon others. Domestic servants, children and women are excluded because 'all these people lack civil personality and their existence is, as it were, only inherence'.[7] To sum up, the requisites of being a citizen include: not being a child, not being a woman, and being 'one's own master'.

Although logically coherent within Kant's discourse, some reflection is due to his assertion that '[a]ll resistance against the supreme legislative power, all instigation to rebellion, is the worst and most punishable crime in a commonwealth because this destroys [its] foundation'.[8] For example, it could be argued that the USA would have never been created if strict adherence to Kant's views had been upheld.

By freely abandoning the state of nature, individuals decide to renounce their 'lawless freedom' in order to be ruled by 'lawful freedom' within the state. This requires their submission to the 'general legislative will' of which they are a part. It also entails obedience to what are described as 'the only principles according to which a state could be constituted [and be in keeping with] the rational principles of the external law of man'.[9] However, Kant ignores both the possibility of political corruption and the need for social change within a given society. As a result, his theory excludes questions such as: How should individuals react to the eventual corruption of their ruler? What mechanisms would be necessary to effect social change? How should moral norms be adjusted to unavoidable societal transformations? Within his framework there is no response to the demands either for women's right to vote or in favour of the abolition of slavery, for example. In my view, Kant's theory of freedom and autonomy is, at least, questionable, for two reasons: its static conception of society and the unquestionable attribution of righteousness to the supreme legislative power.

At the core of Kant's theory is the idea that man is an end in himself, and not a means to anything not himself. He strongly condemns exploitation as a situation in which men are used as means, rather than as ends in themselves. His work includes a plea for self-determination and the insistence on the development of moral freedom. Obligation to submit degrades the individual because it deprives him of freedom: that is, of the ability to choose and enjoy self-government and autonomy, as the key feature that distinguishes 'man' from other creatures.

Kant believed that individuals are endowed with reason. He stood in favour of allowing people to enjoy a right to the free and unrestricted public use of their reason by placing themselves beyond the limits – rules, prejudices and beliefs – set up by their polities and by acting as members of a 'cosmopolitan society' defined by its openness. The entitlement to enter the world of open, uncoerced dialogue was adopted and developed in his concept of 'cosmopolitan right'.[10] Kant regarded universal reason as the guarantor of answers about what is to be done and how life is to be lived, leading to a harmonious arrangement of peace and democracy.

A substantially different approach conceives freedom as the ability to limit desire and emanates from Kant's Lutheran, pietist, anti-Enlightenment upbringing. Isaiah Berlin illustrates this as follows:

> The tyrant threatens to take away my property – I will train myself not to want property. The tyrant wishes to rob me of my home, my family, my personal liberty – very well; I shall learn to do without them: then, what can he do to me? I am the captain of my soul; this, my inner life, no outside force can touch . . . .[11]

I argue that this approach lacks an evaluation of the price of repressing desire. Individuals' struggle to get rid of desire has enormous consequences and impacts upon their life experiences. Even the determination to remain independent comes at a price. Individuals are their own masters; they exert self-control on emotions and desire, but they are unable to enjoy any of the things which they have decided to renounce, not because they do not enjoy them, but because they want to avoid the excruciating pain of losing them while being at the mercy of the 'tyrant'. Individuals' options become restricted as a consequence of their own decision to evade pain. But in this situation they are not fighting to destroy the tyrant, to avoid him; rather they are inflicting pain upon themselves in order to retain freedom while ruling out – if possible – the prospect of pain inflicted from the outside; a pain over which they have no control. Almost inevitably individuals will be consumed by a terrible sense of loss and alienation emerging from their renunciation.

Michel Foucault

> The public execution was the logical culmination of a procedure governed by the Inquisition. The practice of placing individuals under 'observation' is a natural extension of a justice imbued with disciplinary methods and examination procedures. . . . Is it surprising that prisons resemble factories, schools, barracks, hospitals, which all resemble prisons?
>
> Foucault, *Discipline and Punish*[12]

Foucault's objective is to study how the self is actively constituted through what he refers to as 'practices of the self', while arguing that those practices are not invented by the individual; rather, 'they are models that he finds in his culture and are proposed, suggested, imposed upon him by his culture, his society, and his social group'.[13] This assertion can be interpreted as a confirmation of the power of belonging as a key element in the construction of self-identity. It also points to the relevance of 'models' found by individuals in their culture, society and social group. Socially constructed models are appropriated by the individual through 'practices or technologies of the self' applied and administered to the self by the self itself.[14] Following the models imposed by culture, society and social group has a disciplining effect upon the individual, who is expected to conform to the norms. In this context, difference becomes an anomaly.

Foucault argues that in Christianity freedom of the corporeal self was perceived as necessary in order to attend to more elevated, non-worldly matters. Asceticism was conceived as a purifying strategy based upon a renunciation of the material world. In this respect, the Christian self stood up against a part of itself. Foucault speaks of the task 'to create ourselves as a work of art', while emphasizing that care of the self may contribute to human freedom.[15] He conceives relations of power as mobile, reversible and unstable, and affirms that power relations require a certain degree of freedom on both sides. He rejects the idea of one side having 'total power' over the other to the point of eliminating freedom, and he believes in the strength of resistance; a key concept in his theory.

I regard Foucault's assertion as a defence of the pervasive role of freedom and the value and scope of agency in modern societies. His discourse is enabling insofar as it acknowledges that 'there are relations of power in every social field, this is because there is freedom everywhere'.[16] The coexistence of power and freedom generates a never-ending tension between the two because neither power nor freedom is ever absolute. The dispersion of power makes resistance difficult but it also enables resistance by opening up some new spaces within which alternative discourses challenging dominant regimes can be heard. The battle for freedom is fought in different scenarios, with different methods.

According to Foucault, there are no agents in whom power is concentrated, but only techniques, regimens, regulations and measures that establish a distinction between the normal and the pathological. In this context a shifting balance of power becomes a real possibility. To assess this, the pervasive existence of power and freedom needs to be qualified by the different degrees at stake in each particular case.[17] According to Foucault, 'Ethics . . . is the practice of freedom'; a view that connects him with Kant's idea that moral norms also require freedom.[18]

Contrary to thinkers such as Jean-Paul Sartre and René Descartes, Foucault appears to support the view that self-discipline can only be understood as a mode of discipline encouraged and even demanded by culture and society. He maintains that subjects always have the power to interpret norms and commands and always have the possibility to resist discipline. But what are the motives that prompt individuals to 'resist' power and authority by devising resistance strategies while they live under the social, cultural and political influence and requirements of their own societies? A tentative answer responds to Foucault's concept of power as something that 'circulates': it is never localized, it can never be appropriated in the way in which wealth or a commodity can be appropriated. A key original point refers to his idea that 'power is exercised through networks' and that individuals 'are never inert or consenting targets of power'.[19] Outside a disciplining society, resistance, as a distinctive and important form of freedom, would be unlikely to emerge. The individual is a product of society and so is resistance.

In contrast with Christian asceticism, Stoics and Epicureans taught that one should strive 'to delight in oneself, as in a thing one both possesses and has before one's eyes', and they prompted individuals to 'learn how to feel joy'.[20] Foucault vindicates the body as self-constructed and considers it as an arena of freedom. Care of the body and intervention in the body are part and parcel of the process of turning it into 'a work of art'. Foucault's approach has opened up a completely new avenue by enabling the self to engage in its self-construction – agency is at play here.

The construction of the self through self-discipline care may contribute to individual freedom from the control of disciplines imposed by society insofar as self-discipline acts as an enabling and empowering mechanism, but this is not always the case. For example, earlier on we referred to the slave who, through self-discipline, manages to limit desire in order to avoid the pain of loss imposed by the master. Self-discipline is not *per se* an enabling mechanism here; on the contrary, self-discipline is employed to benumb, to avoid – if feasible – the possibility of pain inflicted from outside the self – pain over which the slave has no control.

In his lectures at the Collège de France, Foucault defined 'biopolitics' as a discipline dealing with the population; both as a political and as a scientific problem. He locates the emergence of techniques of power centred upon the individual body in the seventeenth and eighteenth centuries. In the second half of the twentieth century, Foucault identifies a shift from individualizing to massifying, from 'anatomo-politics' of the human body to 'biopolitics' of the human race.[21] This is relevant for our analysis here insofar as it poses some crucial challenges to human freedom by establishing a link between scientific knowledge of both biological and organic processes: that is, of population and the body.

In this novel scenario, 'medicine becomes a political intervention technique with specific power effects'.[22] Biopolitics aims at 'taking control of life and the biological processes of man – as species – and of ensuring that they are not disciplined, but regularized'.[23] The concept of 'the normalizing society' refers to a society in which the norm of discipline and the norm of regulation intersect, and, according to Foucault, these are on the advance. In his view, the recourse to sovereignty against discipline will not enable us to limit the effects of disciplinary power. The only alternative is looking for a new right, which is both anti-disciplinary and emancipated from the principle of sovereignty.[24]

Foucault studied the ways in which freedom as an experience is to be expressed in the face of the new enclosures that have been constructed around it with the aim of controlling the conditions of its manifestation. In so doing he pointed to the resentment of those feeling threatened by the openness to others, a feeling 'exacerbated to the extent that their claims for the privilege of their protected freedom, freedom as a product of enclosure, are challenged'.[25]

Erich Fromm

Freedom entails freedom of speech, as a key victory against traditional limitations to express individual views; however, Fromm argues that while modern individuals may express their thoughts, on the whole, only a few have 'acquired the ability to think originally'.[26] I will refer to this as the '*fiction of original thought*': the belief that one is 'speaking one's mind' while only repeating the views that have been instilled in one by public opinion and the media.

Constraint and dependence

Freedom came at a high price; it was only in a small number of cases that the individual 'gained freedom in the sense of realization of his individual self'.[27] Fromm points to the fascination felt by modern individuals when considering the growth of freedom from powers outside themselves and which ruled their lives in the past. At the same time he stresses their blindness to 'the fact of inner restraints, compulsions and fears which tend to undermine the meaning of the victories freedom has won against its traditional enemies'.[28]

Therefore, while freedom has brought independence and rationality to individuals, it has often left them with feelings of isolation associated with a sense of anxiety and powerlessness. In this context many persons find themselves in search of alternatives to escape the 'burden of freedom' by surrendering to new dependencies and to submission.

It is important to establish a distinction between *constraint* and *dependence*. I understand the former as a limitation to act: individuals are constrained by institutions such as the state and the church; they are also constrained by norms, dogma, law, tradition, public opinion, threats, family expectations, the community or group they belong to and the self. Lack of knowledge also acts as a constraint – even if the individual is not aware of it – because it limits the individual's ability to discern and make an informed choice. In my view, living under conditions of hunger, pain and illness also counts as a constraint to individual freedom and raises fundamental issues about the consequences of inequality within modern societies and, in particular, inequality between different parts of the world.

Dependence negates freedom; it refers to a state of relying on or needing someone or something for aid, support or permission.

What makes the slave un-free is having a master, because while the slave has a master, all his actions are permissions.[29] Dependence implies following orders and advice arising from the 'master'. The individual's life and wellbeing become a part of a wider 'superior' project: that of fulfilling the master's will. Crucially, dependence involves renouncing one's own will in order to follow the master's will. It also entails renouncing one's self-development and fulfillment in order to serve the master's project. The slave may follow orders willingly or may just follow them to avoid punishment; he may obey mechanically or he may become fully engaged in the task he is performing to fulfil the master's plan. In some instances, lack of freedom is internalized as a 'natural state' – put simply, the individual cannot even imagine or desire freedom – and the idea of a possible emancipation may come to be regarded by him as an act of disloyalty to the master and, as such, deserving punishment.

Belonging and submission stand as two strategies usually employed by modern individuals in their quest to avoid the painful experiences of aloneness as a situation that may lead to mental disintegration. Fromm makes clear that

> relatedness to others is not identical with physical contact. An individual may be alone in a physical sense for many years and yet he may be related to ideas, values, or at least social patterns that give him a feeling of communion and 'belonging'. On the other hand, he may live among other people and yet be overcome with an utter feeling of isolation . . . moral aloneness is as intolerable as the physical aloneness.[30]

The individualist and competitive nature embedded in capitalism has contributed to the pervasiveness of a spirit of manipulation and instrumentality among individuals. The laws of the market dominate social relations. Individuals are regarded as mere instruments and indifference has become commonplace; otherwise they would be unable to fulfil their economic tasks, involving, whenever necessary, the destruction of the competitor.

Impersonality, interchangeability and speed are key in the development of economically efficient modern societies, and freedom has a negative rather than a positive connotation. According to Arthur Schlesinger, today freedom 'means a release from external restraints rather than a deep and abiding sense of self-control and purpose'.[31] To many, freedom has taken away the old securities and has brought with it a certain sense of frustration and isolation; an anxiety illustrated by Søren Kierkegaard's declaration, 'Anxiety is the dizziness of freedom.'[32] Later on, Jean-Paul Sartre was to reflect on freedom when drawing his own theory of existentialism. Man is condemned to be free and he is responsible for the way in which he uses freedom: 'by making choices, man makes himself: creates or destroys his own moral personality'.[33]

The freedom to belong

I understand freedom as the power to act, the power to pursue an option without interference. There are different types of interference, the most important being physical, political, religious, cultural and ethnic in nature, and related to social class and age.

I understand belonging by choice as a prerogative of individuals living in modern societies, who, up to a point, are able to choose. In traditional societies, agency was predetermined by the state, the church and the family, and the individual was expected to obey, to comply and follow established traditions and norms; there was little or no scope for free choice. However, this does not imply that dissidence, rebellion, protest and other challenges to established power did not exist. On the contrary, acts of disobedience and unwillingness to conform pointed to various sources of conflict and tension in traditional societies and, as such, deserved severe punishment; mostly public physical punishment, but also pecuniary compensation, exclusion and ostracism. These were designed as deterrents.

Frequently, acts of disobedience and transgression open up avenues for social transformation, generally taking place after pioneers in various fields of thought, inquiry and work have been condemned at one point, to be firmly reinstated later on. Breaking societal norms was in some instances an instrument of social modernization and progress. The unthinkable and outrageous at one stage might become common practice and even be strongly praised in the future. For example, the new public profile of women, the abolition of slavery and the emancipation of blacks in the USA can be portrayed in this manner.

To 'choose' always involves the risk of making the 'wrong choice'; it also includes the commitment to select one option – or none at all. Barry Schwartz[34] argues that eliminating consumer choices has the potential to reduce anxiety for shoppers, echoing an idea formulated earlier on by José Ortega y Gasset in *The Revolt of the Masses*.[35] The act of choosing inevitably results in the need to drop the other options. Individuals do not always select the 'best option' – sometimes they go for the 'easiest option', the one available to them with little or moderate effort; nevertheless it is an option that they expect will be able to provide immediate and sufficient rewards. In a way, it could be thought that, for these individuals, this is 'the best option' because it accommodates their needs and aspirations with the amount of effort they are prepared to invest to achieve them. In contrast, others are likely to select more challenging options involving a higher degree of risk and effort, options where failure is a real possibility. They do so attracted by the possibility of success and the higher material or non-material benefits associated with it. Among the latter are: recognition, influence, power and prestige, wealth, increased self-esteem and the moral high ground.

The act of choosing empowers individuals to decide upon their destiny, but it also suggests a certain sense of loss because, in choosing, they abandon the options that have not been selected. In time, some individuals may come to the conclusion that they have made the 'wrong choice'; and responsibility for it lies exclusively with the free individual.

Modern society has replaced freedom from traditional external authorities by a more subtle role carried out by anonymous authorities including 'public opinion', the media and 'common sense', which, as mentioned earlier, contribute to generate what I refer to as 'the fiction of original thought', having the ability to influence and mould our views while convincing us that these are the outcome of our own rational thinking. Ultimately their role is to promote the internalization of a set of norms, values and feelings – instilled from the outside and subjectively perceived as one's own – to be invoked at particular times. The aim of these processes is to foster a degree of conformity among an otherwise diverse population. As such, it involves an effort to make social behaviour predictable so that fairly accurate expectations about how individuals may react in specific circumstances can be known and, if deemed necessary, controlled and changed.

In modern societies, conformity not only applies to the acceptance of values and norms but also grants relevance to life-styles, including dress codes, make-up and the presentation of the body, which in some cases achieve a quasi-cult status. For instance, let's consider the influence of labels in clothes and accessories as well as the rigid norms applied to dress codes such as 'goth' or 'punk'. People moving within those circles see their value assessed by the degree of conformity with the trends of the particular group within which they seek acceptance. Their entitlement to being recognized as 'group members' depends on adjusting to the traits, rules, doctrine, laws and life-style of the group in question; their status within the group will benefit from a high degree of conformity and commitment.

Often individuals are not fully aware of the renunciation of freedom associated with the choice they have made. On some occasions, they are convinced that their newly acquired status as group members is the outcome of an act of freedom – even when it results in a costly renunciation of freedom revealed in their submission to the group's directives. Although the group induces their feelings and actions, they subjectively regard them as their own, so that they can maintain the 'illusion' of being free. Individuals no longer feel alone because they have fused themselves with the group and they speak and act as group members. So far, they have escaped freedom by submitting their will to outside powers capable of erasing feelings of aloneness and powerlessness in exchange for surrendering freedom.

To be fair, we should acknowledge that the fear of freedom felt by a significant number of people, ready to sign up to new dependencies, is counterbalanced by the freedom cherished and enjoyed by those individuals prepared to take up the challenge of deciding upon their own lives, thoughts and actions, even if all of those – up to a point – are inevitably influenced by public opinion and the pressure to conform.

Individuals feel compelled to act in a certain manner in order to fit in; this is the price they have to pay for avoiding aloneness, being cast away and ostracized. Modern society seeks to create and control the spaces allocated to expressions of difference and 'acceptable deviance'. In so doing it relies upon a certain degree of conformity as a condition for its own survival. However, a fine balance is to be struck between conformity and non-conformity since the latter is also indispensable to guarantee a degree of social dynamism and progress. Ideally, some kind of equilibrium between the level of conformity necessary to build a shared sense of identity, common goals and the emergence of bonds of solidarity among individuals has to be balanced with providing sufficient space for transformation and change so that society does not become solidified, static and unable to respond to new challenges.

Alienation, fear of irrelevance and group membership

A certain degree of alienation pervades economic and social relations and individuals feel the pressure to sell themselves as a commodity. If 'desirable' to the market, this increases their value; if there is no demand for what they have to offer, then they become 'irrelevant'. In this context, 'popularity' acquires great importance and to be popular often insinuates a degree of 'performance'. Individuals feel compelled to construct a public image of themselves, one that they consider will have a positive appeal; however, they cannot control the success of their endeavour and, more importantly, they do not know whether the self-image they have aimed to create will be positively received or not. Failure, if it takes place, is bound to impact upon their professional life and their self-esteem is likely to suffer.

This partly explains why in market societies individuals have a tendency to display their possessions and their attributes with two main – conscious or unconscious – objectives in mind: these are to palliate 'failure' and to enhance 'success'. Yet a non-attractive personality or physique may be counterbalanced by a display of power, wealth, status, possessions, contacts, travel or other attributes having market 'value', with the aim of increasing the worth of the individual involved. If unsuccessful, the individual becomes 'irrelevant'. In this situation, the threat of 'irrelevance' and the constant urge to succeed are to generate feelings of insignificance and aloneness repeatedly accompanied by *ressentiment*.

A sense of belonging provides the strongest antidote against alienation and aloneness. Membership of a group – be it the nation, a faith or any other type of community or organization – offers a point of reference to the individual, who is now able to transcend his or her own limited existence by sharing some common interests, objectives and characteristics with fellow-members.

Identification with the group enhances both the self and the qualities of the group in the individual's own eyes. Accordingly, he or she is prepared to surrender freedom in exchange for the perks of membership, including companionship, status, identity, prestige and power. Invariably, individuals assume the superiority of their own group above others. Group narcissism operates as a mechanism allowing them to identify with the body in question as valuable, important, outstanding, worth sacrificing for. This generates a transfer of the group's attributes onto the individual, who now becomes enhanced by its qualities. Belonging breaks the sense of isolation and provides psychological support to individuals. Consequently, the higher the degree of the individuals' identification with the group, the greater their ability to transcend feelings of isolation and aloneness.

Escaping into new dependencies: addiction

Several strategies to avoid freedom have proliferated in recent years. These include three types of dependence: submission to a leader, compulsive conformity and addiction. To conclude this section, I examine various types of addiction; the other forms of dependence will be considered in chapter 4.

Freedom does not arise if you do not have power or if your power has been taken away, as was the case in traditional societies, where norms and dogma predominated, such as those primarily imposed by nature, the church and the absolutist state. The conquest of freedom from traditional limitations gave the life of modern individuals rationality and independence. However, the empowering effects of freedom 'from' should be counterbalanced by the sense of aloneness experienced by some individuals forced to fend for themselves in a competitive environment run by the values of market capitalism. The sense of security provided by traditional societies has disappeared and learning to be free is proving a challenging and, for some, daunting task. In this environment some individuals actively seek novel forms of dependence destined to avoid the 'burden of freedom'. For them, the need to choose, to take responsibility and effect their free will is proving too demanding.

In this milieu, many individuals have reacted by escaping into new forms of dependence, including various types of addiction, for example drug addiction, addiction to work, sex, risk, gambling, the internet or eating, among many others. Addictions involve a 'patterned habit that is compulsively engaged in, withdrawal from which generates an unmanageable anxiety. Addictions provide a source of comfort for the individual, by assuaging anxiety, but this experience is always more or less transient.'[36] In what follows, I briefly examine a sample of addictions that have become quite frequent in modern societies. Here my aim is to identify some common trends among them.

Drug addiction. According to *The Lancet,* 'an estimated 149–271 million people used an illicit drug worldwide in 2009: 125–203 million cannabis users; 15–39 million problem users of opioids, amphetamines, or cocaine; and 11–21 million who injected drugs', adding that levels of illicit drug use seem to be highest in high-income countries and in countries near major drug production areas, although data for poor countries were not available.[37] According to the National Center on Addiction and Substance Abuse at Columbia University (CASA), 90 per cent of Americans suffering from addiction started using before the age of 18. The CASA report reveals that 75 per cent (10 million) of all high school students (in the USA) have used addictive substances, including tobacco, alcohol, marijuana or cocaine; one in five of them meet the medical criteria for addiction. In addition, one in four Americans who began using any addictive substance before age 18 are addicted, compared to one in twenty-five Americans who started using at age 21 or older.[38]

Workaholism. The term 'workaholic' became widespread in the 1990s. It refers to a person working excessively and compulsively in order to reduce anxiety and the feelings of guilt that he or she gets when not working. The workaholic profile points to a person who either enjoys his or her work or who feels compelled to do it while sacrificing all other aspects of his or her life, for example relationships. It is argued that workaholism is a form of addiction and, as such, it masks anxiety, low self-esteem and intimacy problems, and it is often related to other addictions, for example to alcohol, drugs or gambling.[39]

Sex addiction manifests itself in loss of control, failed attempts to stop unwanted sexual behaviour, and a pattern of negative consequences, including anxiety and depression. Sex addiction is common among people experiencing some type of personality disorder emerging from different causes. For example, victims of childhood sexual abuse often repeat patterns of abuse in a subconscious attempt to gain control over their childhood trauma while substance abusers frequently develop sexually addictive behaviour.

In turn, bipolar disorder sufferers tend to engage in high-risk sexual activities during manic states, while people with borderline personality disorder and those with dependent personality disorder, or love addiction, can become sexually addicted as well.

Sexual addicts are those who engage in persistent and escalating patterns of sexual behaviour acted out despite increasingly negative consequences to self and to others. They become addicted to the neuro-chemical changes that take place in the body during sexual behaviour.

To be seen as an addict is to be seen as being inferior or defective, and it is quite common for an addicted person to be considered 'weak' or lazy.[40] According to Roschbeth Ewald,

> Sex addicts don't necessarily enjoy sex more than other people. In all reality, the sex addict is compelled to act out sexually. The addiction is often mistaken by the sex addict as 'love,' but love really has nothing to do with it. What passes for love is really a progressively negative and intrusive behavior that takes away all of the addict's self-esteem. It has little to do with true intimacy, but more so involves exploration and use of power or manipulation. Sex addicts have no comprehension of the risks they are taking. They feel their life is out of control. To deal with the pain, the addict may resort to other addictions such as alcoholism, eating disorders, and abusive drugs.[41]

Internet addiction. It is curious to observe that a whole series of games are advertised as 'addictive'. This is quite alarming because it is presenting addiction as a positive characteristic of the games; moreover, it assumes that the 'addicted' person does not have a 'problem' but a 'quality'.

A study to investigate whether some on-line users were becoming addicted analysed 396 dependent internet users (Dependants) and a control group of 100 non-dependent internet users

(Non-Dependants). Qualitative analyses have identified significant behavioural and functional usage differences between the
two groups. According to this study, Dependants 'gradually developed a daily Internet habit of up to ten times their initial use as
their familiarity with the Internet increased'. This is a feature that
can be connected with the tendency among alcoholics to stead-
ily increase their consumption of alcohol in order to achieve the
desired effect. In contrast, Non-Dependants reported that they
spent a small percentage of their time on-line with no progressive
increase in use. According to Kimberley S. Young, this suggests
that excessive use may be a distinguishable characteristic of those
who develop a dependence on on-line usage.[42]

In turn, Nicola F. Johnson argues that she is not convinced
that internet addiction exists since 'in light of our dependence on
digital technologies for work, for leisure and for everyday life, we
must remember that dependence does not signify addiction. The
elements of choice still remains.'[43]

In my view, all forms of addiction share the following
characteristics:

- They compel individuals to act in a specific manner; addiction can
  both constrain and encourage individuals' actions by creating dependence and the need for a fix. However, it can also be argued
  that, in the early stages, individuals may regard addiction as an act
  of freedom, as a choice and as a challenge.
- Individuals tend to require a stronger/higher dose of their addiction
  with time; in so doing, their freedom becomes restricted. Dependence grows to a point at which individuals may become unable to
  exercise free will: that is, unable to act as their own master.
- Dependence involves physiological and psychological consequences
  for individuals and almost invariably affects the lives of those close
  to them.
- Escaping into dependence has the potential to seriously restrict
  and even eliminate the ability of individuals to manifest their free
  will. They lose the capacity to commit themselves to other people
  and to successfully engage in various tasks while under the influence of the object of their addiction. They become slaves to the
  subject of their addiction.
- Addiction emerges out of the individual's need to engage in the
  reflexive project of the self only available in modernity; this is a
  project in which the individual is able to decide on patterns, habits

and life-style options unavailable in traditional societies, where these were already predetermined.

- Addiction, at least for many, entails an internal struggle. Individuals love and hate the object of their addiction; their mood is unstable and depends on the highs and lows of their feelings. Ambivalence towards the object of their addiction is experienced as pain and anxiety, also as a desperate cry to escape a situation which they are unable to control.

Summary

Traditional bonds provided security anchored in a sense of belonging, but they also limited individual choice. In modern societies, individuals enjoy freedom of choice and this makes them responsible for their actions. This chapter has explored the ambivalent nature of freedom as both enabling and constraining individuals, thus adding a constant tension to their lives.

Kant firmly believed that all individuals are endowed with reason and this prompted him to assert their equal worth and deserving of equal respect. In his theory, the defining feature of humans, which distinguishes them from other creatures, is their freedom to choose, enjoy self-government and autonomy. According to Kant, submitting to moral norms is the outcome of our decision and we can also break them; so we choose at the price of acting irrationally. However, Fromm insists that independence and rationality have left some individuals with feelings of isolation associated with a sense of anxiety. To alleviate the 'burden of freedom', some individuals have opted to surrender to new dependencies such as different forms of addiction and submission.

Foucault argues that individuals actively engage in processes of self-construction by adjusting, copying and obeying cultural and social models suggested and imposed upon them by their culture, society and social group. This has a disciplining effect upon individuals, who are expected to conform to the norms established. He emphasizes that, while self-discipline is always encouraged and demanded by culture and society, there is always a possibility to resist it because both power and freedom are everywhere. Foucault defines relations of power as mobile, reversible and unstable, and requiring a certain degree of freedom on both sides.

In his view, neither power nor freedom is ever absolute. Foucault firmly believes in the strength of resistance and conceives of power as exercised through networks.

By examining the tensions between freedom and constraint, this chapter emphasizes that belonging to a group or community does not invariably function as an enabling mechanism; rather, quite often, belonging acts as a constraining and limiting force on individual freedom. Yet belonging and submission stand as two strategies being employed by modern individuals in their quest to avoid the painful experiences of aloneness, which they expect to overcome by means of joining a group or community, offering them security, support and a sense of familiarity within a friendly environment. Obviously, these traits are subject to substantial variations in their manner and intensity depending on the group one decides to join. Finally, to avoid freedom, some individuals surrender to various forms of dependence, including different types of addiction.

We shall now move on and focus upon the resurgence of authoritarianism and its connection with the rise of radical right populist anti-immigrant political parties across Europe and beyond. These parties advocate the return of ethno-politics by establishing a sharp division between those who 'belong' and 'outsiders', those who are to be permanently excluded.

4

The New Radical Right and the Resurgence of Authoritarian Politics

The rise of authoritarianism

In recent years two new forms of dependence have emerged in modern societies: submission to a leader (which in some instances is reminiscent of Fascism and Nazism) and compulsive conformity (i.e. blind acceptance of the values, norms and even the fashion dictates of a distinct community or group, be it political, religious or other).

Submission or obedience to a political ideology or religious faith viewed as powerful seems to fulfil individuals' need to acquire a sense of purpose and strength that they are unable to find within themselves. Often this explains their readiness to give up personal autonomy – freedom – and surrender to an external power with the aim of seizing or at least participating in its magnitude.

Submission to an external powerful force generates three main reactions. First, it fosters a sense of security by offering individuals a role of which they can feel proud. Second, it confirms their status as 'insiders', as belonging to the group; individuals are no longer alone. Third, it opens up access to an environment within which, in theory, individuals should be able to trust fellow-members and be trusted by them. Of course, this is not to underestimate rivalry and conflicting interests as permanent features that almost invariably emerge among members of the same group competing for perks, jobs and recognition.

Submission to an external force is connected with masochism[1] as a means of allowing one 'to lose oneself' and to get rid of feelings of inferiority and powerlessness.[2] Masochistic strivings have two sides: the annihilation of the self and the attempt to fuse oneself with a superior, more powerful, external entity. In the words of Erich Fromm:

> The masochistic person, whether his master is an authority outside himself or whether he has internalized the master as conscience or a psychic compulsion, is saved from making decisions, saved from the final responsibility for the fate of his self, and thereby saved from the doubt of what decision to make. He is also saved from the doubt of what the meaning of his life is or who 'he' is.[3]

Fromm defines the authoritarian character as a combination of sadism[4] – aiming at unrestricted strong power – and masochism – aiming to dissolving oneself in an overwhelmingly strong power while participating in its strength and glory.[5]

During the twentieth century, the rise of Fascism[6] and Nazism highlighted the willingness of thousands of individuals to accept submission to a powerful leader;[7] a decision that in many instances negated the freedom to which many of them had just become entitled. For instance, in Spain women were granted the right to vote in 1931 and abortion became legal in 1932, only to be suppressed by the rise of Franco's dictatorship in 1939. During the dictatorship (1939–75), only women who were considered heads of household were allowed to vote. Since 1976, the year in which the Spanish transition was initiated, women have been able to fully exercise the right to vote and be elected to office.

At present, the twentieth-century emphasis on freedom associated with the proliferation of social movements and revolutions – such as feminism, the civil rights movements in the USA, the Prague Spring or May 1968 in Paris – seems to have been halted by 'the return of authoritarianism'. By this I refer to a form of government and politics which emphasizes the relevance of power as gradually detaching itself from the, until recently, widely held emphasis upon the importance of democracy. Suddenly the emphasis on authority brings renewed significance to notions of order and to the role of the powerful leader able to command obedience, distribute perks, rule and punish – a leader who is not necessarily charismatic but who is always perceived as powerful.

The rise of authoritarianism is connected with both the failure to successfully manage modern societies and the will to control and limit them. It is also associated with what a significant number of citizens describe as a 'need for order, leadership and a sense of purpose', which partly emerges as a response to what is perceived as an unruly world in which ordinary citizens do not matter, are insignificant and disposable.

Since their inception, modern liberal democracies have successfully managed to empower individuals by improving living conditions and progressively introducing universal suffrage, yielding human rights and expanding access to goods, welfare and education; also by making available a range of life-style choices, and enabling freedom to travel and the right to follow different ideologies and religions. However, as these democracies have become multicultural, the diversity that this entails has proven difficult to manage. Right now the global economic crisis is highlighting social inequality, bad financial management accompanied by lack of responsibility and the urgent need to control the power of the markets, which are revealing themselves as alien to ethical principles and values. The rule of markets – impervious to ethical values or principles other than making maximum profit – is constructing a dislocated society in which the nation-state is losing power and influence. Preoccupied with generating a sense of belonging among its citizens, the nation-state struggles to regain their trust, which is indispensable if democracy is to survive. In the meantime, self-regulated markets act as a machine to generate benefits at any price, even at the expense of threatening the very ethos of liberal democracy.

We are living through a period defined by a 'downgrading of democracy', where the name 'democracy' remains, but its original content has been impoverished, its original meaning overridden by abusing it. For instance, the dynamic, progressive nature of democracy is often turned into an ossified set of principles presented, by some, as 'static'. Dialogue as a means of reaching agreements and as a method to resolve disputes is often replaced by arguments and actions forced upon people. To a significant extent, power and not reason accounts for political and economic decisions.

In this context, the basic tenets of liberal democracy – social justice, deliberative democracy and individual freedom – are being challenged by the rise of the new radical right and by political and religious fundamentalism. Their power emerges out of their ability to construct an alternative frame of reference for individuals who feel disenfranchised and dissatisfied within their own communities.

In my view, the return of authoritarianism is expressed through three main phenomena, which have arisen in recent years:

1 The rise of ethno-politics, manifested in the proliferation and strengthening of new radical right populist parties across Europe and beyond.
2 The potency of fundamentalist doctrines applied to various fields, ranging from the market to political ideology.
3 The resurgence of religious fundamentalism as a force with political aims.

It is important to note that in the twentieth century the West had already fought against authoritarian and totalitarian regimes: Fascist Italy, Nazi Germany, Franco's dictatorship in Spain and Soviet Communism are cases in point. In a similar manner, modern society has already fought against fundamentalism – be it of a political or a religious nature – by leading a socio-political transformation rooted in the values associated with the Enlightenment and which prompted the spread of liberal democracy, human rights, ideas of social justice, universal suffrage and the emancipation of women as key achievements.

Today it is particularly frustrating to acknowledge that many of the old evils have not been fully defeated and that old battles have not been completely won. There is an open resurgence of authoritarianism in many European countries, such as Norway, Sweden, Austria, the UK, France, Italy and Hungary, to mention just a few.

Fear of freedom remains unyielding, as significant sections of the population surrender to new dependencies, which are usually portrayed as the outcome of choice, and individuals seem eager to give up freedom in exchange for security, order and a certain degree of affluence. Belonging by choice is generally interpreted as a sign of freedom; however, instead of pursuing an empowering and emancipatory agenda destined to foster the individual's quest for democracy and social justice, choice is geared up to the possibility of a certain degree of self-satisfaction obtained by means of acquiring and consuming. Belonging becomes a matter of owning the right 'valuable' goods and possessing 'must-have' attributes.

In the meantime, power resides in the hands of those prepared to keep freedom to themselves while promoting new forms of authoritarianism.

In what follows, I examine some key factors that contribute to an understanding of the reasons behind the resurgence of authoritarianism exemplified by the rise of new radical right political parties across Europe. These are populist parties that are antagonistic to elites, critical of the status quo and opposed to certain types of immigrants – Muslims in particular. Initially these parties were ignored by mainstream political parties, which considered them as 'unpresentable'; however, this trend is changing with the new parties' ability to attract support and obtain political representation in quite a few – generally affluent – societies, such as Sweden, Finland, the Netherlands, northern Italy and Austria (Table 4.1). The new radical right stands as an example of a return to tradition insofar as it seeks to re-establish and preserve the idea that 'pure identities' are still viable through the exclusion of those deemed 'too different' and 'unfit' to belong. The new radical right advocates assigned membership based upon ethnicity and, in so doing, it closes down the possibility of belonging by choice. This represents a set-back to democracy and clearly stands in opposition to the emancipatory politics promoted by a myriad of social movements in the second part of the twentieth century. I begin by examining whether it is accurate to conflate new radical right parties with traditional fascism.

The new radical right versus traditional fascism

If we examine the fascist regimes of the 1922–45 period, we find a movement – to be precise, an anti-movement, in Juan Linz's view[8] – defined as anti-liberal, anti-parliamentary, anti-Semitic (except in Italy), anti-communist, partially anti-capitalist and anti-bourgeois, and anti-clerical or at least non-clerical. All these anti-positions, combined with exacerbating nationalist sentiments, led in many cases to pan-nationalist ideas, which posed a challenge to existing states and accounted for much of the aggressive expansionist foreign policy of some fascist regimes.

In contrast, the new radical right is primarily liberal. It accepts the rules of parliamentary democracy, in spite of being strongly

Table 4.1 Countries with representation of right-wing extremist or
progress parties in their national parliaments

Country: political party	Percentage	Date
Austria: Freedom Party (FPO)	17.54	28.09.2008
Jörg Haider's List (BZO)	10.70	28.0.9.2008[a]
Bulgaria: Ataka	9.36	07.2009
Denmark: Danish People's Party		
(DPP)	12.3	15.09.2011
Finland: True Finns	19.1	17.04.2011
France: Front National	17.9[b]	21/22.04.2012
Germany: National Democratic		
Party of Germany	0 seats[c]	27.09.2009
Greece: Golden Dawn	6.92	17.06.2012
Hungary: Jobbik	16.7	04.2010
Italy: Lega Nord	8.3	04.2008
	4.08[d]	24/5.2.2013
	4.33[e]	24/5.2.2013
Netherlands: Party for Freedom	15.5	06.2010
Norway: Progress Party	22.9	09.2009
Poland	–	
Spain	–	
Sweden: Swedish Democrats	5.7	09.2010
Switzerland: Swiss People's Party	26.6	23.10.2011
UK: British National Party	1.9[f]	06.5.2010

Notes:
[a] Both results from National Council of Austria elections.
[b] First round.
[c] Federal election.
[d] Chamber of Deputies.
[e] Senate.
[f] Average: percentage of votes ranged from 0.4 to 14.6.

Source: Various sources, including Nora Langenbacher and Britta Schellenberg
(eds), *Is Europe on the 'Right' Path?* (Berlin: Forum Berlin, Friedrich-Ebert-
Stiftung, 2011), as well as national data on referendums held in the countries
cited.

anti-establishment, and although, in some cases, it endorses
anti-Semitism, it doesn't generally do this in an open manner.
Against the corporatist and state-controlled economies defined
by a strongly hierarchical political leadership, the radical right
favours small government. Anti-communism is no longer its key

concern and a major justification for its existence; the collapse of communism and the disintegration of the former USSR after 1989 are responsible for this significant shift. The new radical right accepts market capitalism, and probably one of its main ideological weaknesses is the lack of an alternative economic programme to that of mainstream political parties. It has replaced the fascist traditional antipathy towards the bourgeoisie by antipathy – to put it mildly – towards immigrants, asylum seekers and refugees, in particular if they are non-Western and non-white. The new radical right continues to be mainly non-clerical; however, a number of pro-clerical elements can be found within some radical right populist parties such as the Austrian Freedom Party (FPÖ).[9]

In trying to emphasize its closeness to the people and its rejection of the status quo, the new radical right prefers to define itself as a transnational movement, of which we find representatives in Western Europe, the USA and Australia, which reaches far beyond the scope of mainstream political parties.

In Europe, the new radical right advocates the preservation of Western values, a principle turned into the call for 'national preference': that is, citizens should enjoy priority access to social welfare and the protection of their own culture and language in detriment to those of foreigners. Citizenship should determine a sharp boundary between those who belong and those who do not, and the latter should be excluded from the social, economic and political rights associated with it. According to this line of argument, new radical right-wing parties portray themselves as defenders of those citizens who, in their view, have become vulnerable and marginalized within their own societies.

The Front National in France and the FPÖ in Austria endorse this principle. In the Netherlands, the Lijst Pim Fortuyn (LPF), named after its leader, Pim Fortuyn, who was assassinated during the 2002 Dutch electoral campaign, also emphasized this particular point. Fortuyn did not fit within the xenophobic parameters created by the Front National; his main concern was not the protection of national identity but the establishment of some kind of 'welfare chauvinism' granting priority to Dutch nationals. In this sense, his discourse was closer to that of the Scandinavian Progress parties and to the democratic right advocating radical measures against immigration. His style and discourse – very critical of the political class – struck a chord with some sections of a tradition-ally tolerant Dutch society genuinely preoccupied by increasing immigration and diversity.

It would be a mistake to consider that the new radical right appeals primarily to those negatively affected by globalization. New radical right-wing parties have done particularly well in some of the most affluent areas in Western Europe: for example, in countries such as Austria, Norway, Denmark and Switzerland, and regions such as northeastern Italy and Flanders. In these areas, 'unemployment has generally been significantly below OECD average, and . . . social welfare systems are among the most gener-ous in the world and thus well-positioned to compensate potential losers from globalization'.[10]

Antipathy – and, in some instances, open hostility – towards immigration characterizes radical right-wing parties, which, by definition, do not oppose all immigrants but solely those who are deemed to pose a cultural threat to Western values and culture. In particular, these parties regard the growing number of Muslims settling within Europe and the spread of Islamic fundamentalism as a serious threat to Western culture and values. In their view, Muslims will never belong because some aspects of their religion and culture undermine the very foundations of Western secular societies; the possibility of belonging is closed to them. The new radical right stands in favour of what it regards as the fundamental right of the West to defend its political culture, values, principles and way of life.

Northern Italy's Lega Nord criticizes the fusion between the public and the private sphere, and between religion and politics, which lies at the core of Islam. As Anrej Zaslove argues, they see such an amalgamation as a threat to European democracy.[11] Both the Lega Nord and Austria's FPÖ regard Christianity as a core component of European identity. As the FPÖ put it in their 1997 programme:

> The world order formed by Christianity and the ancient world is the most important intellectual foundation of Europe. The prime intellectual movements from humanism to the Enlightenment are based on them. The cultural character of Christian values and tradi-tions even embraces members of non-Christian religions and peo-ples without any confession.

Who votes for the new radical right?

According to Pippa Norris, 'The comparison of the social class profile of radical right voters, including multiple indicators of social inequality, suggests that they are disproportionately over-represented both among the petite bourgeoisie – self-employed professionals, own-account technicians, and small merchants – *and* among the skilled and unskilled working class',[12] with the exception of Hungary, Italy and Israel, where the petite bourgeoisie prevails and is over-represented. Cas Mudde presents similar findings, and argues that the populist radical right receives support from lower middle-class voters and especially from the self-employed.[13] Norris warns that we should adopt a sceptical attitude towards theories which establish a linear causal relationship between growing levels of unemployment, or increasing dissatisfaction among low-skilled and low-qualified workers, and rising support for the radical right, highlighting that 'the socio-economic profile is more complex than popular stereotypes suggest'.[14]

Moreover, although, as mentioned above, a large percentage of those supporting new radical right-wing parties are to be found among the ranks of the working classes, it is quite striking to note that backing for the new radical right also originates from some well-educated middle-class people. They are not so much driven by economic motivations, but regard the impact of migration as a deadly threat to national identity. Basically, they are concerned about the 'levelling down' of their own cultures as a result of 'hybridization'. The fact that there are substantial differences in the percentage of middle-class educated people promoting the new radical right in countries such as Austria or Denmark compared with the UK, where radical right approval remains a primarily working-class phenomenon, adds to the complexities involved in sketching the socio-economic profile of the new radical right voter.

A recent study by Jörg Flecker et al. also demonstrates that voters endorse the radical right for a multitude of reasons. Three trends were identified: (1) supporters demonstrate 'intensive feelings of injustice from frustrations of legitimate expectations relating to various aspects of work, employment, social status or standard of living'; (2) they share a sense of fear and anxiety that comes from a sense of powerlessness grounded in experiences of 'economic decline, precarious employment, or the devaluation of skills and qualifications'; and, finally, (3) significant backing is a constant among those who have experienced 'occupational advancement' with a strong sense of attachment to the 'company and its goals'.[15]

Norris attributes the radical right's growing support to 'the way in which formal institutional rules set the context of, and thereby interact with, both party supply and public demand in any election'.[16] She claims that no significant relationship exists at national (aggregate) level between the national share of the vote cast for radical right parties and a wide range of indicators of ethnic diversity, while simultaneously arguing that 'at individual level support for cultural protectionism does indeed predict who will vote for the radical right, as expected, with anti-immigrant and anti-refugee attitudes remaining significant variables even after applying a battery of prior social and attitudinal controls'.[17] However, her analysis fails to spell out clearly that it is not the intensity and scope of the social, economic and political transformations that prompt specific reactions; instead, it is the manner in which they are perceived and interpreted by individuals, as well as particular societies, that determines public opinion and voting behaviour.

'White resistance' as a transnational movement

The principle of national preference, combined with hostility towards those considered too different in terms of values and culture, and often skin colour, should be viewed as part and parcel of a wider project of *white resistance* or *cultural nativism* destined to protect what is described as an endangered European identity. From this perspective, Nazism is contemplated as an exemplary case of white resistance against non-Western contamination; such a view is in some cases accompanied by statements denying the Holocaust. Also, within radical right-wing circles, some claim that the Waffen-SS should be considered as the first proto-European army and a predecessor of NATO owing to its vanguard role against the advance of communism on the Eastern Front during World War II.

The precursors of contemporary white resistance and cultural nativism are to be found in some of the reformulations of Nazi and Fascist ideas that took place in the 1960s. In 1962 George Lincoln Rockwell (leader of the American Nazi Party, or ANP) and John

Colin Campbell Jordan (leader of the British National Socialist Movement, or BNSM) founded the World Union of National Socialists (WUNS) with the aim of uniting the efforts of neo-Nazi activists in Europe and the USA. In their view, fear of communism and Soviet expansion could work in their favour. Rockwell and Jordan defended the idea of Europe as a spiritual and racial entity encompassing those territories – including Europe and beyond – inhabited by white people. It was Rockwell who invented the term 'White Power' as a response to the 'Black Power' nationalist movement in the USA.[18] Currently the WUNS website defines its membership as follows:

> All groups participating within W.U.N.S. will remain Sovereign and National Identity retained within their own groups. No Organization will compromise their own individuality within this formation. W.U.N.S. will consist of many different NS [national socialist] and NS related groups, many of which will vary greatly in tactics, but all will have the same end goal, a National Socialist State within our various Homelands. The purpose of the Reformation of W.U.N.S. is simple, we intend to bring together all National Socialist groups Worldwide together within W.U.N.S. as an International bulwark against international Zionism, and all other enemies of our collective cultures.[19]

The new radical right exhibits a cultural nativism tinted with populist overtones that connects with the dream of a 'white Europe'. The transnational character of this populist nativism reaches beyond nationalism by defending the preservation of European culture and values.

In different European countries, some loose associations of right-wing extremists are active at both local and regional level and cooperate across borders. In Eastern Europe, the use of violence appears to be higher than in the West: 'In Eastern Europe local paramilitary groups play a specific role. With the *Hungarian Guard* or the "*Militia*" for instance, the *Jobbik* party created an instrument to fight against and expel the Roma population.'[20]

The transnational character of the new radical right includes the existence of a right-wing subculture influenced by global or at least European right-wing extremist networks. This subculture includes right-wing music, attendance at concerts and demonstrations connected with right-wing groups, as well as an active use of the internet. All these actions and activities are geared up to the building of transnational alliances and cooperation with the aim of promoting a movement of white resistance. According to The Local, an English-language Germany news website:

> It is thought that Europe's populist right-wing parties are building a network in preparation for the 2014 European elections. Established right-wing political parties like the FPÖ, the Vlaams Belang of Belgium and the Dansk Folkeparti of Denmark need a similarly strong populist party in Germany in order to build a faction that can challenge in the European parliament.[21]

A further example of transnational right-wing extremist mobilization is the alliance Cities against Islamization, launched in Antwerp in 2008. The project was presented by representatives from the Vlaams Belang, the FPÖ, Pro Köln and the Republikaner Partei (both from Germany) and Alsace D'Abord (from France).[22] Cities against Islamization stands against multiculturalism, it opposes the official recognition of Islam, and the subsidizing of Islamic associations, Qur'an schools and imams. It argues that 'the institutionalization of Islam will lead to the creation of an Islamic socio-political group which will slow down the integration of the Muslim community'.[23] It stands in favour of freedom of religion, including Islam; however, it maintains that freedom of religion cannot be employed to introduce undemocratic or discriminatory customs or acts. It also opposes policy makers' concessions towards Islam and 'resists the introduction of Sharia law as a replacement for the European rules of law'.[24]

The novelty of the new radical right stems from its adoption of the emerging identity politics discourse to suit its own interests; it is in this respect that, in spite of its links with the traditional extreme right, it is able to offer a fresh message. The new radical right presents itself as an alternative to traditional political parties and centres its programme upon a critique of democracy, a protest against elites and a concern about the cultural preservation and integrity of national identity understood as part and parcel of European identity. It justifies itself by appealing to the image of a world hostile to Western values and culture. It brings ethno-politics to the forefront and contributes to a revival of ethno-nationalism, by which I mean a type of nationalism based upon ethnicity.

The rise of ethno-politics

The most important item in the new radical right's political agenda concerns its hostility towards immigrants, asylum seekers and refugees.[25] Their success here reflects the inability of mainstream parties to face and deal with such a controversial issue in a manner that is considered 'fair', 'just' and even 'patriotic' by a considerable sector of the population, who in turn are prepared to guarantee electoral support to the new radical right. Once again, it should be stressed that support for the new radical right is not restricted to blue-collar workers, the petite bourgeoisie or poor countries.

Today, establishing common legislation affecting migrant workers from Eastern Europe, Africa and Asia is one of the major challenges faced by the European Union.[26] It puts into question moral and economic principles and brings to the fore national differences and interests. A further and extremely important issue related to the accommodation of immigrants to Western societies concerns the conditions for acquiring citizenship. So far, European citizenship is solely granted to those who are already citizens of a EU member state; however, in the future it is possible to envisage the establishment of some kind of European citizenship – detached from membership of a specific nation-state – allowing for the free circulation of some individuals entitled to restricted economic, political and social rights probably linked to their status as 'free-floating labourers' within the EU.

Within the nation-state, usually the 'majority' has the power to decide upon the status of minority groups' members. The 'majority' regards as natural and legitimate its ability to determine the minority's status and perceives its power as grounded in its unquestionable superiority, although popular sovereignty and democracy are invoked with variable intensity depending on each particular case. Patronage and condescension are likely to emerge in a context in which those considered as inferior play an active part in the established economic structure of production. Yet a cheap, unproblematic labour force willing to perform any type of job and passively accepting submission is easier to tolerate. The communities of migrant origin settling in Western Europe, which are increasing in size and strength, have the capacity to progressively transform this by organizing themselves politically, culturally and economically. In European countries, mainstream political parties are eager to obtain the support of ethnic communities of immigrant origin entitled to vote, in particular where such communities are of sizeable dimensions.

Notwithstanding, this is a factor which is also regarded with suspicion and resented by the new radical right, which is sceptical about the idea that immigrants and refugees could make any valuable contribution to their society. The new radical right is anxious about the potential ability of citizens of immigrant origin to influence the political agenda while challenging national identity.

In times of crisis, minorities tend to receive a harsher treatment. They are blamed for the misfortunes affecting the whole society. They are considered guilty because of their 'inefficiency', 'laziness' or 'lack of culture', 'propensity to crime', 'arrogance' or 'economic success'. Any excuse seems appropriate to emphasize their condition as outsiders and negatively charge it. Racism gains recruits in hard times, when the pre-eminent status of a group is under threat. But economic turbulence is not the only feature which may favour racism; rather, some ideological factors, such as the perception of a cultural threat capable of endangering national identity, are responsible for raising alarm among the 'dominant' group.

On racism

Floya Anthias and Nira Yuval-Davis define racism as an ideological discourse based upon the exclusion of particular collectivities because of their biological or cultural make-up.[27] The specificity of racism lies in its constant invocation of a difference that attributes superiority to one group to the detriment of another, and favours the growth of hostile feelings towards those who have been defined as 'different'. Racism, as pointed out by Michael Banton,[28] involves a negative evaluation of the other that requires an active censorship of any tendency to regard him or her as an equal. This process generates the emergence of boundaries that change over time in response to concrete economic, political or ideological conditions. Those subscribing to racism often invoke cultural preservation, fear of the unknown and, above all, the maintenance of a political-economic status quo. The use of stereotypes contributes to what is presented as a clear-cut distinction between individuals who are classified and attributed a set of positive or negative characteristics depending on their race.

The key role of racism, since its early manifestations in colonial times, has been the denial of social, political and economic participation to certain collectivities and the legitimation of various forms of exploitation. As stated by Michel Wieviorka, racism is embedded in power relations.[29] It reflects the capacity of a certain group to formulate an ideology that not only legitimizes a particular power relation between ethnic communities but also represents a useful mechanism for the reproduction of such relation.

In the last fifteen years or so, prejudice, fear and resentment towards immigrants and refugees have been growing within Western societies. The notable influx of refugees from Eastern Europe and Africa in the 1990s gave rise to talk of an 'invasion of the poor' and expressions such as 'storming Europe'. Currently some of the economic, social, political and cultural arguments regularly cited to justify a negative attitude towards immigrants include the following:

- They alter the labour market by offering cheap and often 'black market' work force.
- They contribute to rising unemployment among the native working-class population.
- They claim welfare benefits, thus stretching an already tight system.
- They generally have high birth rates – higher than those of the native population – and this involves greater demands on welfare and has the potential of altering the political system in the medium term, when communities of migrant origin obtain the right to vote. There is also the possibility that higher birth rates among the newcomers – if these were to remain unchanged – could reduce the indigenous population to a minority status.
- They contribute to a rise in violence and crime.
- Their cultures, languages, traditions and ways of life are alien to the indigenous population and they are often regarded as a threat to national identity. Yet not all foreign cultures are perceived as menacing to national identity, and among those who do, there is a clear gradation. At present, and after the wave of Islamophobia generated by the 9/11 terrorist attacks in New York and Washington, Muslims are singled out as posing the most serious threat to Western civilization and they are often portrayed as the most alien and difficult to assimilate.

The nation: conflicting views

At a time when a sizeable number of Western citizens question whether all foreign cultures should be evaluated as a source of cultural enrichment and argue that excessive diversity irremediably leads to the levelling down of native and foreign cultures alike, a bitter debate about whether multiculturalism offers a valid integration model for immigrants has emerged.

Two conceptions of the nation are at stake here. First, there is a traditionally French idea of the nation as a voluntary union of individuals able to create a general will and present itself as sovereign. Second, there is a German idea of the nation conceived as a *Volk*: that is, an entity with an organic character that pre-exists and transcends the life of its members.[30]

According to the traditionally French conception of the nation, *ius soli* determines citizenship and national identity as the outcome of the will of the individuals who constitute the sovereign nation at any specific point in time.

In contrast, the nation as a *Volk* implies being born and socialized into a well-defined culture with its own language, customs and traditions capable of fostering a sense of belonging among those sharing a distinctive national identity. It follows that only those who belong – or are prepared to belong – can attain citizenship.

Neither of these ideal types of the nation is found in its pure form within contemporary Western societies; rather, a mixture of the two seems to prevail. Present concerns on how to maintain social cohesion within societies experiencing an intensification of cultural diversity have opened up a debate on the elements which constitute the core of national identity. Against political theories which base social cohesion solely on adherence to certain civic values and principles – exemplified by Jürgen Habermas's theory of constitutional patriotism[31] – the idea that this is not sufficient to either promote a shared national identity or encourage a sense of solidarity among fellow-citizens seems to gain relevance. For instance, David Miller is sceptical about constitutional patriotism as a substitute for nationality because 'it does not provide the kind of political identity that nationality provides. In particular, it does not explain why the boundaries of the political community should fall here rather than there; nor does it give you any sense of the historical identity of the community.'[32]

In Western Europe, the new radical right has reacted to greater awareness of a rising presence of immigrants and refugees by promoting an organic conception of the nation, which regards 'foreign bodies' as a threat to its life and health. Thus, against the idea of society as the outcome of a social contract or the free will of its members, the new radical right considers that it is ontologically impossible to integrate foreigners if they do not assimilate.

In France, Marine Le Pen, new leader of the Front National since 2011, came third in the first round of the 2012 presidential election, scoring 17.9 per cent of the vote. The 2012 FN electoral programme proposes: 'the reaffirmation of our republican model and its values against Anglo-Saxon multiculturalism. Assimilation, through the school system has to become the norm, and comunitarianism would be banned. France will write in its Constitution: "the Republic does not acknowledge any community".'[33]

A similar point had been made by Jörg Haider, founder of the FPÖ,[34] who argued that 'Austria does not certainly need a "foreign legion made in Austria"', and maintained that 'the social organization of Islam stands in opposition to Western values'.[35] More recently, one of the electoral posters featuring the current FPÖ leader, Heinz-Christian Strache, read: 'We believe in our youth, not immigration.'[36]

The new radical right exploits a mounting hostility towards immigrants and refugees and has managed to attract the support of significant sectors of the population who, in other circumstances, would have never considered voting for an extreme right-wing party: people who feel disappointed, neglected and betrayed by mainstream political parties. They are tired of unfulfilled promises and convinced that politicians are primarily concerned about their own personal and party interests. In this environment they become receptive to the new radical right's message; a message based on national issues such as unemployment, welfare entitlements, the protection of a sense of community and national culture.

At the heart of the Front National's conception of identity is the idea that France is not only a territory, so that being French cannot be based exclusively on *ius soli – droit du sol*. Such a view would presume a 'materialist assumption ignoring the intellectual, linguistic, cultural and spiritual heritage of the nation while neglecting the true nature of human beings', since, as General Charles de Gaulle argued, 'France is a country of white race, Greco-Latin

civilization and Catholic religion. Foreigners wishing to become
French ought to assimilate, start by knowing the language, the history and the practices.'[37] According to the Front National:

> Uncontrolled immigration is a source of tension in a French
> Republic unable to assimilate the new French people. The ghettoes,
> inter-ethnic conflict, community demands and politico-religious
> provocations are direct consequences of massive immigration
> challenging national identity and leading to an ever more visible
> Islamization accompanied by more demands. Communitarianism
> is a poison against social cohesion.[38]

The Front National condemns the practice of granting citizenship
to individuals who do not identify as French and insists on coincidence between citizenship and national identity. Therefore, in its
view, allowing for naturalization to precede assimilation is a serious mistake since, in adopting such a practice, the French nation
is failing to defend its distinctive national identity.[39] According to
the former Front National leader Jean-Marie Le Pen, 'the most
serious danger for France is losing its independence for the sake of
Europe and losing its identity for the sake of immigration'.[40]

From biological to cultural exclusion

After World War II, a shift from biological to cultural racism took
place. In adopting this view, the new radical right sought to distance itself from skinheads and neo-Nazi groups still keen to make
open references to biological racism.

The *Nouvelle Droite*'s concept of the 'right to cultural difference' constitutes a fundamental ideological and philosophical
influence on this new paradigm, whose main figures are the French
philosopher Alain de Benoist and the French think-tank GRECE
(Research Group for the Study of European Civilization).[41] They
oppose racism but share a staunch defence of cultural difference.
This, in turn, assumes the need of all cultures – European or not
– to maintain their 'purity' by being free from alien influences and
avoiding hybridization.

The *Nouvelle Droite*'s paradigm assumes that cultural difference involves separation, exclusion and what Benoist refers to as
the 'right to difference'.[42] Benoist has subsequently argued that

he never intended his theory to be employed against immigrants. In contrast, and while making use of a dialectic familiar to critical theory and phenomenology, he has argued that immigrants, with their natural differences, provide a dialogue against which one defines one's identity. In short, the other is seen as a threat to one's own cultural purity and portrayed as a 'quasi-enemy' against whom to construct one's own identity.

The term 'ethno-pluralism' has been coined by the new radical right to advocate respect for cultural and ethnic differences while maintaining that the best strategy to protect them is to avoid their mixing with each other. By adopting this term, it has appropriated and transformed the definition of 'difference' traditionally employed by the left to promote multiculturalism and respect for diversity. At the same time, the new radical right has skilfully abandoned references to racial or ethnic superiority and presupposes a post-racist discourse based on the preservation of national identity and culture.[43]

Ethno-pluralism, as defined by the new radical right, stands for the protection of national culture and identity while arguing that the national culture and identities of immigrants should also be preserved. To do this successfully, different cultures and identities should not be mixed because it is in the mixing that culture and identity are weakened, levelled down and eventually destroyed.

The new radical right defends the idea of a 'fortress Europe', which it argues is compatible with the protection of national cultures and identities as well as with economic prosperity. It exploits the fears and anxieties of citizens who feel threatened by socio-economic changes and resent a rise in the number of immigrants, asylum seekers and refugees entering their countries. For many of these citizens, national identity operates as the last resort, able to sustain an already damaged sense of self-esteem. For them, identification with the nation offers a source of pride which they do not experience as a result of supporting any of the mainstream parties.

By emphasizing the 'politically incorrect' and 'unpresentable' discourse and ideology of the new radical right, mainstream parties have underestimated the extent to which their arguments resonate with the public and have tended to reject the possibility of these parties becoming real contenders for political power. Of course, such assumptions are beginning to change as new radical parties have entered into coalition governments in various European countries, have gained a significant number of seats in the European Parliament, and are making progress at the local level in countries where they previously had no support, such as in the UK.

The electoral success of the new radical right requires a careful analysis of its discourse; in particular, its critique of the functioning of democracy in European societies and the way in which the governments of most liberal democracies tend to deal with immigration. All things considered, the new radical right offers strong arguments destined to foster a sense of togetherness among citizens accompanied by a renewed emphasis upon the consolidation of a sense of belonging to the nation and the practical advantages as well as the emotional warmth deriving from it. But the new radical right's offer comes at a high price: the exclusion of those considered 'too different', those who will never be permitted to belong, and the request for them to 'stay away'.

Summary

The urge to belong prompts some modern individuals to enter into novel forms of dependence, including addiction, submission to a leader and compulsive conformity. A trend confirming a certain devaluation of democracy in the minds of Western citizens seems to go hand in hand with a renewed emphasis upon notions of order and the role of a powerful leader. At present, liberal democracy is being challenged both by the ascent of radical right populist parties and by the rise of fundamentalism affecting various milieux, including markets, politics and religion. The rise of the new radical right in Europe partly reflects a marked increase in public disaffection and disenchantment with the established political parties and the political system in general.

Authoritarianism is creeping back as new radical right parties bring about a renewed emphasis upon ethno-politics, which establishes a sharp distinction between 'members' and 'strangers', those who belong and the rest. It is precisely the centrality attributed to 'difference' as a reason for 'exclusion' that is already encouraging the resurgence of non-democratic forms of nationalism across the

West. We should now move on and examine the meaning, the power and the key role of symbols and ritual in both fostering a sense of belonging to a community and becoming an indispensable tool to constitute power; and not just to reflect power that already exists.

5

The Rituals of Belonging

The power of symbols

Belonging to a community or group is effected through symbolism and ritual. Symbols embody entities such as the nation, by providing them with distinct attributes destined to highlight their unique character. In a similar manner, belonging to a faith is also expressed through symbolism and ritual.

Symbols are necessary to legitimize and strengthen political power; however, they are also indispensable in processes aimed to challenge and overthrow a particular political order. In such situations, the emerging new elite's success in attaining and consolidating power will depend, to a considerable degree, upon their ability to either radically challenge and replace old symbols by new ones, or manage to imbue old symbols with a different meaning akin to support the emerging status quo.

Symbols stand for ideas, values, worldviews, all of them defined as 'things that matter' to such an extent that individuals are often prepared to give up their own lives to preserve them. Symbols are powerful because they are able to prompt strong emotions, and emotions stand as a potent trigger for social action, including political mobilization.

Symbols only have value, meaning and power for those who are able to recognize what they stand for. Among the most effective symbols are those that indicate belonging to a particular group, be it the nation, a faith or any other group or community. Even so it is not the same to be aware of the meaning of a symbol as to identify with a symbol. Yet where a group member regards a particular symbol as a sign of strength, a reference to the enactment of old battles, and the remembrance of shared injustice, suffering and fear, the non-member sees a material object free from the distinctive character, meaning and value that members attribute to it. Only those who identify with symbols and are aware of their meaning feel offended by acts of disrespect towards them. In a similar manner, only they, by challenging certain symbols, can make a statement of dissidence capable of questioning the status quo.

In multicultural societies, a significant number of people are competent to identify symbols belonging to various cultures; however, they are only moved and feel emotionally attached to those symbols endowed with what I refer to as a 'sentimental meaning'. By this I refer to some kind of emotional identification with a symbol beyond cognitive definitions and historical explanations of its origin and intent. Cognition may contribute to an understanding of the meaning of a symbol, but it can never communicate the emotional dimension attached to it and experienced, with different nuances, by different people. The richness and complexity of symbols tolerate a degree of ambiguity in their definition, one that allows for a certain measure of emotional creativity on behalf of individuals while constructing their own sense of belonging.

Respect and reverence for symbols derive from the content and meaning attributed to them within distinct communities and groups. Sharing certain symbols and being moved by them unites individuals. It also contributes to generate a sense of community and to foster feelings of solidarity among them. In addition, symbols act as organizers of social roles within the community and impose a sense of hierarchy and structure.

Experimenting cultural difference through emotions

I recall visiting the Lama Temple in Beijing in 2007 and being enchanted by its beauty, but also feeling surprised by the bright colours of its golden Buddhas, in particular their red lips. I felt detached from these huge and not particularly delicate statues being worshipped by those who were burning long incense bars, some of them kneeling down, while others, standing, joined hands and bowed from the waist three times. The display of fruit, plastic flowers, money, candles and incense burners at the Buddha's feet signalled cultural similarities with and differences from my own Western culture. It was my ignorance of the meaning of the symbols and rituals being performed together with contact with a different culture that alienated me from that situation and prevented me from sharing the emotion clearly being displayed by the worshippers. The symbols and values inspiring their prayers, their beliefs, their faith, was totally alien to me, as alien as those Buddhists may feel when visiting Western cathedrals such as Westminster, Cologne or Gaudí's Sagrada Família in Barcelona. Where believers find meaning, non-believers see art; a type of art that often obeys different canons of beauty across time and place.

While symbols unite group members, they also alienate foreigners unaware of or sceptical, curious or indifferent towards the meaning attributed to them. Symbols ring-fence communities using a range of 'visible and invisible markers'. Among the former are uniforms, badges, hairstyles, dress codes and salutes. Among the latter are private rituals generally anchored in experiences of past or actual persecution and discrimination: for instance, pogroms endured by Jewish people, genocide in Bosnia, repression of Catholics in Northern Ireland and of Catalans in Spain during Franco's dictatorship.

In order both to make sense of a new socio-political environment and to transform or advance a novel worldview, we need either to construct new symbols or to re-create old ones by charging them with 'relevant meaning' for contemporary individuals. Symbols play a critical part in collective life; they offer a distinct interpretation of the world and they also become anchor points in individuals' life by sending specific messages that are routinely modified to fit new social needs. The process of constructing, modifying and identifying with symbols involves a strong emotional investment.

The role of symbols: regime change in a reunited Germany

After World War II, Germany was divided into four military sectors controlled by France, the UK, the USA and the USSR. On 23

May 1949, the sectors controlled by France, the UK and the USA became the Federal Republic of Germany and stayed in the area of American influence and the capitalist economy. On 7 October that year, the sector controlled by the Soviet Union became the Democratic Republic of Germany and adopted communism. The Cold War divided Germany into two halves and prompted the construction of the Berlin Wall with its checkpoints as the key symbol of the separation between Western and Eastern Europe.

On 9 November 1989, Berlin civil society mobilizations called for political reform; the checkpoints between East and West Germany were opened and people were allowed to travel freely. This date marked the 'fall' of the Berlin Wall. An extremely complex process of economic, political and cultural reunification followed, culminating in the creation of a single, federal Germany on 3 October 1990, the anniversary of which is celebrated every year. This 'Day of German Unity' is a public holiday marked by political speeches, cultural events, communal meals, fireworks and other festive activities. Each year a different city hosts the national celebrations.

The Brandenburg Gate, the Berlin Wall and the German Unification Treaty have become key symbols of a reunited Germany. After the fall of the Berlin Wall in November 1989, many East Germans cut the coat of arms out of their flags, as Hungarians had done in 1956. The widespread act of removing the coat of arms from the East German flag sought to portray the plain black–red–gold tricolour as a symbol for a united and democratic Germany.

At present the old black–white–red tricolour of the German Empire is still used by monarchists and those members of German royalty who long for the peaceful reintroduction of a German democratic monarchy. However, the use of the old flag has been taken over almost completely by its prevalent use by the far right; since the swastika is illegal in Germany, the far right has been forced to forgo any Nazi flags and instead use the old tricolour, which the Nazis themselves banned in 1935. The ban on Nazi symbols in Germany and some other countries is the main reason why many computer games related to World War II do not feature the Nazi flag, sometimes replacing it with the anachronistic flag of pre-1918 Germany, or the modern tricolour. The utilization of the old imperial tricolour by the far right and its attempts to associate the tricolour with its antidemocratic and xenophobic ideals are strongly objected to by the modern German population.[1]

The role of symbols in the Spanish transition to democracy

In 1936 a coup d'état effected by General Francisco Franco against the legitimate government of the Second Spanish Republic provoked the Spanish Civil War (1936–9) and nearly forty years of dictatorship. It was only after the dictator's death in 1975 that the Spanish transition to democracy was starting by allowing for a new democratic Constitution in 1978. One of the key challenges of the newly democratic regime was to get rid of the symbols of Francoism that had divided Spaniards between 'winners' and 'losers' of the Civil War. This was a process starting in the 1970s but not systematically accomplished until 2007, when the Socialist government of Prime Minister José Luís Rodriguez Zapatero presented the Law of Historic Memory to the Spanish parliament with the aim of effecting the complete elimination of hundreds, if not thousands, of Fascist symbols reminiscent of the Franco era from public buildings. The Bill sought to make reparations to the victims of the Spanish Civil War and ensuing dictatorship. It aimed at the removal of all statues, street names and symbols associated with the dictator and his supporters; even plaques and stained-glass windows showing the Falange symbols of the yoke and arrows or the eagle would have to be replaced.

Besides the statues of Franco, there still exist hundreds of other references to the Fascist regime, with streets, colleges and roads named after Franco and his generals. The most controversial of these is the *Valle de los Caídos* (The Valley of the Fallen) near Madrid, commissioned by Franco as his final resting place. The *Valle* is an underground shrine inside a mountain, topped with a 500-foot-high stone cross, which can be seen from a distance of 30 miles. Prisoners of Franco, many of whom lost their lives in the process, were forced to quarry this huge cavern, 250 metres deep into the rocks of the mountain of the Sierra de Guadarrama. It was begun in the early 1940s and completed in 1959.

While supposedly housing the dead from the Civil War,[2] it is a monument to Franco and his regime. It houses the graves of

Franco and José Antonio Primo de Rivera, the founder of the Fascist political party Falange. Around 450,000 visit it every year, most of whom are foreign tourists; however, in recent years it has been frequented by groups of Falangists and supporters of the old regime coming to pay tribute to the dictator.

Demands for either the closure of the monument or the removal of the bodies of Franco and Primo de Rivera from the site are piling up, while some suggest the shrine be turned into some sort of museum where the barbaric actions of the dictatorship could be exhibited.

The meaning of symbols

Symbols accompany individuals by infusing their lives with specific messages. Symbols embody aspirations and values; they evoke moments of defeat and joy. They stand as the pillars of individuals' identity by helping them to make sense of their own personal life as well as of the life of the community to which they belong. In order to fulfil such an ambitious task, it is crucial for symbols to retain some ambiguity, allowing for a variety of meanings. Symbols and ritual are employed to mark transition points in the individual's life. A wide range of initiation rituals are performed with the aim of imbuing an unknown or challenging transition with order and predictability. Fear of the unknown generates potent feelings that are channelled through ritual and often involve a series of tests on the suitability of the individual to rise to a new status, be it as an adult, a leader or a group member.

The ability to redefine existing symbols and construct new ones is heavily influenced by the distribution of resources. Powerful and influential individuals, states, churches and corporations invest heavily in the generation of a symbolic universe making sense of the world, and it is through the manipulation of symbols that they reinforce their authority.[3] However, not all symbols stick in individuals' minds, and not all symbols fulfil the aims of their creators. There is a measure of unpredictability regarding the level of success achieved by powerful entities and individuals seeking to create a symbol capable of generating people's loyalty and fervour.

Belonging to a group can only be represented through symbolism. Taking an oath, wearing distinctive clothes, cutting or arranging hair in a certain way, singing a song, adopting a specific salute, wearing a uniform, a badge or a ring – these are all symbols connecting the individual to a specific group or community.

As David I. Kertzer notes, during the French Revolution, '[d]ifferent costumes came to represent different political positions, and wearing the wrong color, the wrong trouser length, or the wrong hat could lead to a street brawl'.[4] Lynn Hunt, the French historian, notes that these everyday symbols did not just express the individual's political position but, by 'making a political position manifest, they made adherence, opposition and indifference possible'.[5]

It is through symbolism and ritual that a collectivity defines itself as a named group, for example 'the English', 'the Jews', 'the Masons', 'the Catholics', and so on, and establishes its own self-image. Thus, by praising the group to which they belong, individuals are praising themselves.

Symbols provide the content of ritual as a powerful instrument not only to preserve tradition but also to innovate and transform whenever it is felt necessary. As Mary Douglas writes: 'It is impossible to have social relations without symbolic acts.'[6] Symbols are sacralized through ritual.

Ritual and power

Ritual is 'a religious or solemn ceremony consisting of a series of actions performed according to a prescribed order'.[7] A ritual is acted mainly for its symbolic value and it is often associated with the specific traditions of a community. Arnold van Gennep defines a ritual as a 'device provided by society to help the individual to achieve a new adjustment': for example to overcome a life crisis.[8]

A wide range of symbols and rites may be included in ritual; these encompass worship rites generally connected with organized religions and cults, rites of passage, purification rites, oaths of allegiance, coronations, marriages and funerals, sports events and graduations. Rituals also include jury trials, the execution of criminals and mundane activities such as Halloween parties and hand shaking.

Here I focus upon the social and political role of ritual in both fostering a sense of belonging to a community and becoming an indispensable tool to constitute power; and not just to reflect power that already exists. Ritual communicates authority by organizing people according to hierarchy: that is, by establishing clear-cut distinctions between the status, power and role of those involved. Ritual is also routinely employed to validate tradition and reinforce the status quo.

One of the functions of symbols is to identify status: the length and colour of a gown reveal a difference between undergraduates and graduates at Oxbridge; the wearing of the crown and tiara identify the monarch; a ring may be used to single out a married person, and it is also employed to indicate having a particular status within a group, as in the case of the pope, bishops and other religious officials in the Catholic Church. The wearing of a uniform and the specific features added to it – such as stars to signify military rank within the army – also stand as a symbol of belonging. Ritual sends a clear message to society members by identifying the elite, establishing an organizational structure and defining individual roles.

Sometimes ritual has the aim of exalting a leader, a political system, an ideology, a distinct society or group. On other occasions it aims to instruct or to generate a sense of closeness and solidarity among those participating in it and, in some instances, ritual is intended to instill terror.

Ritual is necessary to legitimize power and, as such, it fulfils a major role in structuring social and political relations, be it within a nation, a group, a secret society or any other form of community. As Émile Durkheim argues, people worship their own society through ritual,[9] so it follows that legitimacy is a feature of all stable societies and that ritual plays a major role in nurturing and conveying this social consensus.[10] Durkheim expresses this as follows:

> [T]here is something eternal in religion which is destined to survive all the particular symbols in which religious thought has successively enveloped itself. There can be no society which does not feel the need of upholding and reaffirming at regular intervals the collective sentiments and the collective ideas which make its unity and its personality. Now this moral remaking cannot be achieved except by the means of reunions, assemblies and meetings where the individuals, being closely united to one another, reaffirm their common sentiments; hence come ceremonies which do not differ

from regular religious ceremonies, either in their object, the results
which they produce, or the processes employed to attain these
results.[11]

Often presented as anchored in tradition, ritual is employed
as an instrument to legitimize the status quo. For this reason, it
is frequently argued that ritual, when allied with tradition, has a
conservative role. This interpretation ignores the transformative
capacity of ritual and its ability to reinvent and create novel social
and political structures with the aim of legitimizing a radically
fresh view of society. Ritual remains indispensable as a tool to
present political leaders and political power as rightful, genuine
and lawful. It also plays a decisive role in the consolidation of new
regimes and new leaders. Crucially, 'ritual can recognize, define,
explain, and thus control change'.[12]

The Arab Spring

In search of new symbols

For instance, this is the case in revolutionary times, such as the
so-called 'Arab Spring', which brought regime change to some
Middle Eastern countries in 2011–12. The leaders of four nations,
Tunisian President Zine El Abidine Ben Ali, Egyptian President
Hosni Mubarak, Libyan leader Muammar Gaddafi and Yemeni
President Ali Abdullah Saleh, were driven out, sentenced or killed.
A fifth Arab leader, Syrian President Bashar Assad, appears, at
the time of writing, to be fighting for his survival. In most of these
countries, regime change has already been initiated and conflicts
between the old and the new are evident: for instance, in the case
of Egypt a power struggle between Egypt's first civilian leader –
Mohamed Morsi – and the Mubarak-appointed generals is already
manifest. This case illustrates the tension between legitimacy and
the rule of law as opposed to revolutionary legitimacy.

I distinguish three key symbols of the Arab Spring: first, the
mass demonstrations in Tahrir Square; second, the rise of the
Muslim Brotherhood; and, third, the unprecedented engagement
of women in the protest movement.

Although the vast gatherings in Cairo's Tahrir Square appeared
emblematic of Egypt's revolution, in Peter Beaumont's view, a

more potent signal confirming political life in post-Mubarak Egypt was '[t]he relocation of the offices of the Muslim Brotherhood, the once banned party, . . . [from] shabby rooms in an unremarkable apartment block on Cairo's Gezira Island, situated behind an unmarked door to gleaming new accommodation in the Muqatam neighbourhood, in a dedicated building prominently bearing the movement's logo in Arabic and English'.[13]

This ascendancy of political Islam has cast doubt that the role played by women during the uprising will be sustained. 'Women in frontlines but not in parliaments' is how this was characterized by Italian Senate Vice-President Emma Bonino,[14] aiming to highlight the contrasting uncertain future for women's rights and political participation in the newly emerging regimes in countries south of the Mediterranean now claiming to be engaged in a transition to democracy. Similarly, Shirin Ebadi, winner of the 2003 Nobel Peace Prize, has expressed her concern by pointing out that, while Tunisia is equipped with strong civil institutions that increase the hope that democracy can take hold there, in Egypt: 'Many political actors are talking about returning to Islamic law, which could result in a regression of rights for women and girls similar to what we experienced in Iran in 1979.' This need not be a foregone conclusion, however. She continues: 'There are interpretations of Shariah law that allow one to be a Muslim and enjoy equal gender rights – rights that we can exercise while participating in a genuinely democratic political system. Shariah law and women's rights do not have to be mutually exclusive.'[15]

Commenting on the Arab Spring, Stephan Rosiny notes that in some countries, the demonstrations began on deeply symbolic days.

> In Egypt, 25 January is 'Police Day'; it was after violent attacks by the police that the young protesters came together on that day. In Bahrain, 14 February was the anniversary of the 2001 referendum on a national reform charter, the implementation of which the demonstrators urged. In Libya, several people demonstrating against the Muhammad caricatures had been shot on 17 February 2006. A gathering of the victims' relatives on the anniversary of their murder escalated into violence and marked the beginning of the Libyan revolution. Moreover, the opposition movements named themselves after special dates: for instance, the '14 January Front' in Tunisia, named after the day that Ben Ali left the country. The

'14 February Movement' in Bahrain, the '20 February Movement' in Morocco, the '15 March Movement' in the Palestinian territories and the 'Youth of 24 March' in Jordan named themselves after the initial, taboo-breaking mass demonstrations in their respective countries.

Demonstration days were given proper names. The *Day of Anger* (*Yaum al-Ghadab*) marked the beginning of the wave of protests in Egypt, Palestine, Bahrain, Iraq, Libya, Jordan, Yemen and Saudi Arabia. The repetition of the same name generated immediate connections between protests. The creation of further named days mobilized and escalated the protests: there was thus the *Day of Dignity*, the *Day of Regret* (on 7 March 2011 in Iraq) and the *Day of the Country's Protectors* (27 May 2011), which was directed at the Syrian soldiers to motivate them to change sides.[16]

The power of cyber-revolutions

The speed of recent political change across North Africa and the Arab world has been extraordinary. What began as a relatively small popular protest against long-term authoritarian regimes had in just a few days turned into a mass movement capable of prompting regime change.

The visibility of these revolutions was unprecedented, the speed and success of the insurgents was also impressive, even the willingness of political leaders to relinquish power was incredibly fast. What made a difference? Much has been said about the role of Facebook, Twitter and the internet in spreading protest messages, images and news. Still I find it extraordinary that thousands of people can be mobilized by strangers: people they have never met or heard of; people who may be using a fake identity; people whose intentions and credibility have not been checked; people who, in some cases, are now being portrayed as 'heroes' but who tomorrow may be turned into 'villains', depending on how things evolve.

It has been absolutely baffling to witness the readiness of large numbers of individuals prepared to blindly 'trust' the messages posted on Facebook and Twitter to the point of considering them much more reliable than the information facilitated by news agencies, governments or non-governmental organizations, for example. For the sake of this argument, let's accept that the media may be indeed serving some political and economic interests, but even so, why should people believe that the messages posted on

Facebook and Twitter are legitimate, objective and free from interests?

Such unusual behaviour among people who use the internet and social media is a product of the belief – conscious or not – that they belong to some kind of community of equals, people who can be trusted, good ordinary people acting within a novel environment free from the constraints of the media and other interested parties.

Cyber-messages create the illusion of privacy since they are received through a personal gadget – 'I have received this message on my mobile phone with its personalized ringtones and screen saver' – they use plain language containing some specific words known to those who belong to the social network; and the message is presented as a direct communication to 'you' and it requires 'you' to respond to it. These types of messages appeal to the need of individuals to be able to trust others and be trusted by them. To do so they construct a shared illusion of forming a community created to fight for what they regard as a just common cause. They become engaged in a collective legitimate action. In the case of the Arab Spring, this was the fight for democracy, which was a powerful task to accomplish while the world was watching. If only for a limited period of time, individuals left their seats in front of their computers, galvanized by the élan associated with the mission bestowed upon them personally via a cyber-message.

Politicians have noticed the effectiveness of cyber-communications, in particular their ability to generate the 'fiction' of closeness and trust while adding a personal touch; features that a public statement or a press release cannot deliver. This was recognized by Barack Obama, whose effective use of social media was key to his 2008 and 2012 presidential campaign victories.

Ritual and emotions

The emotional bond is aloof from rational imperatives; it evolves at a completely different pace and level. However, its significance must not be underestimated, because emotion impacts upon beliefs and, in so doing, it has the ability to promote social action.

Frequently, somebody compelled to act following his or her emotions is described as being 'carried away'; this implies that while emotionally aroused, individuals pay less attention to other issues, they restrict their focus, neglect rational analysis and critical thinking. Arousal transports them to a different universe governed by emotions. This is not to ignore that, up to a certain point, which is different for each person, emotions are omnipresent in individuals' life; so much so, that time and again we attempt to disguise the actions prompted by our emotions by covering them with a veil of rationality.

Participation in ritual entails acting in unison with fellow-members. This stimulates and reinforces a shared sentiment of belonging while simultaneously highlighting dependence upon the group or community. The emphasis on belonging is aimed at enhancing a sentiment of attachment and loyalty to the group. It is also destined to position individuals within the group's internal hierarchy and to assign them a role. Significantly, ritual contributes to define the boundaries of the group or community.

Only insiders can participate in ritual – except whenever they are included as 'the other': for example, in the sacrificial element present in some rituals. Sacrifice is the offering of objects, foods or the lives of animals or people to God or the gods with the aim of obtaining divine favour or avoiding divine retribution. The term 'offering' usually conveys bloodless sacrifices of food or artefacts, while 'libation' refers to the offering of liquids by pouring.

The leaders of the French Revolution, Robespierre in particular, were conscious of the power of ritual and the need to replace religious ceremonies by secular ones as a key pillar of the new political regime they were aiming to constitute. They sought to establish powerful symbols to communicate strength and attract mass support; however, they did not always manage to achieve their objectives, and some of the 'secular' alternative rituals – for instance funerals – were never fully accepted by the population.

In the twentieth century, Adolf Hitler, aware of the relevance of ritual and its tremendous emotional power in lending legitimacy and building loyalties, wrote: '[T]he individual, lonely when he joins the group as a member . . . receives [in the mass meeting] for the first time the pictures of a greater community, something that has a strengthening and encouraging effect on most people.'[17] By establishing the Nazi salute and using the swastika to represent their movement, the Nazis managed to build two potent symbols equally loved or feared by Germany's citizens, depending on their political standing. The Nazis sought to convert traditional events into occasions to foster and strengthen a sense of unity and loyalty to the regime. For instance, May Day was turned into a Festival of National Brotherhood, and 16 March – Remembrance Day for mourning the dead of World War I – was reinvented as Heroes Remembrance Day and, as such, associated with the rebirth of Germany and the glorification of the military.

Rituals of 'inclusion' and 'exclusion'

I distinguish between what I refer to as 'rituals of inclusion' and 'rituals of exclusion'. The former refers to rituals destined to promote unity within the group and to encourage a sense of belonging anchored in positive terms, for example by fostering a feeling of community and solidarity among group members. The main objective of rituals of inclusion is to turn a collection of individuals into a loyal cohesive community capable of self-sacrifice. Rituals of inclusion emphasize the 'expected' qualities of group members; they enhance the power and the superiority of the group and offer a clear idea of internal hierarchy. Shirin Rai has investigated the ability of symbolism and ritual to frame the functioning of members of parliament in India, South Africa and the UK. In particular, she has focused upon their role in maintaining strong symbols of democracy and power while paying dedicated attention to gendered and racialized dimensions.[18]

To spell out fear is also a key objective of 'rituals of inclusion', one necessary whenever the group is faced with external threats, real or invented, imminent or not. For example, sentiments of strength and unity are fostered whenever the group demands the sacrifice of its members, which in many instances includes their active participation in violent actions such as war.

In contrast, 'rituals of exclusion' seek to identify and punish traitors, to condemn unruly behaviour within the group and to stigmatize aliens and enemies. It is the aim of 'rituals of exclusion' to highlight the price of dissidence and treason by severely punishing those members who have faltered in their loyalty and committed treason. Stigmatizing aliens and enemies involves attributing negative, perverse, abnormal and always 'undesired' qualities to them.[19] In ancient Greece, stigma was a mark signalling those individuals who had to be avoided or shunned. In modern society, stigma, time and again, functions as an excuse to treat certain individuals as non-human. This is a tactic that has been frequently employed to legitimize violence towards those rejected as deviant in physical, moral, ethnic, political, religious or cultural terms.

A 'ritual of exclusion' regularly involves purifying ceremonies, which in many cases include the punishment of members. This has the objective of sending an unequivocal message about members' duty to conform, obey and follow their leader's commands. In turn, punishing enemies will aim to send an unambiguous message about the price to be paid by those who dare to threaten or challenge the power, status and assets of the group. Engaging in ritual has the ability to confer some kind of rationalized explanation for the individual's behaviour while seeking to strengthen his or her loyalty.

Ritual dramatizes the experience of belonging and spells out the duties and perks associated with it. If effective, either it may be employed to reinforce opposition to the status quo or, on the contrary, it may contribute to affirm the power of tradition.

Ritual and symbolism in Francoist Spain

Where the gap between rulers and ruled is greatest, the rituals destined to enhance their power are most elaborate. In such circumstances, rulers tend to appeal to a varied range of arguments to legitimize their power. For instance, some may decide to emphasize the 'divine blessing' that they claim to have received from God as a quality that grants their legitimacy and makes them and their rule unquestionable. In situations of great social inequality, rulers become untouchable by criticism and a huge distance between rulers and ruled divides society.

This became evident in Spain in the aftermath of Franco's coup d'état and the commencement of the Civil War. On 30 September 1936, the bishop of Salamanca, Enrique Pla y Deniel, published a pastoral letter entitled 'The Two Cities', in which he described the Civil War as a 'crusade'. Until then, no ecclesiastic hierarchy had so explicitly expressed its support for the insurrectionist army. The point of reference of this pastoral letter was the blessing by Pope Pius XI of the Spanish exiles in Castelgandolfo (14

September 1936). On that occasion he had established a distinction between the Christian heroism of the 'nationals' (those led by General Franco launching the coup d'état against the Second Spanish Republic) and the barbarity of the 'Republicans'. Pla y Deniel quoted Saint Augustine – author of *Civitate Dei* – to justify the distinction between the 'earthly city' (the Republican zone), dominated by hatred, anarchy and communism, and the 'celestial city' (the national zone), where the love of God, heroism and martyrdom were the norm.[20]

This implied a difference between the 'good' and the 'bad' in the conflict, but even more important was the fact that it provided the emerging regime with ideological legitimacy. The 'nationals', who boasted that they had the blessing of God, fought against the 'reds', the 'infidels', and declared that they were undertaking a war of liberation, a crusade. This proclamation became one of the pillars in the construction of the new Francoist state. On describing the Civil War as a religious crusade, Franco succeeded in presenting himself as the defender not just of Spain, but also of universal faith. As Paul Preston points out, this ability to give the war a religious nature was taken advantage of to attract international support for the rebel cause: 'Many British Conservative MPs, for instance, intensified their support for Franco after he began to stress Christian rather than fascist credentials.'[21]

The pre-eminent role of the Catholic Church was useful both for the 'nationals', who could argue that 'God was on their side', and for the church itself, which acquired great influence over the political and social life of the new regime. Franco constantly insisted on this:

> In accordance with our historical destiny, on 18 July 1936 we were again the protagonist of an enterprise of supranational importance. A great struggle then began on our land to save the fundamental values of Christian civilization. . . . [T]hanks to its religious content and spiritual symbol, thanks to the explicit desire to work in favour of what Christianity is and represents, it was officially designated a Crusade, a just war par excellence.[22]

On 20 May 1939, in a religious ceremony held in the Madrid church of Santa Bárbara, Franco received the blessing of Monsignor Isidro Gomá y Tomás, archbishop of Toledo and primate cardinal of Spain. At the end of the ceremony, the Caudillo drew his sword in triumphant manner and handed it to the cardinal, who placed it on the altar, while Franco declared:

> Lord, please accept the effort of this people, always yours, which, with me, and in Your Name, has heroically defeated the enemy of Truth in this age. Lord God, in whose hand is all Right and all Power, lend me Your assistance to lead this people to the full freedom of the Empire by Your glory and that of Your Church.[23]

There are two important points to be noted in these words: the tacit public and official recognition of the key role played by the church in the new Fascist state and the pre-eminence of symbols and rituals in a political regime that took advantage of its religious character in seeking legitimacy. It is important to note that the Spanish church was divided regarding support for the dictatorship; particularly in Catalonia a very significant sector of the church distanced itself from the dictatorship and actively participated in resistance activities.[24]

Rites of belonging in modern society

The Enlightenment allowed little place for ritual in politics. The effects of passion and emotion were to be avoided and, if possible, eliminated and replaced by rational thinking. It was the aim of the 'Siècle des Lumières' to combat ignorance and to support knowledge.[25] The *philosophes* believed in human progress, promoted a scientific revolution and stood up against intolerance and political absolutism. However, historically, some prominent thinkers have regarded with scepticism the possibility that the majority of people can be convinced or trained to follow rational arguments without taking into account the potent force of emotions as mobilizing agents; a point already discussed in chapter 3. For instance, in the sixteenth century, Machiavelli observed: 'Men in general make judgments more by appearances than by reality, for sight alone belongs to everyone, but understanding to a few.'[26]

In 1915, Émile Durkheim defined religion as 'a unified system of beliefs and practices relative to sacred things, that is to say, things set apart and forbidden – beliefs and practices which unite into one single moral community called a Church, all those who adhere to them', emphasizing that since 'the idea of religion is inseparable from that of the Church, it makes it clear that religion should be an eminently collective thing'.[27] In his view, 'the real function of religion is not to make us think, to enrich our knowledge . . . rather, it is to make us act, to aid us to live'.[28]

He defined society as an 'active cooperation' among individuals. In his view, '[S]ociety cannot make its influence felt unless it is in action, and it is not in action unless the individuals who compose it are assembled together and act in common. . . . Then it is action which dominates the religious life, because of the mere fact that it is society which is its source.'[29] Durkheim emphasizes the power of religion as a tool created by society itself to set up order and structure, to avoid chaos.

Society produces civilization and relies on symbolism and ritual to overcome its fears and awaken strong emotions among those who belong. Society aims to unite its people as separate, distinct and blessed but also as loyal and capable of collective mobilization. The sentiment of belonging is destined to aid us through life by providing a point of reference in social, cultural and emotional terms. It is also instrumental in helping us to overcome feelings of isolation and the sense of vulnerability associated with them. Belonging strengthens individuals by making them part of a group or community that extends well beyond the limited nature of their own lives, and it has the ability to confer a sense of transcendence to individual life. From an ethno-symbolist perspective, Anthony D. Smith has provided a thought-provoking analysis of the roots of nationalism by examining the myths, symbols, heroes, sacred places and memories that contribute to define the nation and sustain a sense of shared identity.[30]

Communities of belonging

It is the argument of this book that belonging by choice has become a distinctive feature of modern societies. Individuals' eagerness to join a group almost invariably requires the acceptance of the group or community one seeks to enter. On some occasions, belonging is strictly hereditary, as in the case of the 'Sabians' – a religion founded by St John the Baptist admitting no strangers[31] – while in most cases, one can only belong if invited to join.

As modern societies become larger, more complex and more diverse, a growing number of individuals turn to what I refer to as 'communities of belonging'; by this I mean groups with a distinct but complex identity, structure and hierarchy within which the individual has a role, is recognized, known, and valued as 'one of us'.

'Communities of belonging' stand against the impersonality and anonymity of living within large modern societies within which individuals become anonymous, powerless and irrelevant, except on those occasions when they are instrumental to either maintain or obtain power, as is the case of war and in electoral contests, for example.

'Communities of belonging' are small or medium size and they do not necessarily require co-presence. For instance, virtual social networks allow for regular contact between individuals living in various parts of the world. Their members are not necessarily homogeneous in cultural or political terms, but they share certain aims and values; in some cases, they are a part of a wider community – one too huge for the ordinary member to matter. Some 'communities of belonging' are organized through branches working at local level which allow for the development of a personal relationship between members. Other 'communities of belonging' encompass membership of a nation, a social club, a secret society such as the Freemasons, a university, as well as membership of a mosque or a youth gang, to mention just a few examples.

Rites of passage

Rituals of passage are portrayed as a 'sacred' mechanism to formalize group membership – although we should be aware of the wide range of groups and societies that exist and also of the different levels of commitment, loyalty and obedience demanded by each one of them.

Belonging by choice is a defining feature of social and political attachments within modern liberal democracies. However, it cannot be ignored that while some individuals wish to belong out of their own free will and conviction, others are compelled to belong by social pressure: that is, to fulfil other people's expectations and will. Arnold van Gennep's seminal book *Rites of Passage*

(1960), following Durkheim, argues that 'the only marked social division remaining in modern society is that which distinguishes between the secular and the religious worlds – between the profane and the sacred'.[32] Van Gennep regards all life as transition, and ritual behaviour is devoted to restoring 'the equilibrium where changes in social interaction impended or had occurred'.[33] He concentrates upon the study of rituals aimed at helping the individual to overcome life-crisis events such as puberty, marriage and death, which consistently involve three stages: separation, transition and incorporation. For instance, while a funeral is a rite of 'separation', an initiation ceremony exemplifies a rite of 'transition'. In turn, marriage or joining a group or community stands as an example of 'incorporation'.

The following quote encapsulates the significance attributed to baptism in the Catholic Church, where it is presented as an act of incorporation involving a transition from the 'old' life into the 'new' life of those baptized:

> We will never fully discover the value of Baptism and its importance for our individual lives. The entire existence of the lay faithful 'has as its purpose to lead a person to a knowledge of the radical newness of the Christian life that comes from Baptism, the sacrament of faith, so that this knowledge can help that person to live the responsibilities which arise from that vocation received from God' (John Paul II Ap Exhortation *Christifideles laici*, n. 10).[34]

In some cases, the individual becomes a full member after a single ritual, while in others the candidate or novice has to progress through various stages: a threshold has to be crossed whereby he or she is considered to have reached the point at which full membership – or incorporation – is acceptable to group members. The Freemasons and Opus Dei exemplify the latter, while becoming a member of the House of Lords in Britain is the outcome of a single ceremony embedded in specific ritual. In all cases, the candidate has to prove worth of becoming a member and often he or she is given a name; a practice that can be associated with the idea of being newly born – at least within the particular group the individual is joining.

Almost invariably – although subject to significant differences in each case and culture – the candidates or novices go through a process of separation from their previous life and enter a transition process in which initiation rites take place. Often these involve a purification of their body and soul. The transition process requires learning the principles, values and doctrine of the group they seek to join. Once this is accomplished, the group has to evaluate their plea and decide whether to accept them or not. If accepted, the ritual of incorporation takes place and they become members.

Membership may be permanent or temporary. It may be easy to leave the group – for example, by stop paying the membership fee – or it may be possible but not easy – abandoning membership of a gang. There are also some groups to which individuals belong for life (e.g. baptized Christians, citizens of a country, alumni of a university), even if at a later stage they decide to renounce their membership or to stop endorsing the group's principles and objectives.

'Exclusive' and 'inclusive' groups and associations

A further distinction can be established between what I refer to as 'exclusive' and 'inclusive' groups and associations. The former usually require some form of separation from society, and, in some cases, they demand a transition or learning period of initiation or induction during which the individual is taught about the association's aims and functioning. The individual is generally invited to join once he or she has been tested and considered 'worthy' of becoming a member; often a new member requires the backing of some already established members to support his or her application. Membership involves a commitment to the group's principles, values and actions.

By and large, 'exclusive' associations and groups generate a stronger sense of identity and belonging than 'inclusive' ones; this is because of the higher degree of identification, loyalty, commitment and expectations – on both sides, that of the individual member and that of the group. Belonging to an 'exclusive' group has a greater influence upon the individual's life and it habitually fosters an emotional attachment to the group. In turn, 'inclusive' groups are easy to join, they are open to the majority of people and it is unproblematic to leave them. 'Inclusive' groups have a lighter hold on the member's life, if any, and do not affect or transform the individual's behaviour in a manner comparable to 'exclusive' groups.

Becoming a doctor of philosophy at the University of Cambridge

For instance, in order to become a doctor of philosophy at the University of Cambridge (UK), one has to successfully comply with the academic requirements of completing an undergraduate degree – generally lasting three years – with top marks at a recognized university and then moving into an active research phase – usually lasting three to four years – in which one is expected to widen one's horizons and write a doctoral dissertation. One must also pay high university fees by means of a scholarship or personal resources.

At the University of Cambridge, the candidate has to submit an original manuscript of no more than 80,000 words and be prepared to defend his or her thesis at an oral examination (the viva) in front of at least two examiners: one internal to the University, the other external. If the candidate's dissertation is satisfactory to the examiners, they recommend it to be awarded a degree of doctor in philosophy by the university. This takes place at a formal ceremony held at Senate House, where the vice-chancellor of the university awards the degree and the candidate receives a title to that effect.

From that moment onwards, the new doctor in philosophy becomes a university 'alumnus' and, as such, is entitled to a series of advantages that mark his or her status as a 'senior member' of the university. The new doctor of philosophy also becomes an 'alumnus' and/or 'senior member' of the College he/she attended while at Cambridge. Belonging to the University of Cambridge alumni community stands as an example of membership of an exclusive community, with restricted access, well-defined rights and expected duties.

In this case, the *separation* from undergraduates is followed by a *transition* marked by the years in which the candidate writes his or her doctoral dissertation, and, if successful, it culminates with his/her *incorporation* into the community of doctors of philosophy at the university.

Becoming a gang member

The emergence of gangs is becoming commonplace in both urban and rural environments. Gang members may be of any ethnic group and they tend to become under gang influence from the early age of 8 on into the twenties. Typically, young males form gangs 'to acquire companionship, gain peer respect, act out biases and express cultural identity'; they may also be motivated by easy access to money, drugs and other perks.[35]

Being a gang member generates a strong sense of belonging by providing social support and community engagement. Gang members are enticed to participate by what they regard as the excitement of gang activity, 'which often involves violence, danger, and outward expressions of cultural biases, coupled with the acceptance given by fellow gang members'.[36]

Incorporation into a gang requires a ritual of initiation which frequently includes 'jumpin' in': this entails a series of beatings over a set period of time by a certain number of members willing to test the candidates' endurance. If the candidates are considered tough enough, they are admitted and become gang members. In other cases, rites of initiation comprise robbery, shoplifting, rape, a drive-by shooting, stealing a gun, assaulting a rival, or self-mutilation.

Once the candidate has been incorporated into the gang, it is hard to quit. Two of the very few options available to those willing to leave the band are being 'beaten down' or 'jumped out': this refers to beatings, which repeatedly result in severe injuries. If a member manages to get out of the gang 'with dignity', the gang will no longer disturb him or her; however, that person will not have protection from former enemies.

While males become gang members for the thrill of it and the power they may gain out of joining in, most girls seek membership to escape loneliness and to find security, warmth and affection, although some may be attracted by the excitement of becoming a gang member. Many of them regard belonging to a group and adopting its ways, dress code and traditions as a symbol of solidarity among group members. Girls may also join a gang to 'express anger and frustration encountered daily in a life fuelled with poverty and joblessness and devoid of hope'.[37]

In the past, although many male gangs allowed females to join, girls' role was mainly limited to being a 'girlfriend', a 'drug-trafficker' and a 'go-between'. In the last few years, girls-only gangs have emerged as a reaction to the sexism and gender inequality found in male-dominated gangs.

To become a gang member, a girl will be subjected to some initiation rites, which might consist of 'a beating with fists and/or clubs, an order to shoot someone, [and] participation in an act of violence, such as assaulting or beating a rival gang member, or an innocent person'. Many females are initiated by being 'sexed in': this involves a young woman agreeing 'to have sex with some or all of the male members and, in some instances, she may be raped. A recently reported trend to being sexed in is to have sex with someone who is known to be HIV positive.'[38] In London, a former gang member has exposed the growing levels of sexual violence against young women who join gangs, saying that 'many are willing to risk being raped in return for the status of membership'.[39] In turn, ritualized rape separates them from their previous life while incorporating them into a new 'restricted environment'. Leaving the gang, meanwhile, is difficult and painful for both males and females; it almost consistently involves beatings and other forms of violence similar to those suffered in initiation ceremonies.

In the cases we have examined, the transition from one stage – separation – to the next – initiation – often, but not always, includes physical pain and a certain degree of violence. It regularly leads the individual to break with the past and start a new life defined by the adoption of a fresh identity attached to some new commitments. The past is to be cut off and there is no way back, or if there is, it is usually a tough way to follow.

Physical punishment and mutilation, present in rituals of semi-civilized peoples such as those studied by van Gennep and others, are also present in a significant number of modern rituals of belonging. For example, the 'covenant of circumcision' (*Brit milah*, also known by the Yiddish word '*bris*') is a Jewish ritual performed on a baby boy eight days after he is born: '[I]t signifies the unique relationship between a Jewish boy and God. Traditionally, a baby boy is named after his bris.'[40] The followers of Judaism and Islam religiously practise male circumcision.

Hazing stands as a rite of initiation to a group, where the transition from novice to member once again is associated with some form of punishment and/or violence, as in the rituals we have already examined. Hazing refers to the practice of various rituals involving harassment, physical or psychological abuse or humiliation, and, in some circumstances, it may include nudity or sexually orientated activities as initiation to membership into a group.

Hazing is common practice in gangs, sports teams, schools, military units, workplaces and fraternities. Although often forbidden by law, hazing continues to go on and sometimes it has devastating consequences on those being subject to it. For example, 'Over 325,000 athletes at more than 1,000 National Collegiate Athletic Association schools in the US participated in intercollegiate sports during 1989–99. Of these athletes: More than a quarter of a million experienced some form of hazing to join a college athletic team, while one in five was subjected to unacceptable and potentially illegal hazing.'[41] In some instances, hazing involves branding individuals: that is, marking them – permanently or not, depending on each occasion – to indicate membership of a group.

Summary

Some kind of initiation remains a constant prerequisite to belong, although we still encounter some examples in which belonging is hereditary. Belonging to a group or community can only be represented through symbolism and ritual. In turn, symbols only have value, meaning and power for those who are able to recognize what they stand for. The richness and complexity of symbols tolerate a degree of ambiguity in their definition, one that allows for a certain measure of emotional creativity on behalf of individuals constructing their own sense of belonging. Symbols unite members and alienate foreigners. They embody aspirations and values, evoke defeat and joy.

This chapter has focused upon the political role of symbolism and ritual as indispensable tools to constitute power and also in fostering a sense of belonging. They are employed by the powerful to reinforce their authority but they also have the capacity to innovate and transform. For this reason, symbolism and ritual are vital in the consolidation of new regimes. Ritual contributes to define the boundaries of the group or community: society produces civilization and relies on symbolism and ritual to overcome its fears and awaken strong emotions among its members.

One of the properties of belonging is that it usually generates a sense of loyalty towards the group or community. In what follows we will explore some of the tensions arising between freedom and loyalty, as well as between freedom and security, that have emerged in Western liberal democracies.

6

Loyalty, Citizenship and the Nation

On loyalty

At present, it has become common practice to request that immigrants wishing to apply for citizenship take an oath of allegiance to the monarch – as in the UK – or to the nation – as in the USA and Canada. On some occasions the taking of oaths has been opposed on religious grounds. For instance, we encounter many cases involving conscientious refusal by members of some religious communities. Jehovah's Witnesses, for example, believe their allegiance belongs to God's Kingdom, which they consider as an actual government. This explains their refusal to salute the US flag, to sing any kind of nationalistic songs and to pledge allegiance to any country; they also refuse participation in the military service – even when it is compulsory.[1]

This raises an important question for Western liberal democracies: should political loyalty take precedence over religious loyalty? This is a complex question, since it is already clear that not all citizens grant preference to political loyalty. It is also the case that a number of citizens are willing to enjoy the perks of citizenship – including welfare – while openly undermining the nation-state and placing their political allegiance elsewhere.

A fundamental feature of Western societies is the separation between state and church and the endorsement of secularism. In spite of that, the influence of religion continues to be significant, although it varies according to specific cases. For example, the Christian Orthodox Church plays a major role in Greece's public sphere; in contrast, the French Republic distances itself from the Catholic Church and other denominations existing within French soil while standing in favour of *laïcité*.

In Spain, the influence of the Catholic Church has been strong and constant for many centuries. In the twentieth century, it acted as one of the most influential pillars of Franco's dictatorship (1939–75). During the Spanish transition to democracy, the privileged position of the Catholic Church was significantly mitigated by the policies of the PSOE (the Spanish Socialist Workers' Party) in power from 1982 to 1996 and from 2004 to 2011. In spite of that, the Catholic Church continues to have considerable weight upon some sectors of Spanish society.

The UK, as a country defining itself as multicultural, offers a distinct example since the monarch is also the head of the Church of England and a number of seats are reserved for bishops in the House of Lords. In turn, religion has a visible and central presence in the political life of the USA, where religious symbols and principles are invoked regularly, in particular during electoral campaigns. Let's bear in mind that presidents of the USA often conclude their speeches with a 'God bless America' and that the sentence 'In God we trust' is printed on US banknotes.

In modern societies the presence and influence of religion, defined as a set of values and a cultural framework, does not usually entail a powerful influence of religious hierarchies upon social and political affairs, nor does it result in their direct participation in politics, except in some particular cases. The content of religion is often visibly social rather than transcendent and it is generally treated as a celebration of community.

Among the reasons that could explain the decline of traditional religious faith and observance are the advancement of science – endowed with tremendous prestige – and its role as the indispensable foundation of modern technology and, thereby, also of modern economy. Secularization is moving forward, and 'where religion contains some vigour, it does so by becoming civic. . . . In North America, religious attendance is high, but religion celebrates a shared cult of the American way of life, rather than insisting on distinctions of theology or church organization, as once it did.'[2]

In contrast, if we turn our gaze towards Islamic countries, we encounter religious principles and hierarchies guiding public political life in an unequivocal manner. Religious law almost invariably becomes the law of the country, and there is no clear-cut distinction between religious and political principles since, in Islam, points of doctrine and points of law are not separated. 'Muslim learned scholars are best described as theologians/jurists.'[3] Today, in Europe, Islam is stronger than a century ago and, to a considerable extent, it remains impervious to secularization.

The increasing presence of Muslims in Western countries has accentuated awareness of the role of Islam in determining the life and politics of its followers. It also highlights the remarkable ability of Islam to generate a robust sense of belonging among its believers.

In Europe, demands for the adoption of Sharia law – based upon Islamic principles – instead of abiding by the law of the country of residence is gaining strength as Muslim communities grow and become more influential. In this novel environment new questions are raised about whether or not political loyalty should stand above religious loyalty, thus reflecting the Western secular principle of separation between state and church, politics and religion. As already mentioned, such a distinction is not valid within Islam, where 'there is no canon law, but simply divine law as such, applicable to the community of believers'.[4]

This clash between religious and national loyalty became poignantly difficult after the perpetrators of the London bombings in 2005 declared allegiance to a form of Islamic fundamentalism, implying that, for them, religious loyalty had taken precedence over their duties as British citizens; an assertion certified by the fact that the bombings primarily killed and maimed British citizens. Since then, the concern with loyalty and, in particular, the possible clash between political and religious loyalties has come to the fore as one of the most complex and challenging issues faced by Western societies.

Three types of loyalty

But what are the main attributes of loyalty? What does it mean to be loyal? Does loyalty involve a free choice or is it the end result of being under pressure?

Loyalty by choice

I understand 'loyalty by choice' as the outcome of a free personal decision that contributes to the individual's self-definition. Loyalty entails a personal option and, as such, it cannot be obtained through force or coercion. Loyalties provide identity and offer a vantage point from which the individual interprets the world and relates to others. Shared loyalties offer a solid foundation for the constitution of communities and groups orientated towards the advancement of common aims. They also facilitate communication among individuals and supply a common ground for their cooperation.

'Loyalty by choice' is an attitude grounded upon the commitment and identification with a person, a cause, an ideology, a community or a group. Loyalty manifests itself by passionate devotion to a cause and readiness to act in order to advance its objectives. In some instances, loyalties have a very precise object – for example, loyalty to a person, be it a family member, a friend, a mentor, a religious or a political leader – while on other occasions, the object of loyalty is much more diffuse and difficult to pin down – for example, loyalty to the European Union.

Loyalty results in specific actions and is associated with intense emotional feelings. It commands a long-term commitment and involves awareness that this may impose significant demands on the individual, who should be ready to place the interests of the object of his or her loyalty above personal aims. 'Loyalty by choice' encourages a strong emotional attachment and affection marked by faithfulness, allegiance, constancy and fidelity that, whenever necessary, may function as a trigger for actions orientated towards fulfilling what is regarded as a higher end.

Acts of loyalty have the ability to lift the individual above a life based on self-interest; his or her qualities are enhanced and he or she is praised and admired by fellow-members. This is an experience which instantly raises the individual's self-esteem. Loyalty translates into an attachment outside the self and, as such, it is associated with a sense of altruism: that is, the disposition to sacrifice one's own wellbeing with the purpose of attaining a 'higher aim'.

Authoritarian loyalty

Whenever some individuals are forced to obey and show loyalty to a ruler, a country or a cause, their actions do not respond to 'loyalty by choice' and are not the outcome of free will. Loyal behaviour emerging out of coercion refers to 'authoritarian loyalty' and does not involve the free act of committing oneself to a cause. Membership of non-governmental organizations, political parties and most religious communities and associations usually responds to a free personal decision; however, in some instances individuals are compelled to pay allegiance to particular principles by joining various groups and associations. For example, in the first half of the twentieth century, Fascist Spain, Fascist Italy and Nazi Germany compelled their citizens to join some parapolitical movements and organizations created or supported by these regimes with the aim of indoctrinating their citizens as well as testing their loyalty.

Loyalty, as an emotion rooted in our deepest sentiments and needs, implies a subject–object relationship founded upon a strong commitment and identification with the object of loyalty. The content of loyalty is determined and transformed by changes in that relationship. Almost invariably, loyalty implicates the idealization of its object in the eyes of the beholder, who is bound to regard it as worth fighting for, valuable and superior. However, individuals experience loyalty with varying degrees of emotional intensity, ranging from blind commitment, devotion and even fanaticism to much more rational expressions.

Instrumental loyalty

Loyalties differ in precision and endurance and a distinction should be established between loyalty as a 'life-commitment' and loyalty as a 'short-term investment'. There are some short-lived loyalties such as those of people supporting a particular athlete or tennis player while he or she is doing well and then shifting to another who might be regarded as more successful, trendy or attractive. On other occasions, we encounter people who are keen to express loyalty to powerful individuals while they are in command but who are also ready to shift their allegiance quickly once those individuals fall from power or are tarnished by scandal, resulting in a diminishing value and regard for their past achievements.

The two cases that I have cited betray the definition of loyalty as a long-term commitment; instead they exemplify what I refer to as 'instrumental loyalty'. By this I mean a type of loyalty defined by a primarily temporal commitment to a specific cause generally accompanied by a feeble willingness to endure adversity and to sacrifice in order to advance its aims.

Those subscribing to 'instrumental loyalty' regard it as an investment and, consequently, if returns are not coming their way they automatically feel uncommitted and ready to shift the present object of loyalty for another one that promises to offer higher benefits. 'Instrumental loyalty' cannot be treated as genuine 'loyalty' since it does not involve endurance in the face of adversity, which I regard as one of the most efficient testing grounds for the concept.

A key question here concerns whether loyalty, based upon free will and conviction, and 'instrumental loyalty', as a strategy for self-profit, will result in similar levels of commitment and willingness to sacrifice for their cause. For instance, would an individual who acquires a British passport in order to participate fully in the social and political life of the country be as committed to Britain as somebody whose sole motivation to apply for citizenship is to become an EU member and, as such, obtain the right to work across the EU? This is a difficult question whose answer is likely to vary depending upon each particular case. Yet, while willingness to acquire citizenship as an entrance card to a particular labour market – the EU – responds to a primarily instrumental motivation, there is no reason to assume that this individual's level of commitment to the country would prove higher or lower than that of another individual who wishes to obtain citizenship with the aim of becoming integrated into and contributing to the political life of the UK. At this stage, however, while we do not know about the levels of commitment of the former, we have a clear indication of those of the latter, even if time could prove us to be misled.

Loyalty, the nation and nationalism

Loyalty is a quality crucial to the construction and survival of the nation, but also important in the evolution of various forms of political mobilization such as nationalist and national liberation movements across the globe.

At present, one of the most potent triggers of loyalty is a strong sense of belonging to the nation as the 'emotional' community able to muster the highest levels of loyalty and energy from its members through nationalist mobilization. However, this has not always been the case and, for centuries, religion took precedence and generated the most passionate examples of loyalty, as well as treason, on behalf of a wide range of people across the world.

When applied to the nation, loyalty translates into patriotism: that is, 'devotion to one's own country and concern for its defence'.[5] Loyalty to the nation involves a strong emotional engagement; so much so that the individual feels as a part of the community and identifies with its aims, rejoices in its achievements and suffers its losses and defeats.

Loyalty does not imply acting according to rational behaviour, nor does it assume complying with the actual laws of the nation – as important as they might be. The emotional intensity associated with loyalty creates a bond between subject and object, a relationship that goes beyond instrumentality.

While, to function properly, the market grants pre-eminence to rationality and depreciates emotion, the nation calls for the emotional commitment of its citizens insofar as it actively seeks their loyalty, solidarity and readiness to self-sacrifice. Rationality encounters a stumbling block when dealing with the generation of commitment, solidarity and loyalty because they require an emotional dimension that solely rational theories, such as constitutional patriotism, are unable to provide. Rationality tends to discard and ignore the power of emotions, the very same emotions that are also present in the often-passionate defence of rationality itself.

Nationalism[6] is the political doctrine defending the right of the nation to decide upon its political destiny – be it as an independent state, a member of a federation or confederation, a unit within a larger nation-state or a part of a state within which the nation is bound to obtain differing degrees of recognition and political freedom depending upon each particular case. Nationalism – as the sentiment of attachment, identification and love for the nation – is prompted by its members sharing five main characteristics:

1 A sense of belonging to the nation based upon the consciousness of forming a distinctive community: for example, 'the English', 'the Greeks', 'the Flemish', 'the Turks' or 'the Catalans'.

2 A shared history crucially based upon the collective memory of the nation.

3 A shared culture, including a specific language, political beliefs and religion, as well as myths, symbols, ceremonies, sacred places, heroes and memories.

4 Attachment to a clearly demarcated territory associated with the life of the nation; a territory regarded as a source of nourishment and resources, as a landscape and also as a site of crucial events in the nation's life.

5 And most importantly, people's right to be recognized as a *demos* able to decide upon their political destiny triggered by their desire to share a common fate.

These characteristics emphasize the image of the nation as a community born out of the shared efforts, experiences of victory and defeat, challenges and projects of its members. The nation is not an eternal and fixed entity; rather, it has evolved throughout time, and it is attached to a demarcated territory that its members regard as 'their own'. Values, beliefs, customs, conventions, habits, languages and practices are transmitted to the new members who receive the culture of a particular nation. Knowingly, nations are not eternal; they are subject to transformations throughout their lives, and while some new nations may emerge, others are likely to disappear.

National identity is constituted by a set of attributes shared by those who belong to a particular nation. The nature of these attributes stems from the specific way in which the nation is defined. Yet, in referring to the nation as a human group conscious of forming a community, sharing a common culture, attached to a clearly demarcated territory and having a common past and a common project for the future while claiming the right to decide upon their political fate,[7] I am implying that national identity has five dimensions: psychological, cultural, territorial, historical and political.

The **psychological** dimension of national identity arises from the consciousness of forming a group based on the 'felt' closeness uniting those who belong to the nation. Such closeness can remain latent for years and suddenly come to the surface whenever the nation is confronted with an external or internal enemy – real, potential or imagined – threatening its people, its prosperity, its traditions and culture, its territory, its international standing or its sovereignty.

The attributes, real as well as invented, sustaining the belief in common ancestry make up national identity and foster a sense of belonging which generally engenders loyalty and social coherence among fellow-nationals. Political leaders and agitators are fully aware of the power of national identity, and it is not uncommon for them to mix rational arguments with the appeal to shared sentiments of belonging and love of the nation while trying to mobilize the population. Calls for action and sacrifice in the face of threats to the nation and of defeat are accompanied by appeals to the 'unique character' and 'qualities' of those who belong, those who should be proud of defending their nation. Such assertions have the capacity to lift people beyond their daily lives and routines, to raise them to a higher level in which their actions are qualified as crucial for the survival and prosperity of the nation.

The selective use of **history** provides members of a nation with a collective memory filled with transcendental moments in the life of the community. All nations evoke some features that make them special and, in a certain way, 'superior' to the rest. They all excel in something, no matter what, that makes their members believe that they are valuable and unique, thus increasing their self-esteem. History contributes to the construction of a certain image of the nation and represents the cradle where the national character was formed. By connecting us with our ancestors, history strengthens the subjective belief of being part of an extended family. History can be employed to instil potent emotions in people's minds by reminding them of past victories and defeats; by infusing them with sentiments of pride, boosting self-esteem and, on some occasions, promoting hatred and a thirst for vengeance. However, I agree with Anthony D. Smith that '"the nation" is not an essence or fixed state that is either present or absent, or that one either possesses or lacks'.[8]

The process of identification with the elements of a specific **culture** involves a strong emotional investment. Two major inferences deriving from this possess a particular significance. First, a shared culture favours the creation of solidarity bonds among the members of a given community by allowing them to recognize each other as fellow-nationals and to imagine their community as separate and distinct from others. Second, individuals socialized within a distinct culture tend to internalize its symbols, values, beliefs and customs as forming a part of themselves.

Territory has traditionally been the people's primary source of nourishment, and even today domestic products and natural resources possess great significance and constitute a crucial component of the nation's wealth. A great shift was required for people to conceive the nation as their home, since large sections of the population had never travelled around their own nation's territory and could not imagine it as clearly bounded and distinct. Print and other forms of media have contributed to individuals being able to imagine their nations and regard them as homelands.[9] In addition, international media and communications have brought awareness of the territorial limits of nations and of the different peoples and cultures inhabiting them.

When turned into landscape, territory achieves a completely different meaning for those who belong, those able to discern particular sites where memorable battles and events took place and to identify particular landmarks and sacred places constituting the distinctive character of the nation. People come to regard the landscape as embodying the traditions, history and culture of the nation they share with their ancestors. The landscape, be it urban or rural, also represents the heritage that we shall bequeath to future generations.

Nationalism is able to cut across gender, class and age boundaries by capitalizing on the consciousness of sharing a sense of national identity, a common culture, history, territory and the will to decide upon the shared future of those who belong to the nation. In addition, if nationalism is committed to democracy and social justice, then it also cuts across ethnic boundaries and may become cosmopolitan in its outlook.[10]

The attachment to the **political** values, culture, principles and institutions of a nation combined with the desire to advance them is generally founded upon a complex mixture of tradition and sentiment, conviction and interest able to foster a sense of common identity and shared loyalty among members of a given community. Loyalty defines the community and preserves its identity throughout time. It encourages a sense of trust among fellow-members and facilitates agreement in the development of common projects. Loyalty is closely connected to trust; only those loyal can be trusted. In turn, trust requires a belief in the permanence of the conditions that make it possible, among which loyalty is probably the most important.

National loyalty in peacetime and wartime

During peacetime, national loyalties seem to weaken and dissolve. They are often portrayed as 'a feature of the past' connected with old traditions which have become obsolete and transcended by cosmopolitanism, the idea of a global world and exceedingly high levels of individualism typical of modern societies. Even so, awareness of a common threat – be it internal or external – has the proven ability to shake individuals' sense of security and to activate nationalist feelings as well as the political loyalty associated with membership of the nation.[11] In these circumstances, a clear-cut distinction between members and 'strangers' takes effect almost immediately since different expectations and duties are associated with them, although the nation cannot assume that all its citizens will be loyal and engage in its defence.

For example, the 9/11 terrorist attacks in New York and Washington, as well as the subsequent attacks carried out in London, Madrid and other cities by Islamic fundamentalists, highlighted the existence of a small number of individuals prepared to kill their fellow-citizens. In so doing they managed to trigger a wave of Islamophobia, which is still present in the Western world. In some quarters, calls for cosmopolitanism have been rapidly replaced by a renewed emphasis on nationalism and the defence of national values and principles.

Some of the most recent challenges to multiculturalism are connected with an emerging mentality of 'feeling under threat' promoted by the new radical right and its anti-immigrant discourse. This is a message which establishes a sharp division between members of the nation and aliens, with the latter described as people 'who cannot be trusted', and who are 'a threat to the nation's life and wellbeing'. It primarily targets certain types of immigrants and citizens disengaged from the nations of which they hold citizenship status – or where they live – and currently paying allegiance elsewhere.

In principle, citizens are presumed loyal to the nation – they can be trusted; it is their duty to defend the nation and show readiness to sacrifice in order to preserve it. In wartime, betrayal and disloyalty are the highest possible offences, the most abhorrent of crimes, and also the ones more severely punished because they endanger the life of the nation, its values and freedom. In law, treason is the crime that covers the more extreme acts against one's sovereign or nation and includes performing overt acts to help the enemies of one's country or government. Outside legal spheres, treason is often used to describe betrayal of one's own nation, political party, ethnic group, religion, community or any other group to which the individual may belong. Historically, the main objective of laws of treason issued in different countries has remained the elimination of political and religious dissenters. In English practice, treason is tightly bound up with private betrayal (husband–wife, serf–lord).

Loyalty is tested in wartime and often it becomes associated with violence as a means to defeat the enemy, as a tool to protect one's own fellow-citizens, country and principles. The use of violence marginalizes democracy and peaceful means, which are, in turn, replaced by the law of the stronger, the one able to defeat by force rather than by providing the best argument. In times of war, self-definition as a member or supporter of a particular nation, cause or principle contributes to the consolidation of nations fighting each other while promoting internal cohesion, solidarity and a sense of common fate. In those circumstances, loyalty and trust become a matter of life and death.

War also opens up the opportunity for heroic actions able to instil feelings of altruism, which raise the individual's sense of self-esteem while enhancing his or her status within the community. Facing a common enemy prompts rising levels of solidarity among citizens and reinforces a sense of community. In difficult times, and in spite of material hardship, people may feel happier about themselves out of the possibility of being useful to others. Challenging times are clearly more demanding on individuals, who are then encouraged to feel proud of acting in a generous, altruistic manner. This partly explains why in wartime both a sense of community and patriotism are reinforced.

But let's not be misled by the generosity and solidarity associated with war efforts. War generates a situation in which the lowest of impulses and all forms of cruelty are often 'justified' as actions to defeat the enemy or to uncover the traitor. War is based upon the use of violence; it brings death, suffering and destruction. Often enemies are downgraded and treated as 'non-human'; violence becomes a tool for victory.

In the context of war, strangers are regarded as outsiders and often portrayed as potential enemies by arguing that their loyalty cannot be taken for granted because it is likely to be placed elsewhere. They do not belong to the nation and are not expected to identify with it. Generally, they are not trusted to contribute to its defence, although there are some exceptions in which armies of foreign nationals have fought side by side with nationals of a different country while defending a common political idea: for example, scores of British and other Europeans formed the International Brigades – around 2,000 men – fighting against Fascism in the Spanish Civil War.[12]

Loyalty programmes in the USA

In the sixteenth and seventeenth centuries, England established a series of loyalty tests and oaths imposed by Catholic governments upon Protestants and by Protestant governments upon Catholics. Historically, loyalty tests have been devised as a means to guarantee the loyalty of citizens, servants, members of specific groups and associations. For instance, in the USA, southern Americans in the Civil War and the Reconstruction periods were required to prove their right to full membership in the American political community by test oaths and loyalty checks. The allegedly 'disloyal' were suspected of owing allegiance to political entities other than the American nation.[13]

After the Spanish Civil War (1936–9), and in addition to the constant and systematic repression and surveillance, a wave of accusations and denunciations of 'reds' was incited by the new dictatorial regime imposed by General Francisco Franco.[14] The 10 February 1939 Law ordered public employees to take an oath of allegiance to the Falange – the Fascist party supporting the dictator – within eight days and to answer a questionnaire on their political and trade union activities both before and after 18 July 1936 (the date of the coup d'état against the democratically elected government of the Second Spanish Republic). Trial judges confirmed the truth of the answers by checking political reports elaborated by the police, the Guardia Civil, the Falange and sometimes the Military Information Service.

During the Cold War period and in the wake of the persecution and conviction of communist sympathizers in the USA, a debate considering the meaning of loyalty and disloyalty within a liberal-democratic state led to strong opposing views.

One of the most controversial issues concerned the division between those against 'loyalty programmes' and those in favour or them. While the former were staunch defenders of freedom, the latter were prepared to renounce some civil liberties in order to guarantee loyalty. The opposition between the two camps was passionately argued. In that tense context the proper standard by which to judge loyalty was spelled out by the 'clear and present danger doctrine' enunciated by Justice Oliver Wendell Holmes. It reads as follows:

> The government is justified in interfering in the realm of ideas *only* if the nature of a specific utterance of the ideas and the circumstances in which they are uttered are such as to give rise to clear and present danger of overt actions which the state may legitimately forbid. . . . [I]t is urged every American must be considered loyal so long as he engages in no actions which the law specifically forbids.[15]

In that context, those against loyalty programmes argued that disloyal actions should be primarily restricted to sabotage, espionage and treason and felt that loyalty measures were non-democratic. One of the main arguments invoked by them pointed to what they saw as pressure to redefine loyalty as conformity: that is, uncritical and unquestioned acceptance of America as it was. Henry Steele Commager argued that to define 'loyalty as conformity' involved the falsification of the former since conformity is a narrow and restrictive concept that denies freedom of thought and of conscience.[16] According to him, the content of loyalty cannot be fixed; it must be larger than oneself and untainted by private purposes or selfish ends. Commager conceives of loyalty as including the possibility to challenge certain provisions of the American Constitution itself. To illustrate this point he refers to the ethically sound decision of some in the South to stand in favour of abolitionism in spite of this posing a challenge to the official position there.

> From 1830 to the Civil War, the South was committed to a position in economics, sociology, politics and philosophy that was all but impervious to criticism. This was the view that slavery was a positive good and that it was the cornerstone of a prosperous South. In defense of this peculiar institution, the South drove out, silenced, or suppressed her critics . . . .[17]

Commager mentions that later on 'historians concluded that anti-abolitionists who back in the 1840s and 1850s subscribed to the "Higher Law" were lacking in loyalty'.[18] He employs this example to demonstrate the value of respecting criticism and diversity of opinions within a society if this is to progress. To strengthen this argument, he cites Benjamin Franklin: 'They, that can give up essential liberty to obtain a little temporary safety, deserve neither liberty nor safety.'[19]

In contrast, those in favour of loyalty programmes argued that 'complete toleration of undemocratic ideas and organizations is a luxury which the nation can no longer afford'.[20] In their view, democratic regimes must be prepared to regulate and curtail freedom of association and expression 'if it is clearly demonstrated that organizations and ideas aim (as Communist organizations and ideas were held to do) at the ultimate destruction of American democracy'.[21]

It was in this milieu that President Harry S. Truman issued Executive Order No. 9835 on 22 March 1947 setting up a federal loyalty programme. For many, that marked a period labelled 'the modern American Witch Hunt', in which the concern with loyalty often 'served as cover for an attack on civil liberties'.[22] Throughout the time that the federal government's employee loyalty programme was implemented, communists were barred from teaching. Truman's loyalty programme set up as one standard for employment and dismissal 'membership in, association with, or sympathetic affiliation with any . . . organization, movement, group or combination of persons, designated by the Attorney-General as . . . subversive'.[23] Those against loyalty programmes considered the so-called 'guilt by association' to be pernicious.

Immediately the confrontation among opposing views emerged. Leonard A. Nikoloric argued that, as stated by President Truman, the loyalty programme was not aimed at discharging employees expressly because of what they had done in the past but rather its aim was to identify the 'potentially disloyal persons' who, because of the attitudes and ideas they entertained at the time or had subscribed to in the past, 'might in the future undertake action contrary to the best interests of the USA'.[24] The intense disagreements between those in favour and those against the loyalty programme resulted in the Internal Security Act 'veto message' issued by President Truman in 1950.[25]

Commager argued that such a doctrine was pernicious in principle, in application and in its consequences since it was based on fear and suspicion, ignorance and bigotry, arrogance and vanity. He regarded this doctrine as destined to 'subvert vital parts of our democracy and of our constitutional system'.[26]

At the heart of this argument was the impact that the 'guilt by association' doctrine might have upon various types of associations and groups which had proved crucial in the development of the USA since the colonization era, when, significantly, the first government of the Thirteen American colonies was called 'The Association'. In the USA, churches remain private voluntary associations, and since the link between state and church was broken by the American Revolution, most crucial reforms, such as the abolition of slavery, the institution of women's rights, prison and penal reform, education, protection of Native Americans and civil rights, have been defended and carried out by associations of individuals. Associations continue to stand at the heart of US democracy.

In 1934, rising concerns about the expansion of communism in the USA, as well as in Europe, prompted a campaign to require a flag salute in American schools as part of a drive for 'patriotic conformity'. In that context, anxiety about loyalty, as well as about a clash of political loyalties, came to the fore and galvanized US public opinion. In 1947, the Board of Supervisors of Los Angeles, following the lead of President Truman, embraced a loyalty programme based on a test oath containing specific disavowals, 'in this case, the loyalty ordinance was clearly adopted as part of a drive for political conformity'.[27]

Nevertheless there were some exceptions: for instance, the Supreme Court of California decided in 1951 – after President Truman had issued the Internal Security Act 'veto message' in 1950 – that the requirement of a loyalty oath was unconstitutional. Court Judge Peek held taking the constitutional oath was sufficient proof of loyalty and that demands for further loyalty oaths would only undermine it.[28]

The argument that 'no loyal American could possibly object to making an affirmation of loyalty in which various foreign allegiances and "subversive" doctrines are repudiated' was defended as a response to those critical of the American government loyalty programme. However, as John C. Wahlke points out, checking on people's loyalty requires investigation and surveillance. 'It also implies disabilities and penalties other than sentences for perjury.' In his view, 'measures for testing loyalty are invariably developed outside the existing legal framework'.[29]

Scapegoating and dissent

Often the drive to set up loyalty programmes appears in periods defined by social, economic and political maladjustments. On other occasions, they spring out of a sense of insecurity within a particular political system. In both cases, rather than tackling its causes, it is possible to identify a tendency to suppress criticism and dissent; it is also quite common to turn a particular group into a scapegoat: that is, to be made to bear the blame for others. It should be noted that scapegoating seems to be a universal and perennial phenomenon sometimes stimulated by frustration. However, we should not confuse 'scapegoating' with 'heresy hunting', the latter being as a set of measures intended to identify those deemed to pose a threat to the nation.

The machinery of persecution without exception relies upon denunciation as a mechanism that emphasizes the power of accusers; however, every time some concerns about the truthfulness of informers comes into view. As informers become frightened of the consequences of their perjuries, their accusations become bolder and a culture of informers informing on informers emerges. This promotes a sense of fear, insecurity and lack of trust. Ordinary people are constantly urged to prove their loyalty through a system of symbolic actions, including participation in public ceremonies and other events aimed at confirming and reinforcing their allegiance to the political regime.

Whenever peace breaks up or a threat is perceived as serious and imminent, loyalty becomes a key issue and almost automatically it triggers the launch of loyalty campaigns. Consistently, loyalty campaigns feed society with fear and suspicion and, in so doing, they challenge the trust that fellow-citizens should be able to share; a sense of trust that is the backbone of cooperation and solidarity among them and that, once broken, it is exceedingly hard to restore.

Countries that have experienced authoritarian regimes, such as the former USSR,[30] China during the 'Cultural Revolution'[31] or Chile, Greece, Portugal and Spain, during periods of dictatorship, have vivid memories of the meaning of loyalty campaigns and the mechanisms created to identify, control and punish dissent.[32] While those regimes lasted, citizens became accustomed to living in fear and under a constant threat of denunciation. Their experience of living within a surveillance state, eager to identify and punish opposition – for its own sake but also as a deterrent for those who might be tempted to betray or challenge the regime – has marked their lives forever. Trust in their fellow-citizens was lost at some point in the past when their own society was divided between friends and foes. For them it has become extraordinarily hard adjusting to a free democratic society.

Freedom versus conformity

Commager argued that if some 'dangerous ideas' are to be silenced, then one must establish what ideas are safe. His approach appealed to Tocqueville's argument in *Democracy in America* that, in modern societies, legal censorship has been replaced by public opinion as the most effective instrument of control. His main concern was that the power of public opinion has the potential to produce a situation where independence and originality simply do not emerge, a society in which 'first-rate men and women will not and cannot work under conditions fixed by those who are afraid of ideas'.[33] Coherently following this principle, he stood against disloyalty tests and described them as 'futile in application'.[34] In his view, to impose loyalty as conformity was 'a confession of fear, a declaration of insolvency',[35] and he cited the USA's harsh treatment of Japanese Americans deemed as suspect of disloyalty in World War II. It should be noted that only two Japanese Americans were tried for treason after

World War II: Iva Toguri, known as 'Tokyo Rose', and Tomoya Kawakita.[36]

Commager stood up against the idea of loyalty as conformity, as passive acquiescence in the status quo, as a blind preference for everything American over everything foreign. Loyalty could never justify or involve ignorance of other countries and institutions. In a similar manner, he argued that loyalty should not be equated with the indulgence in ceremony – a flag salute, an oath of allegiance – and warned of the risk of judging loyalty by gestures and ceremonies rather than by conduct.[37]

He went even further to stress that loyalty did not designate a specific creed, a version of history, a body of economic practices and a particular philosophy. Instead, he defined loyalty as a tradition, an ideal and a principle.[38] He portrayed freedom in academia as a necessity, not in order to indulge error but as the only effective strategy to discover truth. Commager pointed out that if the system of freedom crucial to the US Constitution were to be weakened, then it would result in a society in which freedom of inquiry, criticism and originality would not flourish. 'For whatever may be the balance of military resources . . . there is one realm where our superiority is beyond challenge, and where it cannot be lost except by our own will. Ours is a system of freedom.'[39] He conceived democracy as intrinsically connected with freedom and regarded criticism and dissent as essential: '[I]f our democracy is to flourish it must have criticism, if our government is to function it must have dissent. Only totalitarian governments insist upon conformity and they – as we know – do so at their peril.'[40]

Arthur M. Schlesinger Jr shares this view. For him, 'Americanism is not a totalitarian faith, which can impose a single economic or political dogma or require a uniformity in observance from all its devotees.' A democratic society is invariably formed by a multiplicity of groups to which individuals belong and to which they are loyal. Shared loyalties are the building blocks of community, and freedom must entail the 'right to choose and act for oneself, it means absence of compulsion . . . for where compulsion begins, responsibility ends'.[41]

At present, one of the main challenges faced by modern societies is how to construct an environment of toleration and acceptance of the internal diversity of beliefs and loyalties coexisting within their borders. The coexistence of different groups entails some competition among them with the aim of attaining the loyalty of free citizens. It is precisely this political framework that fosters democracy and freedom itself, since while competing for citizens' loyalty no group can afford the stigma of being labelled as undemocratic or authoritarian.

'Authoritarian' versus 'democratic' loyalty

The authoritarian view of loyalty regards it as conformity, as obedient service characterized by unreflective acceptance of principles, orders and values, which often include the threat of punishment if these are either questioned or challenged. It absolves the individual from personal responsibility for actions performed in the service of political superiors: for instance, when soldiers, in a context of war, decline responsibility for their actions by claiming that they are following their superiors' orders. It is understood that in such cases it is the 'superiors' who take up responsibility and not the soldiers following orders. However, recently some instances have emerged in which the lack of responsibility of some soldiers carrying out orders that clearly infringe human rights has been challenged in court.[42]

'Authoritarian loyalty' is generally presented in terms of reverence for a particular narrative, the preservation of the status quo and the defence of traditionalism. As John H. Schaar writes, '[I]ntrinsic to the authoritarian conception is a belief that the object of loyalty is full and entire in itself, a finished product that cannot be improved and that must not be bared to critical examination'.[43]

In contrast, 'democratic loyalty' is a dynamic principle defined by a 'voluntary and wholehearted devotion to the best interests of the object of loyal attachment'.[44] As such, it tolerates critical examination of political authority with the aim to better it. The object of loyalty is no longer regarded as complete, perfect and unquestionable, as in authoritarian forms of loyalty, but as open to questioning and change. Democracy is considered as a dialogical process and there is no blind acceptance of the status quo, nor is there unreflective adulation or automatic participation in ceremony. Loyalty emerges out of a personal choice, and, as such, it implies responsibility and commitment on behalf of the citizen. Liberal democracy seeks to embody it when assuming that 'its own superiority may be established through open inquiry into its own principles and practices',[45] rather than through blind obedience and conformity.

The argument for the superiority of democracy rests upon the conviction of citizens that 'the democratic way is worthy of devotion because, in the light of intelligence, it is superior to its rivals'.[46] As a political ideology and as a principle of government, liberal democracy affirms the inherent value of human personality, its authority is based upon consent, and it defends equality of rights and equality before the law as well as majority rule. It also encourages diversity of association.

Of course, such a definition could be interpreted as a recipe for practical and moral conflict between individual liberty and group authority, echoing the debate between individual and collective rights. For instance, how to discuss ethical questions without a shared system of values? This is an issue which brings to the fore a crucial challenge facing liberal-democratic societies in today's world. A diversity of political ideas, a multiplicity of religious and ethical conceptions and varying definitions of democracy and social justice have fostered different, and sometimes radically opposing, loyalties. As a result, significant questions and conflicts about how to manage diversity within the modern nation-state have emerged. For example, should individual loyalties be allowed full expression, even at the risk of injury to collective unity? Can the nation-state require loyalty from those who do not accept its tenets and who refuse to give their consent to the democratic system? These are major dilemmas that become emboldened whenever individuals are forced to choose between two loyalties.

To those questions, Schaar concludes:

> Just as the person who has consented to the system of democratic authority cannot morally be compelled by that authority, so also does he himself lack any moral basis from which to impose his own demands upon the state. In short, where voluntary consent is lacking, relations between state and citizen are essentially relations of war in which both sides use stratagems and implements of battle, and in which either may or may not grant quarter to overpowered opponents.[47]

This resonates with Thomas Jefferson's Declaration of 1776,[48] arguing that 'faith and loyalty are owing only to a government founded on contract and consent and working for the common interest', in what became to be regarded as an influential theory of loyalty challenging the ancient English notions while building 'anew on consent rather than tradition, on individual judgment rather than forced conformance'.[49] However, this novel conception of loyalty founded upon consent and individual judgement, was already being questioned in the 1950s. Schaar illustrates this point by referring to the Supreme Court's shift in opinion when considering *Dennis* v. *United States*:

> It appears that the right of revolution, the core of the early American conception of loyalty, and once official doctrine of the land, is now repudiated by the Court on the argument that the existing order provides techniques of peaceful change and is therefore justified in adopting measures for its own defense against projected violence. Note the following quotation from a recent case: 'Whatever theoretical merit there may be to the argument that there is a "right" to rebellion against dictatorial government is without force where the existing structure of the government provides for peaceful and orderly change. We reject any principle of governmental helplessness in the face of preparation for revolution which, carried to its logical conclusion, must lead to anarchy. No one could conceive that it is not within the power of government to prohibit acts intended to overthrow the Government by force and violence' (*Dennis* v. *United States*, 341 U.S. 501 (1950)).[50]

In the 1950s, the USA experienced an important shift from freedom to security, thus initiating a trend which gained unprecedented support in Western societies after the 9/11 terrorist attacks in New York and Washington. Since then, awareness of new global risks, such as the threat of terrorism posed by some forms of 'Islamic fundamentalism', global pandemics, climate change and organized mafia, among others, has become potent and widespread.

Currently the omnipresence of what are described as 'uncontrollable threats' has exacerbated the desire for security: that is, the need to build a safe environment within which the individual feels protected. Many individuals feel the urge to belong, the need to become members of a community within which they matter and feel safe; a community from whom they expect to receive support and within which they will be granted certain rights in exchange for their commitment and loyalty; a community entrusted to distinct values and objectives which individuals are prepared to endorse.

At present, the nation is the most potent community able to provide a sense of security and welfare in return for loyalty. This takes place at a time when the nation-state is recasting its nature under the pressure of global forces, including the proliferation of novel mechanisms and actors of global governance. In this unprecedented context, individual freedom is often exchanged for security and the pressure to conform.

The great challenge: turning immigrants into Americans

The USA has an impressive track record regarding the integration and, in some cases, the assimilation of immigrants from a wide range of backgrounds. Table 6.1 reflects the diversity of their origins.

One of the key challenges facing the nation-state is how to transform immigrants into loyal citizens. In the first instance, becoming a citizen refers to the legal bureaucratic process leading to the adoption of citizenship; however, it is not limited to it. Often, a passport is viewed as an entrance card to a specific labour market, be it the USA or the EU, to mention only two examples. The

Table 6.1 Legal permanent resident flow (%) by region of birth: fiscal years 2009 to 2011

Region	2009	2010	2011
Africa	11.2	9.7	9.5
Asia	36.5	40.5	42.5
Europe	9.3	8.5	7.9
North America	33.2	32.3	31.4
Caribbean	12.9	13.4	12.6
Central America	4.2	4.2	4.1
Other	16.0	14.6	14.7
Oceania	0.5	0.5	0.5
South America	9.1	8.4	8.1
Unknown	0.1	0.1	0.1

Source: Randall Monger and James Yankay, 'US Legal Permanent Residents: 2011', Annual Flow Report, April 2012, Table 3 (Office of Immigration Statistics, Policy Directorate, US Department of Homeland Security) (http://www.dhs.gov/xlibrary/assets/statistics/publications/lpr_fr_2011.pdf, accessed 20 February 2013).

greatest of challenges for the host nation consists of earning the loyalty of newcomers by awakening their desire to identify with their new home nation and to become full members of the political community while maintaining their own cultural roots and a sense of pride binding them to their community of origin.

This requires a difficult and long process, which depends on the political culture and the attitudes of the host society towards immigrants as much as on the immigrants' own readiness to respect and learn the language and culture of the host nation, to value and show consideration for its institutions and laws. Access to education is the major source in the socialization of immigrants into a new society and generally integration takes place in the second or third generation.

The loyalty of immigrants cannot be fostered when the conditions that nourish it are absent. A weak sense of community and a strong emphasis on difference based upon ethnic, social, religious or other attributes invoked as arguments to justify discrimination, together with excessive levels of inequality, represent major obstacles in the integration of immigrants. Inability to access the labour market will cause frustration and *ressentiment*. To attract its citizens' loyalty, the nation-state offers them a shared sense of national identity based upon its distinct culture, language and history, the beauty and the symbolic content of its territory. A democratic nation-state is also able to offer a political system where human rights, freedom, social justice and diversity are respected and promoted.

Loyal behaviour may be forced upon some individuals; however, this is likely to be short-lived and would certainly not stand the passing of time. Once those imposing loyalty become weaker, individuals will exit in search of new attachments – if possible – of their own choice. To many people it may sound old-fashioned to speak of loyalty; modern societies and their emphasis on individuality have fostered an environment within which few have ever had a personal experience of genuine loyalty. The long-term commitment, the altruism, the solidarity, the readiness to sacrifice one's own interests for a higher aim and the faithfulness associated with loyalty do not prevail.

On the contrary, today individuals prepared to shift and change allegiances are described as flexible and ready to adapt to an ever-changing marketplace and working environment. People are not educated and socialized to invest too much in others and a certain degree of doubt is built into all types of relationship, probably as a self-protection mechanism. This makes trust much more difficult to achieve and, as a consequence, the bonds of community become weaker and instrumentality comes to the fore. In this atmosphere, loyalty is seldom praised and rarely spoken about and it is easier for individuals to fall prey to populist doctrines offering a clear-cut view of the world with well-defined enemies and friends, with readily available responses to their questions, with a promise of security and, above all, with the authoritarian populist's commitment to grant preference to those who belong; all in exchange for renouncing freedom. The tragedy of modern societies is to have attained an unimaginable degree of freedom – when compared with that experienced by previous generations – just in time to give it up in exchange for scant promises of security and relative comfort.

Summary

This chapter has established a clear-cut distinction between 'authoritarian loyalty', as a type of loyalty emerging from coercion; 'loyalty by choice', as the outcome of a free personal decision that impacts upon the individual's self-identity; and 'instrumental loyalty', as a temporary commitment to a specific cause generally regarded as an investment, as a strategy for self-profit. 'Authoritarian loyalty' refers to those situations in which the individual is forced to obey and show loyalty to a cause or leader. In contrast, 'loyalty by choice' is the outcome of free will and it implies personal responsibility and commitment. 'Instrumental loyalty', in turn, responds to the individual's self-interest and is conditional on it providing expected rewards.

One of the most potent triggers of loyalty is a strong sense of belonging to the nation as the 'emotional' community able to muster the highest levels of loyalty and energy from its members through nationalist mobilization. Shared loyalties provide a solid foundation for the constitution of nations and groups endowed with a common sense of solidarity. While the market defends its internally generated rationality at the expense of depreciating emotion, the nation relies on the emotional attachment of its citizens as a source of their loyalty, solidarity and readiness to self-sacrifice. Nationalism is a political ideology defending the right of nations to decide upon their political destiny; it is also a sentiment of love and identification with the nation as a community with a shared name, culture, history, territory and fate. However, at present, the nation cannot assume that all its citizens will be loyal and engage in its defence, if this was ever the case. Different political allegiances coexist and compete within a single nation and a renewed emphasis on the benefits of sharing a common national identity often comes to the fore.

Loyalty is tested in wartime. During the Cold War and in the wake of the prosecution and conviction of communist sympathizers in the USA, a debate considering the meaning of both loyalty and disloyalty generated passionate opposing views. For instance, some stood up against the idea of loyalty as conformity while denouncing the way in which the concern with loyalty often served as a cover for an attack on civil liberties. Whether to support loyalty campaigns or not became a dividing issue, which translated into the debate about whether freedom or conformity should prevail.

We shall now move on in the final chapter to explore the relevance of emotions as a trigger for political mobilization. In so doing, we shall examine the relationship between emotion and social action.

7

Emotion and Political Mobilization

So far, the role of emotions in face-to-face interaction has received considerable attention, while its significance in large-scale or macroscopic social processes has been largely neglected. This chapter studies the role of emotions in selected processes of political mobilization, thus opening up a novel avenue to the study of social movements and complementing other approaches. The originality of the argument advanced here resides in the assertion that the emotional dimension of belonging not only functions as a trigger of social action – including political mobilization – but also plays a major role in the way in which actions are evaluated by individuals and groups. This is not to assume that emotions are either the 'only', the 'most important' or the 'indispensable' trigger for any type of political mobilization. Instead, I argue that emotions have the power to modify, transform and change the ways in which circumstances, actions and objectives are evaluated by individuals and groups, thus affecting their disposition to act.

Emotion and social action

Belonging includes an emotional component; it implies a certain degree of commitment and identification with the group's objectives, ideals, practices and categorization of other individuals and groups as both 'friends' and 'enemies'. Those who belong to a group tend to emphasize its positive qualities while excluding negative information and experiences capable of distorting an optimistic image. In this context, fellow-members are considered superior to outsiders, and their qualities are almost routinely exaggerated, although the tendency to in-group competition-fighting as well as the creation of internal factions and sub-groups should not be underestimated.

Generally, group members tend to adopt a favourable view of fellow-members and to be more lenient when judging their faults, mistakes and crimes. This tendency to understand, explain and justify the deeds of fellow-members stands in stark contrast with a harsher attitude displayed when judging the deeds of 'outsiders'. Ruth Wodak has argued that the discursive construction of 'in-groups' and 'out-groups' often involves positive 'self' and negative 'other' presentations which tend to be employed as a justification and legitimation of exclusionary practices.[1]

For instance, members of political party A tend to feel committed to their party and are prone to overlooking or even undermining the importance of some questionable political behaviour which they would be criticizing if performed by a rival party member. On some occasions, accusations of impropriety on behalf of some political leaders regarding the abuse of some prerogatives – for example, using an official car to attend personal engagements – may be overlooked when it concerns one's own party leaders, while being actively denounced and highlighted as an abuse of authority and taxpayers' trust if performed by politicians of another party. In both cases, the party member is bound to express his or her feelings and, generally, these are strongly influenced by whether the individual is a member of that group or not. One's own standing as a 'member' of or as an 'outsider' to the group in question contributes to the emergence of differing views when assessing discourses and practices.

Emotions are intrinsic to social and political attachments and, as such, are essential to an understanding of belonging. However, this does not mean that all behaviour is determined by emotions. Rather, as Thomas Scheff has argued, it shows that emotions, like perception and cognition, are present in most behaviour while highlighting the relevance of 'non-verbal behaviour'.[2]

Emotions are central in social structure and social processes; even so, they are often neglected or studied as a negative and disruptive element capable of blinding actors to the advancement of reason and rationality. This approach prevails in the social sciences and has resulted in the emphasis being placed upon cognitive and behavioural approaches which favour beliefs, casting away emotions, considered disruptive of dispassionate/rational social action. For example, Talcott Parsons referred to 'strains [which may] eventuate in deviant motivation' as an endemic force present in social systems.[3] He considered them unavoidable and impossible to eliminate, though containable.[4]

Advanced societies confine or suppress emotions by often expelling them from secondary institutions while being allowed free expression in primary institutions of society such as the family and friendships. Social order is constructed out of a delicate balance between deviance and control. In my view, this interpretation highlights the connection between emotions and the sentiments and values – rational or not – regarded as the guiding principles of a given society or group.

From a constructionist perspective, emotions are described rather than explained. They are presented as a consequence of other forces and their capacity for influencing social processes is neglected, if not implicitly denied. J.M. Barbalet observes that emotions are almost invariably qualified as a negative force, as an attitude that openly neglects the study of 'socially efficacious emotions', which are likely to be experienced below the threshold of awareness. He writes:

> In our day-to-day experiences, therefore, we tend to ignore those emotions, which the prevailing cultural conventions do not designate as 'emotions'. The constructionist approach cannot assist us in uncovering those emotions which are crucial to social processes, such as implicit trust or bypassed shame, when they are not given social representation in the prevailing culture, along with love and hate, for instance, as emotions.[5]

Emotions should not be treated as a cultural phenomenon, although it is true that the time-frames of emotional experiences and the manner in which they are conceptualized and expressed are influenced by culture. As pointed by Barbalet: 'Before anything else, emotions must be understood within the structural relations of power and status which elicit them. ... [T]his discussion is not to deny the cultural aspects of emotion but to reassert its non-cultural basis.'[6] He understands them as 'a necessary link between social structure and social actor'; as a phenomenon provoked by circumstances and experienced as a transformation of dispositions to act.[7]

Emotion and the rational imperatives of market capitalism

The effort to establish a clear-cut distinction between rational and emotional behaviour became predominant during the Enlightenment, even though our contemporary focus on rationality and the effort to erase emotion as a potentially distracting and dangerous force tends to neglect that philosophers such as David Hume – and psychologist William James over a century later – offered a much more nuanced view of human nature that acknowledged the relevance of both reason and passion. Hume in his *A Treatise of Human Nature* (1739–40) stressed the importance of feelings, rather than abstract moral principles, as a base for ethics. He argued that 'reason alone can never be a motive to any action of the will . . . reason alone can never oppose passion in the direction of the will'.[8] This is why, in his view, reason is, and ought only to be, the slave of the passions. Hume pointed to the role of passion in directing action and claimed that reason alone 'can never immediately present or produce any action by contradicting or approving of it'.[9] He maintained that actions are emotionally motivated and executed by means selected with and applied through reason. This assertion contrasts with Max Weber's idea that spontaneous and impulsive forces, which distract a person from his or her purposes, create 'disorder' in human affairs.[10]

William James in his essay 'The Sentiment of Rationality' (1897) also exposes a much more integrated view of human nature, implying that reason and emotion are not opposed phenomena. He argues that intellect, will, taste and passion necessarily support each other.[11] Cooperation with others is based upon trust, and trust is therefore essential in social relations; these ideas presage their future development by Richard Sennett (cooperation) and Niklas Luhmann (trust).

As Luhmann points out,[12] the decision to trust relies on faith or belief. It is only in the future that the outcome of a commitment to trust can be assessed by whether trust has been honoured or broken. Luhmann acknowledges the emotional nature of trust, and it is precisely as an emotion which overcomes the uncertainty of the future that trust is rational. He writes: '[T]o show trust is to anticipate the future. It is to behave as though the future were certain. . . . [T]his problem of time is bridged by trust, paid ahead of time as an advance on success.'[13]

Yet there is a clear contrast between the terrain of trust – as an emotion compelling to action – and the rational imperatives of market capitalism together with the distinct emotional pattern that the market promotes, including the 'thrills and dangers' associated with it. In his work, Georg Simmel, writing at the turn of the twentieth century, highlights the increasing dependence of modern individuals upon others who are completely alien to them; it is almost shocking to realize the degree of trust in the honesty of the alien other that pervades modern societies. As the market economy becomes more complex and our dependence on scientific knowledge guides our decisions, we 'presuppose the confidence that we will not be betrayed'.[14]

Individuals, to protect themselves emotionally from the intense pressure associated with rational calculability and exactness, adopt what Simmel refers to as the 'blasé' outlook: that is, an attitude that pretends to be free from emotion. Simmel notes that the instrumental nature of market capitalism has displaced emotion as a motivating force; however, in my view, 'to displace' is not the same as 'to eliminate'.[15]

Modern society is the product of constant collaboration and trust among individuals who often do not know each other and who have very few, if any, reasons to trust each other. In spite of that, they pull forces to run a complex web of relationships resulting in a high degree of interdependence. This provides a robust argument to reinforce the thesis defended in this book that solidarity prevails over division; the readiness of individuals to collaborate and trust each other – as an indispensable foundation of modern society – proves it.

At this point, it is relevant to offer a clear-cut definition of three key concepts associated with the expansion of democracy and the consolidation of the nation-state that were crucial to the development of a novel political framework allowing for the emergence of social movements. These are the 'state', the 'nation' and the 'nation-state'. By 'state', taking Max Weber's definition, I refer to 'a human community that (successfully) claims the monopoly of the legitimate use of physical force within a given territory',[16] although not all states have successfully accomplished this, and some of them have not even aspired to accomplish it. By 'nation', I refer to a group conscious of forming a community, sharing a common culture, attached to a clearly demarcated territory, having a common past and a common project for the future and claiming the right to rule itself.[17] This definition attributes five dimensions to the nation: psychological (consciousness of forming a group), cultural, territorial, historical and political. The nation-state is a modern institution characterized by the formation of a kind of state which has the monopoly of what it claims to be the legitimate use of force within its borders and seeks to unite the people subject to its rule by means of cultural and linguistic homogenization.[18]

Liberal democracies appeal to the nation as a source of political legitimacy for the state. To be or not to be recognized as a nation entails different rights for the community which claims to be one. Moreover, defining a specific community as a nation involves the more or less explicit acceptance of the legitimacy of the state which claims to represent it, or if the nation does not possess a state of its own, it then implicitly acknowledges the nation's right to decide upon its political future comprising some degree of political autonomy, which may or may not lead to a claim for independence.

In her work, Agnes Heller has focused upon the transformations experienced by the meaning of emotions under the force of market conditions. She posits a distinction between the domain of the market, associated with instrumental rationality, and the domain of the family, defined by its emotional 'inwardness'. While both domains may coexist within a single individual, there is an institutional basis for one or the other domain to predominate.

Heller's analysis moves beyond conventional accounts establishing that reason suppresses emotion; instead she focuses upon the transformations suffered by the meaning of emotions in market society. In her own words: '[E]motions do function in rational processes but are seldom acknowledged to be emotions (we tend to see them becoming attitudes); and . . . the emotions which are acknowledged as such constitute a limited range of emotions (only certain emotions are regarded as emotions).'[19] As Barbalet points out, instrumentalism always relies on under-conceptualized emotions, citing that, for instance, 'the instrumental rationality of market competition cannot function without emotions, which are background to the impersonal pursuit of commodities, and as a background these are simply assumed, taken for granted and unacknowledged. And, if acknowledged, they are not regarded as emotions.'[20] According to Heller, before the full development of capitalism, a much larger range of feelings associated with emotions was available. For instance, Adam Smith, who had read Hume's *Treatise on Human Nature*, argued that 'moral sentiments' determine the way in which we evaluate an action as right or wrong. Smith refers to 'sympathizing' as our capacity to 'feel with' someone else: that is, to understand or not the motives prompting a person to act in a certain way.[21] Alexis de Tocqueville examined the 'intense passions' animating public life and defending liberty in France and America:

> I think democratic peoples have a natural taste for liberty; left to themselves, they will seek it, cherish it, and be sad if it is taken from them. But their passion for equality is ardent, insatiable, eternal, and invincible. They want equality in freedom, and if they cannot have that, they still want equality in slavery. They will put up with poverty, servitude, and barbarism, but they will not endure aristocracy.
>
> This is true at all times, but especially in our own. All men and all powers who try to stand up against this irresistible passion will be overthrown and destroyed by it. In our day freedom cannot be established without it, and despotism itself cannot reign without its support.[22]

Market society permits individuals to create their own inner life but not without imposing certain conditions. Crucially, market society limits the range of instruments available to individuals willing to create their own inner life by restricting them to the institutional and cultural resources available; all of those have been previously shaped by the priorities of the larger social system. In this context, reason narrowed to market rationality is matched by emotions of isolated subjectivity. The forms of alienated emotions found in capitalist society are described by Heller as 'the inner life of feeling "wrapped in itself" that turns its back to the tasks of the world . . . the unfettered exercise of egoist passions . . . false sentimentality or sentimental convention'.[23] In what she refers to as 'the bourgeois era', the contradiction between reason and emotion also appears in the division of labour between the sexes: male rationality versus female nurturing emotions.

In modern societies there is evidence of a clash between the rational and instrumental needs of market capitalism and the aims of one of the most powerful agents of political mobilization: that is, the emotional power of belonging to the nation as a 'political community of choice'. While the market requires calculative thinking, and a restraint or displacement of emotions, modern liberal democracies cannot survive without the legitimacy emanating from the consent of their citizenry. The latter entails the support of a people sharing a sense of common identity and belonging to the same nation. To be effective, a sense of belonging should accomplish two conditions: to be shared by a substantial part of the population and to be capable of instilling loyalty towards the nation as well as feelings of solidarity towards fellow-citizens. I regard these as indispensable attributes to fostering a sense of community and necessary to construct a cultural basis for the nation-state.

This does not mean that everyone experiences a sense of belonging in a similar manner, or focuses his or her feelings of attachment upon the same elements or with the same intensity; however, it assumes that a sense of common purpose involving a shared fate generates an emotional bond among fellow-citizens. Sharing a sense of belonging does not imply a homogeneous citizenry, since a certain degree of difference remains a constant.

Currently, most Western liberal democracies are multinational and/or multi-ethnic and contain some groups that regard themselves as alien and detached from both the nation and the state because of choice, exclusion or marginalization, or for economic, social, religious or political reasons. Whenever the proportion of alienated people within a nation-state grows and turns into what I call a 'significant group' – that is, a sizeable number of citizens ready to act as a political actor – the legitimacy of the nation-state is questioned and its sense of community, social cohesion and ability to build a common future is fundamentally challenged.

In such situations, a democratic nation-state is expected to react by seeking some kind of accommodation of internal differences through the building of democratic inclusive political institutions and also by engaging in dialogue and responding to the demands of the 'significant group'. But in some cases, the nation-state may decide to ignore, undermine and even criminalize the 'opposition' movement. All will depend on the level of popular support obtained by the 'significant group', and the willingness to negotiate and reach a peaceful agreement on both parts. Of course, geopolitical and strategic reasons connected with the interests of the international community will have to be taken into consideration and are bound to play an important role in the final outcome.

To survive and prove its legitimacy, according to democratic credentials, the nation-state engages in nation-building strategies destined to foster a sense of belonging and loyalty among its citizens. The construction of national identity fulfils this particular task through the implementation of a set of strategies, the most important of which are the following:

- The creation and dissemination of a certain image of the 'nation'.
- The manufacture and spread of a set of symbols and rituals charged with the mission of reinforcing a sense of community among citizens.
- The advancement of citizenship, involving a well-defined set of civil and legal rights, political rights and duties, as well as socio-economic rights. By conferring rights upon its members, the nation-state facilitates the rise of sentiments of loyalty towards itself. It also establishes a crucial distinction between those included and those excluded: that is, between those entitled to citizenship rights and those deprived of them within the boundaries of the nation-state.
- The construction of common enemies. For example, the prosecution of war has proven vital to the emergence and consolidation of a sense of community among citizens united against an external threat, be it imminent, potential or invented.
- The progressive consolidation of national education and media systems as key instruments in the dissemination of a particular 'image of the nation', with its symbols and rituals, values, principles, traditions and ways of life, and common enemies, and, more crucially, a definition of a 'good citizen'.[24]

'Taming' emotion and the construction of 'healing spaces'

In Western liberal democracies, the social dimension of emotion is often neglected, although it plays a fundamental part in public collective gatherings. Emotion is primarily considered as a matter restricted to the private domain. Nevertheless, certain emotions such as grief or joy are allowed free expression within designated public spaces where some ceremonies and rituals break the monopoly of reason prevailing outside.

For instance, public displays of grief are embedded within certain pre-established rituals, such as funerals and remembrance ceremonies, which acquire different patterns according to the culture and society within which they take place. The framing of emotional displays within collective rituals has the ability to tame emotions by controlling their expression, so that, after participation in the ritual, the individual feels released from the original tension and emotional distress or joy. Participation in ritual provides an occasion to express and share emotions; in addition, the cleansing quality of ritual acts as an effective mechanism capable of washing away strong emotions challenging the individual's psychological wellbeing.

In modern societies, it is accepted that individuals will offer a generally restrained public display of emotions expressing their sadness, vulnerability, isolation and loneliness when confronted with the death of a loved one. Yet, while such displays are considered normal within the framework of rituals and ceremonies of mourning, a similar behaviour would be regarded as a sign of depression or as reflecting some abnormality of character if performed outside the social framework constructed to express grief. Public ceremonies and rituals circumscribe expressions of grief in space and time. They also establish generally unwritten rules about the nature, intensity, duration, spaces, symbols as well as the personal and social behaviour associated with the public expression of emotions. In doing so, they fix the boundaries of what is to be expected as a 'proper' expression of grief, and this varies according to different cultures.

In a similar manner, expressions of joy have also become tamed. Society invents the ceremonies and designates the spaces destined to host public displays of joy, ranging from quasi-private rituals and ceremonies, such as the celebration of a newborn baby, a marriage or the completion of a university degree, to public ceremonies, many of which celebrate the nation's success. Among the latter are the welcoming of a victorious sports team, the winning of a war and the achievement of national independence. Cases in point are the warm welcome for British athletes (Team GB) after the London Olympics in 2012 and for the Spanish football team after their World Cup victory in 2010, the jubilation that greeted the end of World War II in allied countries in 1945, and both the 4 July annual commemoration of the Declaration of Independence of the USA (1776) as well as the celebrations linked to the independence of Kosovo in 2008 and of the Czech Republic in 1993.

The construction of rituals and ceremonies to channel emotions of grief and joy obeys the need to establish some public areas within which certain emotions can be displayed and dealt with. By 'healing spaces', I refer to sites within which individuals are permitted, and sometimes even encouraged, to free themselves from the constraints of rationally calculated behaviour and allowed to loosen up, even if only for a limited period of time. Those who cross the limits may be considered ill and in need of healing, abnormal, weak, mad or unstable; the assessment will depend on the parameters utilized by those having the power to set up the rules.

The institutional effort to hide uncontrolled displays of emotions in Western liberal democracies points to the resolution to maintain order. The innovative character of my argument highlights that, so far, the public display of domesticated emotions has neglected their important role in acting both as a trigger for political action and as the invisible cement indispensable in the construction of social and political attachments.

Emotion and political mobilization

In our societies we encounter numerous examples signalling the persistent strength of emotion to initiate political action insofar as it is able to transform the ways in which we assess, judge and evaluate different scenarios: for instance, emotion is crucial to how we evaluate risk. Emotion has the ability to transform the manner we feel about people, specific projects and ideas, objects, actions, circumstances and even the way we feel about ourselves. That is, emotion has the capacity to 'move', and being moved implies that a person is acting under the influence of feelings and sentiments, which have the power to displace or weaken the strength of rational thinking.

Here I am not assessing the ethical or moral content of emotions, I am only stressing their ability to *modify, trigger or stop our disposition to act in specific circumstances*. In a similar manner, I am not arguing that emotion is the only, the main or the indispensable trigger for political mobilization. I also acknowledge that emotions are often tempered by rational arguments involving a varying degree of calculability into the consequences of our actions; this depends on the individual in question, the specific circumstances he or she is faced with and the intensity with which these are felt.

Emotional versus rational arguments: an example

In August 2011, news emerged of the deal on raising the debt ceiling agreed between US Democrat President Barack Obama and the Republicans; a deal that would avoid a US default. At the time it was unclear whether credit ratings agencies would consider this deal as improving the USA's fiscal position, thus avoiding a downgrade of the nation's triple-A sovereign debt rating.

Undoubtedly, rational arguments – the need to avoid a US default – placed tremendous weight on the shoulders of both Democrats and Republicans and compelled them to reach an agreement. But surely the possibility of a US default generated potent emotional arguments too, concerning how this could challenge the USA's status as a world leader, its citizens' pride at 'being American' and the assessment of President Obama and his government.

An eventual default could have triggered feelings of shame and anger among the citizenry but also feed some further resentment against credit ratings agencies. In that environment, new unknown enemies of America might have come to the fore or be constructed to remove attention from economic matters. It could also strongly influence the way in which political leaders would be regarded by citizens while further undermining the current lack of trust in politicians and the political system alike, not to mention the massive blow that would have been inflicted against liberal democracy. The reasons for avoiding an American default were unquestionably rational; however, it is undeniable that potent emotional arguments also played a crucial part in the decision to avoid it. In early 2013, the renewed battle over raising the nation's borrowing limit again came to the fore as President Obama clashed with the Republicans while the same mixture of rational and emotional arguments were discussed and analysed. This example confirms my point that emotions, even if unrecognized as such, play a fundamental role in politics.

Pre-modern political mobilization: the Revolt of the Catalans, 1640

Pre-modern forms of political mobilization focused on public displays of protest or opposition. According to Charles Tilly, pre-modern popular protest was *parochial*, that is, local; *particular*, in the sense of addressing very specific and pressing issues such as food shortages and what were regarded as unjust situations and events; and *bifurcated*, in a context in which there was a clear distinction between local and national issues within which claims were addressed to local authorities.[25] Hank Johnston argues that 'the pre-modern protest repertoire was local in focus, limited in duration, and often quite dramatic in how it took direct action about grievances and claims'.[26]

I shall now examine one of the early examples of political mobilization, the so-called 'Revolt of the Reapers' (*Revolta dels Segadors*), which took place in Catalonia in 1640 and was prompted by a combination of rational and emotional factors.[27] The Catalan Revolution has a wider relevance since it illustrates the struggle between the centralizing aspirations of monarchs and the traditional and zealously defended rights and liberties of their subjects – most of them living within smaller and autonomous political units such as the Principality of Catalonia. This was a trend that was ranging all over sixteenth- and seventeenth-century Europe, and which prompted the emergence of the absolutist state.

The independence of Catalonia, or, more accurately, of the House of Barcelona, was first recognized by a French monarch in 1258 when James I the Conqueror and Louis IX signed the

Treaty of Corbeil. By this treaty, Louis IX of France renounced claims to the counties of Roussillon and Barcelona, while James I of Aragon gave up his aspirations to the fiefs of the viscounties of Carcassonne and Narbonne, thus reducing Catalan dominion north of the Roussillon.

The union of Catalonia and Aragon in 1137 was the result of a pact allowing both parties to maintain their separate political identities: that is, their territorial integrity, laws, habits, institutions and rulers. The Counts of Barcelona – rulers of Catalonia – became kings of Aragon, and from this moment onwards the historiography refers to their possessions as the Crown of Aragon.[28] During the thirteenth and fourteenth centuries, Catalonia built up a powerful Mediterranean empire of a primarily commercial character. It included Valencia, Majorca, Sardinia, Corsica, Sicily, Naples, Athens and Neopatria, as well as French territories beyond the Pyrenees, particularly Roussillon and Cerdagne. When Martin the Humane died without a successor in 1410, Fernando de Antequera, from the Castilian family of the Trastámara, was elected to the throne (Compromise of Casp, 1412) and confirmed the pactist character of the Catalan Principality. However, the joint rule of Isabel, queen of Castile, and Fernando, king of Aragon, over their territories from 1479 placed two very different nations under the same monarchs. As J.H. Elliott argues, the gulf between the two was made still wider by their differing political traditions and institutions. Yet while the Castilian courts had never attained legislative power and emerged from the Middle Ages as isolated and weak, those of Catalonia, Valencia and Aragon (the component parts of the Crown of Aragon) shared the legislative power with the Crown and were well buttressed by laws and institutions which derived from a long tradition of political liberty.[29]

In practice, the equality between Castile and the Crown of Aragon did not long survive the death of King Fernando and a gap began to widen between Castile and all the other territories, including the states of the Crown of Aragon. A radical change in Castilian policy towards Catalonia took place when Felipe IV appointed the Count Duke of Olivares as chief minister in March 1621. His objective was to create a powerful absolutist state. Clashes between Catalan and Castilian culture and institutions intensified when Felipe IV, in need of fiscal revenues to cover extensive debt generated by his military campaigns, extended centralized control.

The increasing tension between Castile and Catalonia reached its climax in 1640 with the Revolt of the Reapers, which would acquire a particular significance in the Catalan nationalist literature. Scholars of Catalan history argue that, at this early date, the Catalans led what can be described as one of the first nationalist revolutions in Europe. The Revolt of the Reapers stands up as an example of political mobilization against what was regarded as an unfair treatment of a people by its rulers.

The Catalans united against Castile's conduct, emphasized their difference from Castilians and stressed their Catalan identity associated with a sense of belonging to a particular territory. If they did not object to the figure of Felipe IV as their king, they demanded that he had to acknowledge and respect Catalan institutions, law and customs, since monarchy had a pactist character.[30] At the time, a distinctive sense of Catalan identity was strongly connected to the existence of a Catalan Code of Civil Law. Catalonia was being treated as an outsider by Castile – except when its financial contributions were demanded – as illustrated by the Castilians' decision to exclude Catalan merchants from taking part in the lucrative trade with America.[31]

This case-study identifies a mixture of rational and emotional factors acting as a trigger for the Revolution of the Reapers. Political and economic arguments were employed to show that Catalonia was unjustly treated by Castile, among them: the Castilians' unilateral violation of the agreement based upon the equality between Catalonia and Castile; the specific policies of Count Duke of Olivares towards the Catalan Principality; and the high financial demands placed on the Catalan people.[32] Notably, discontent was not restricted to modest Catalan citizens but also pervaded the Catalan elites; a feature which reinforced the idea that those incipient nationalist grievances were fostering political mobilization cutting across social boundaries. Elliott writes:

> Twenty-five years before, when anarchy threatened as a result of the activities of the bandits, the [Catalan] ruling class had rallied around Alburquerque [representative of the Spanish Crown], even though this meant an increase in royal authority in the Principality, and a corresponding diminution of the country's traditional liber-

ties. In 1640, when anarchy actually came, the ruling class was not inclined to accept a comparable reassertion of royal authority as the cure for its ills. This striking difference between the attitude of the Catalan oligarchy in 1615 and 1640 is a measure of the extent to which the policies of the government in Madrid during the intervening period had succeeded in alienating the Catalan ruling class from the Court of Spain.[33]

The quest for rights: an overview

In modern societies, political mobilization seeks to address grievances, vindicate causes and advance specific demands that do not seem to get the attention and/or recognition of governments. Political mobilization involves protest and opposition to the status quo, and different political actors encompassing social movements, clandestine organizations and groups, as well as spontaneous associations, are ready to use it. In what follows, I analyse the novel political framework created by the expansion of democracy and the rise of the nation-state and its impact upon the emergence of social movements.

Historically, the modern state has evolved owing to demands and pressure exerted from below. For instance, the achievement of citizenship rights was by no means a process which could be taken for granted: a sharp contrast between its defence among certain intellectual circles and the strong resistance to it on the part of the more privileged sectors of society illustrates this. The attainment of citizenship rights should be viewed as a slow process launched by the French Revolution, a process that took a step backwards with Bonapartism and the 1815 Restoration, but continued to be present since the French ideals of citizenship and constitutional government provided the template upon which European liberals of the early nineteenth century modelled their demands.

The degrading conditions of the proletariat brought about by the Industrial Revolution provided both the opportunity and the motive for a growth of political consciousness which expressed itself in the formation of different sorts of organizations, some of them fighting for economic and social reforms, for example trade unions. One of the more powerful reasons why demands for and concessions to reform were successful was fear of the violent consequences of continued resistance. As David Heater argues, memories of 1789 were vivid, and were in any case refreshed by the 1848 revolutions.[34]

The achievement of political rights, especially the right to direct engagement in the process of ruling, had to be struggled for. In most European countries, enfranchisement was limited to male citizens owning a certain amount of property – France in 1830 had a population of some 30 million while boasting an electorate of a mere 90,000. But wealth, although it was the main restriction on the franchise, was by no means the only one. Religion, too, could disenfranchise a man, particularly if he were a Catholic in a Protestant state, or a Jew. In Britain, Catholics had to wait until 1829 and Jews until 1858 for the right to vote.

In the USA the issue of citizenship gained complexity owing to the constitutional and legal problems of the federal–state relationship and the institution of slavery. It was not until 1865 that the Thirteenth Amendment abolished slavery, destroying any basic distinction between black and white, and the Fifteenth Amendment was necessary in order to confirm that 'the right of citizens of the United States to vote shall not be deemed or abridged by the US or by any state on account of race, colour or previous condition of servitude'.[35] However, the struggle to achieve complete equality between individuals of different ethnicity and colour is far from a resolution in today's world.

The universal franchise for men was mostly obtained by the early years of the twentieth century, while women had to wait longer. Marie Gouze, a leader of one of the women's clubs created in Paris after the French Revolution, drew up a statement entitled 'Declaration of the Rights of Women', based upon the 'Declaration of the Rights of Man and Citizen', the main constitutional document of the Revolution.[36] However, it received a less than positive response from the male revolutionary leaders – she was executed in 1793. The intensity of the prejudice against the involvement of women in public affairs continued in the nineteenth century, as crudely illustrated by the fact that when Napoleon codified French civil law, they were explicitly excluded from such legal rights together with minors, criminals and the mentally deficient. The legacy of the French Revolution was manifested in equality before the law, freedom of religion and the abolition of feudalism. However, men and women remained unequal. For instance, married women were forbidden from selling, giving, mortgaging or buying property and were obliged to obey their husbands. In France, as late as 1965, married women needed the permission of their husbands to work.[37]

Feminism became more advanced in the USA. At a meeting at Seneca Falls in 1848, a feminist movement was launched by issuing a 'Declaration of Sentiments', consciously echoing the 'Declaration of Independence', which proclaimed as a self-evident truth that all men and women are created equal.[38] Despite this initiative, few real gains in improving the social and political position of women were made during this period, until the Nineteenth Amendment conceded female suffrage on a par with men in 1920.

In Britain, Mary Wollstonecraft's *A Vindication of the Rights of Women* (1792) stands as a predecessor of the feminism that later flourished. This would come to fruition in 1866 when a petition signed by 1,500 women was presented to Parliament demanding that the electoral reforms then being discussed should include full voting rights for women. The petition was ignored, and its organizers responded the following year by setting up the National Society for Women's Suffrage. The campaign for parliamentary suffrage yielded a bitter struggle that only achieved successful results in 1918 when women were conceded voting rights because of the crucial role they had played in World War I. Women in Belgium, France, Italy and Japan had to wait until after World War II to be able to vote, while such an advanced country as Switzerland denied women participation in federal elections until 1971.

'Liberating' versus 'regressive' social movements

As I have tried to show above, the whole process of translating the concept of popular sovereignty into universal adult suffrage required a long and hard struggle during which the ideas of 1789 began a slow but compelling process, and permeated to varying degrees first the educated classes and then the masses in the various European countries. Pressure from below in favour of a wide range of rights gave rise to 'liberating movements' across the globe. As Richard Bellamy writes, 'Citizens are far more likely to identify with laws in which they have had some say. Of course, that say may be very small and be outweighed by what most others say. But the entitlement to have as equal a say as everyone else is the essence of being viewed as a bearer of rights.'[39]

Since their emergence in the 1960s, modern social movements have been defined as 'liberating movements' fostered by both state and non-state actors. These movements aim to promote political mobilization around the specific issues they are seeking to address. They obey the desire to defend, highlight, transform, eliminate or create a new socio-political or economic environment and enlist a wide range of strategies, which vary according to the objectives, means and resources available in each particular case. In some instances, political mobilization revolves around a single issue – achieving universal suffrage, for example. In other cases, political mobilization poses a challenge to the status quo and works to overturn and replace it by a different political system.

'Liberating social movements' defy the status quo and often pursue progressive goals aimed at fostering socio-political change. However, in the last ten years or so we have witnessed the emergence of what I refer to as 'regressive social movements'. These denote a new brand of social movements based upon the defence of authoritarian politics – often anchored in some kind of reinterpretation of tradition – which, in some instances, become connected to ethnopolitics. The rise of the populist new radical right as well as the return of fundamentalism, not only applied to religion but also to markets, stand as two major examples of emerging transnational regressive social movements cutting across national boundaries and using the technological methods advanced by globalization.

In contrast, the advent of a liberating social movement generally takes place whenever the state does not respond or listen to the demands of particular groups. It also arises in situations when institutional political channels are either closed or unresponsive. Political mobilization is associated with the existence of a democratic deficit reflected in low levels of access to political representation. Liberating social movements seeking political mobilization act within the context of the nation-state and adopt different strategies in tune with its changing nature. However, their local or national character has been largely challenged by the proliferation of transnational global movements which have managed to gather support for various causes, such as the defence of women's rights and the protection of the environment.

In order to promote a visible political mobilization, Charles Tilly has suggested that a social movement should demonstrate the worthiness of the cause it is defending; display a unity of purpose; attain massive support; and show a strong commitment on behalf of its members to invoke responsiveness of the state.[40] Nevertheless, in order to achieve media attention and thus influence both the public and policy makers, a movement may turn to extreme tactics, such as the use of violence. While such a strategy may boost the visibility of its cause, however, it is also bound to trigger a reaction from the state; and violence may be employed to contain and eliminate opposition.

Writing in the mid-1970s, Peter Eisinger distinguished between what he referred to as 'open' and 'closed' political opportunity structures as a key factor in the emergence of collective violence associated with political mobilization. This has since been expanded to include all forms of social and political movements. Eisinger sought to explain why some US cities experienced intense rioting in the 1960s while others did not. In his view, decisive in those cities experiencing minimal or no civil disorder was the accessibility of political participation in their municipal governments. When aggrieved populations perceived opportunities to influence political decisions through established, institutional channels, they chose to do so rather than engaging in protest. The perceived costs were far lower, as, unlike protest, there was no risk of being jailed, injured, or losing time at work.[41]

Key emotions in the quest for political mobilization

Emotions fulfil a key role in the crystallization of social and political mobilization aimed at generating collective actions destined to effect social and political change. In these processes the role of leaders is important. Thus charismatic leaders tend to emphasize the possibility of success; they also highlight the impending impact of their actions. The prospect of political change is portrayed as a real possibility. Charismatic leaders appeal to the emotions of their followers through their speeches, meetings and writings. They instil passion, hope and trust among their supporters while seeking to convince them that political change is imminent and depends on them, since only they have the ability to trigger that change. In turn, state actors may exaggerate their power and willingness to repress in order to deter political opposition and protest. In some instances, however, state actors choose to react and employ various means – including violence – to demonstrate that they are in control and have the capacity to repel opposition.

Among the key emotions often invoked by leaders in their quest for political mobilization are vengeance, *ressentiment*, fear and confidence. In what follows, I examine how these emotions tend to play a key part in prompting political mobilization and illustrate them with reference to some examples.

Vengeance is a likely reaction to humiliation, subordination, unfair treatment, injury, repression or denial of satisfaction of a need. The latter include physical, nurturing needs as well as the need for society. The leaders of a socio-political movement may feed a desire for retribution already present in their followers' consciousness. Barrington Moore highlighted the importance of violent political transformation in the establishment of viable liberal societies: 'Revolutionary violence may contribute as much as peaceful reform to the establishment of a relatively free society. . . . But not all historically significant violence takes the form of revolution.'[42]

Vengeance is then interpreted and presented as the action of 'setting things right': that is, as a moral and just action. Vengeance means retaliation against the agents of subordination and humiliation opposed by social movements asserting the dignity and rights of those they are seeking to liberate or empower. Vengeance seeks a reassertion of human dignity or worth after injury or damage; however, 'there is no such thing as a complete restoration of injuries once inflicted. Vengeance may be the most primitive form of moral outrage. But if primitive, it is also highly contemporary.'[43]

Throughout history, political movements aiming to redress what they consider immoral and unjust situations have employed various degrees and forms of violence. Among such movements are the struggles for universal suffrage, for equality between men and women, for equality between people of different colour, for the recognition of the rights of peoples to self-determination – exemplified by the end of colonialism – and for recognition of national and ethnic minorities across the globe.

Ressentiment may be defined as the condemnation of what one secretly craves but cannot achieve. Friedrich Nietzsche refers to *ressentiment* as a self-destructive form of anger which, in reinforcing a passivity in those subject to it, functions anaesthetically to deaden the pain of injury.[44]

Nietzsche establishes a distinction between three classes: the nobles, the slaves and the priests. The nobles are people of a strong physique, naturally well endowed, confident and convinced of their superiority, who always emerge on the top of the social hierarchy; they are well connected socially. They enjoy a challenge that measures their own strength and confirms their higher status. Here we can identify a compatibility with Jean-Paul Sartre's concept of 'inter-subjectivity', which refers to 'the other' as the condition of his own existence. The individual cannot be anything unless others recognize him as such.[45]

The slaves are powerless; they are worse off than the others, inferior or suppressed. They depend on the nobles' command and are subject to them and regarded by them with contempt: 'While the noble man is confident and frank with himself, the man of *ressentiment* is neither upright nor naïve, nor honest and straight with himself.'[46]

The priests wish to rebel against their subordinate position. They despise the nobles but cannot confront them because they are inferior and unable to better their situation; however, they are not 'willing to accept a subordinate position in the social hierarchy'. If they were to rebel, conflict would become unavoidable and they would lose because they are weaker. The priests, aware of their weakness, react by turning inward. Their strategy for survival involves renouncing their desires and their emotions and suppressing their energies and aggressions, at a price. Frustration takes a toll and materializes in feelings of *ressentiment* against the nobles. As a way out, the priests design an alternative story according to which they are the strongest, the best. To do so they effect what Nietzsche refers to as a 'transmutation of values': that is, turning the values that define their weakness into the most important virtues. However, to expect that strength will not manifest itself as strength and as the desire to overcome is absurd. Nietzsche writes: 'One should ask who is actually evil in the sense of the morality of *ressentiment*. The stern reply is: precisely the "good" person of the other morality, the noble, powerful, dominating one, but re-touched, re-interpreted and reviewed through the poisonous eye of *ressentiment*.'[47]

By introducing the concept of free will, the priests portray the nobles as responsible for their own acts, pointing out that their might and strength generates violence and suffering for the other classes. The new morality of the priests gains support and comforts the slaves; it provides hope of a better future. However, Nietzsche, while acknowledging the victory of the slave morality – which he interprets as emerging out of *ressentiment* – expects a future resurgence of noble values.

T.H. Marshall introduces a moral viewpoint in his definition of *ressentiment* by describing it as the action or inaction of those experiencing the emotional apprehension of undeserved advantage. Generally class conflict has been associated with interests and consciousness; however, Marshall establishes a link between class conflict and *ressentiment* against inequality. In so doing, he signals the existence of an emotional basis for social conflict and clearly places social emotion within a political and economic framework. In his view, feelings of *ressentiment* emerge out of three distinct processes: comparison, frustration and oppression.[48] *Ressentiment* may be conscious or unconscious.

Jonathan Cobb and Richard Sennett have developed the notion of sacrificial contract to refer to the sacrifices that some workers are prepared to make in order to improve the life chances of others and, in particular, of their family members, with the expectation that they will receive their gratitude in return.[49] In such situations, *ressentiment* may emerge when those who have sacrificed themselves for the sake of others do not receive the recognition and gratitude that they feel they deserve. In my view, this example could also be applied to those sacrificing for the country, to be faced with the indifference and hostility of those ignoring or even criticizing their efforts.

Fear may be caused by insufficient power or lack of one's own power and excess of the other's power. Human fear frequently arises in social contexts within which the source of fear cannot be fled from; generally human fear emerges as a reaction to a threat not to individual wellbeing but to social wellbeing.[50] A climate of fear tends to isolate people from one another; they do not know whom to trust, where to be safe. There is one exception: the existence of a common well-defined enemy threatening the life and existence of a group acts as a magnet for unity. This situation encourages solidarity and camaraderie among the group's members since their own unity is an indispensable precondition in their attempt to overcome the 'other'.

Fear is the emotional response to danger or threat understood as the prospect of injury or harm. Fear may act as a paralysing force leading to subjugation, but in some instances it can also trigger insurgency, rebellion and revolution, involving violence and radical desperate actions. Common reactions to fear when confronted with a direct physical threat include withdrawal (flight) or counter-challenge (fight).

Elites may attempt to contain fear by accepting some degree of political and economic change in an effort to provide the impression that they are managing the situation, that they have created mechanisms to control the sources of danger and threat. This process assumes the introduction of innovation and development with the aim of managing the risks emanating from the sources of fear. At this point I would like to stress the difference between the object of fear and the cause of fear, while insisting upon the view that we feel threatened because we fear, and not the other way round. The availability of resources is crucial to determine possible responses to fear. Thus containment and rebellion require greater resources than subjugation. To be sure, subjugation is often the option left to powerless groups and communities. Having said so, mass mobilization is the most potent asset in the hands of those lacking other types of resources; it attracts media attention and, often, global awareness. Massive support for a common cause cannot be overlooked when assessing resources.

The original meaning of **confidence** is 'to have trust or faith in an object or person'. It is an emotion which encourages one to go one's own way; it reflects a state of self-projection and it arises from a situation in which the individual is able to overcome uncertainty. Feelings of confidence originate whenever the individual receives acceptance and recognition. Confident persons are those who have a general trust in themselves, people who display consistent behaviour or beliefs over a period of time. The main function of confidence is to promote social and political action, and the leaders of social movements are fully aware of it. This accounts for leaders' efforts to instil confidence among their followers and often downplay the power of the state and the resistance that they are likely to encounter when seeking to advance their cause. The main objective of confidence is to bring a possible future into the present, providing a sense of certainty and prompting people to act and become engaged in social action to bring it about. As Barbalet writes,

> Action brings a possible future into the present, and as the future is unknown and therefore information about it unavailable, reason as calculation cannot provide the basis for action. All action is ultimately founded on the actor's feeling of confidence in their capacities and the effectiveness of those capacities. The actor's confidence is a necessary source of action; without it, action simply would not occur.[51]

Charismatic leaders seek to mobilize the population by transmitting what Randall Collins refers to as 'emotional energy'[52] through their words and deeds. To be effective, their discourses should be able to touch upon the feelings of their audience by appealing to rational as well as emotional arguments capable of enhancing their confidence and enthusiasm.[53] While remembering past achievements will instil collective pride, invoking past collective experiences of humiliation, subjugation and defeat are likely to trigger political mobilization with the aim of redressing their current situation.

Focusing upon past defeats is painful and produces feelings of impotence, which need to be replaced by confidence in the future. Only confidence – regardless of whether it is founded upon objective or subjective reasons and assumptions – will have the power to prompt political mobilization. If those who follow the leader believe in his or her discourse and are convinced of their own capacity to effect change, this will automatically increase their possibilities because their actions will reflect the *élan* that only deeply felt emotions are able to spark.

The emotional distance between outsiders and those who belong

At this stage, a wide gap emerges between the beliefs and perceptions of those committed to the cause and those opposing it: that is, between those belonging to the political movement and identifying with it, and outsiders who may be either indifferent or openly hostile to the movement's aims.

The indifferent may dismiss the objectives of the political movement as impossible, out of place and bizarre. In turn, those opposed to the movement are likely to castigate its objectives and discourse as ludicrous, and deserving rejection, and may even propose some form of threat or punishment to force activists to abandon their demands. However, rising tension between those in favour and those against the objectives of the movement holds the potential to consolidate and strengthen the former by reinforcing the sense of purpose and conviction of its advocates.

Engagement in political mobilization creates a sentiment of belonging to the movement; it also nurtures attitudes of camaraderie among fellow-members sharing common objectives and views as a feature that presumes a certain degree of complicity, agreement and disposition to act.

The individual is likely to feel a sense of closeness to fellow-activists, to trust them. Of course, rivalries and disagreements remain a feature of social movements; however, I regard them as an intrinsic characteristic of group dynamics where internal power structures are being created, discussed, challenged and/or imposed according to the nature of the movement in question.

Involvement in a social movement opens up the possibility of enhancing one's own wellbeing by accessing a friendly environment defined by a certain degree of closeness to others. The individual feels stronger as a member of a group defending a set of ideals considered worth fighting for. He or she identifies with the achievements and strength of the group, and this will undoubtedly increase his or her self-esteem. Membership of a group often results in the construction of what is perceived as a safe environment for the discussion of common objectives and values.

Obviously, there are enormous differences concerning the nature of the environment within which political mobilization takes place. It is not the same to act within a democratic nation-state upholding human rights, tolerant of diversity and prepared to stand by its citizenship as to act within a nation-state unprepared to tolerate dissent and ready to threaten and/or use force against those peacefully challenging the status quo. A much more difficult situation emerges whenever political demands are defended by clandestine political movements operating within authoritarian regimes. Membership is often confined to secrecy since activists are constantly exposed to significant physical risks, including torture and even death.

Summary

The originality of the argument advanced here is based upon the assertion that the emotional dimension of belonging not only acts as a trigger for social action – including political mobilization – but also plays a key role in the way in which actions are evaluated by individuals and groups. Emotions are often looked upon as a factor distracting individuals from their rational objectives while, at the same time, establishing afresh what their purposes are. However, my assertion does not assume that emotions are 'the decisive', 'indispensable' or 'necessary' trigger for any type of political mobilization.

There is evidence of a clash between the rational and instrumental needs of market capitalism and the aims of one of the most powerful agents of political mobilization, namely the sentiment of belonging to the nation. To be sure, sharing a sense of belonging does not imply a homogeneous citizenry, since a certain degree of difference remains a constant. Each individual is bound to experience the common identity in a slightly different manner. Moreover, nation-states are culturally, economically and socially diverse. Whenever a 'significant' number of people do not identify with the nation-state of which they are citizens, feel alienated and do not share feelings of solidarity towards fellow-nationals, we are faced with the rise of a 'significant group'. By this I mean a group that questions the legitimacy of the nation-state and may engage in the organization of political opposition and protest. That is why nation-states struggle to build and uphold a common national identity among their citizenry: they are aware that consciousness of forming a community is a condition for their own survival.

In modern societies, emotions are tamed and their public expression is restricted; some 'healing spaces' mark the boundaries within which joy and grief are allowed. Collective regular rituals and ceremonies are destined to 'tame emotions' so that order can be preserved and, in some instances, challenged. There are occasions on which political leaders and agitators appeal to emotions while opposing the status quo, questioning power and aiming at regime change by means of political mobilization. The unleashing of emotions has some risks, though, since those who promoted them in the first instance may find them hard to control. The opposing forces at work in modern societies are illustrated by the contrast between 'liberating' and 'regressive' transnational social movements that employ the new technologies brought about by globalization. This emphasizes the value-free character of technological progress and the neutral nature of globalization. It also accounts for the radically different aims that may be pursued while employing similar technological instruments. In this context, crucial importance should be given to the values and objectives informing social movements, as well as to the degree of power they enjoy, because the latter will determine, to a very significant extent, their ability to promote their cause and ideas at a global level.

To conclude, this chapter examined some of the most important emotions generally present in processes of political mobilization, such as vengeance, *ressentiment*, fear and confidence. Here it is not my intention to argue that emotions are the only trigger for political mobilization, or that political mobilization is invariably the product of emotion. Rather, my aim is to highlight the need to combine rational arguments (such as proven economic stagnation of a people as a result of discrimination, exploitation or lack of political representation) with emotional arguments which are often present but rarely acknowledged when analysing the collective behaviour of groups engaged with or seeking political mobilization.

Conclusion

A sense of belonging generates the strongest antidote against alienation and aloneness. Belonging offers a point of reference to the individual, who is now able to transcend his or her own limited existence by sharing some common interests, objectives and characteristics with fellow-members. Belonging breaks the individual's sense of isolation and provides psychological support, which is crucial to overcome feelings of anxiety connected with the uncertainty and political alienation experienced in day-to-day life.

The power of belonging springs from its ability to generate an emotional attachment capable of fostering a sense of shared identity and loyalty among members of a given community, which generally results in the emergence of solidarity bonds among them. The predisposition to belong to a myriad of groups and associations highlights the social dimension of individuals' lives and poses a fundamental challenge to the idea that individualism stands as the key feature of modern societies. Throughout this book, I have tried to demonstrate that the intensity of the feelings compelling individuals to belong is so strong that, often, it makes them ready to renounce freedom in exchange for the perks of group membership. Belonging implies a reciprocal commitment between the individual and the group. In the case of the nation, it also requires a certain degree of familiarity with the culture, language, history, aspirations and life of the community, its attachment to a particular homeland, and the key features that sustain a distinction between members and strangers. Individuals are invited and expected to participate in the nation's achievements, thus replacing the focus upon their own lives – and the, at times, unfulfilled expectations and insecurities that go with it – by identifying with a larger and more powerful entity.

In pre-modern societies, individual life was governed by tradition. Individuals were expected to comply, and although in some cases they sought to adopt attitudes of opposition and dissidence towards mainstream society, the majority were prepared to conform and fulfil assigned roles throughout their entire lives. These roles were not the outcome of free choice but a duty, an expectation, something to be done, and questioning them never crossed their minds. Individuals just had to go along with them; choosing was not an option.

The advent of modernity brought about an unprecedented emphasis upon the value of freedom as a prerogative that should not be restricted to the powerful and the wealthy. In Europe and the USA, around the 1960s, a range of new progressive social movements that quickly became transnational engaged in calls for freedom which resulted in the emancipation of women, blacks, colonial countries, gays and lesbians – among many others. Freedom from traditional sources of power was on the rise and the willingness to participate in politics reached an all-time high. Simultaneously, informed by the writings of Sigmund Freud, an unprecedented relevance was attributed to the concept of the self, its construction and functioning.

The emphasis upon freedom acted as a potent transformative force reshaping power structures at a social and political level. It is precisely in this context that 'belonging by choice' – that is, the recently acquired individual right to ponder and decide among various options – became available. Freedom was placed in the hands of the individual and it was his or her concern to manage it. To some, this prompted an active engagement in the construction of self-identity according to newly chosen personal values and life-styles; to others it caused enormous anxiety.

In this book I have explored the meaning, impact and consequences of 'belonging by choice' as a distinctive feature of modern society; one that points to the importance of freedom as an attribute of individuals able to engage in the construction of their own identities. Belonging exerts a very significant influence upon the construction of individual and collective forms of identity by bringing in the frequently neglected force of emotions to modify and transform the ways in which people, circumstances, actions and objectives are evaluated and also by affecting individuals' disposition to act.

In modern societies, belonging by choice is turned into a consequence of free will, and, for this reason, it entails a degree of personal commitment absent from assigned forms of membership where individuals are constrained either to satisfy other people's expectations or to follow the norms imposed by tradition; in particular those of powerful and influential institutions mainly represented by the church, the nation and the family.

At first glance, belonging by choice can be strictly regarded as a tool contributing to the empowerment of modern individuals by prompting them to transcend assigned forms of membership. However, this book shows that, in some instances, freedom is eagerly traded for the companionship, security and solace associated with joining a community or group – although I am aware that communities and groups are fertile ground for competition and jealousy. In other cases, individuals feel haunted by fear of making the wrong choice. They are unsure about their options; they hesitate and doubt. They are conscious of the risk inherent in the exercise of free will at the heart of the idea of being able to choose. It seems to me that the real paradox here lies in the tension between the freedom to choose and the perils of making the wrong choice. Yet, while the former yields anxiety about deciding on what is the best option, the latter triggers apprehension about the fact that to choose one option demands abandoning the others. In the end, the individual may discover that he or she has made the 'wrong choice' and 'the best option' is no longer available.

Freedom has brought independence and rationality to individuals; however, it has often left them with feelings of aloneness. To escape from them many have turned to new forms of dependence, including addiction to drugs, work, sex, risk, gambling, the internet or eating, among many others. Further to these, I regard submission to a leader and compulsive conformity as forms of dependence which are gaining addicts at a considerable pace. However, giving up freedom, even if this is the outcome of a personal and free decision, is always a source of pain; the individual each time loses something valuable in trading freedom for the comfort and the security offered by the sense of belonging to the community. I perceive a strong ambivalence and tension between, on the one hand, individuals' willingness to comply, obey and conform and, on the other, their desire to maintain freedom and independence. All things considered, many modern individuals tend to opt for the former.

But where does the fascination with submission come from? Obedience to a political ideology or religious faith holds the potential to foster a sense of security based upon membership of a community perceived as powerful and of value within which individuals are considered as 'insiders' having access to the advantages – material and immaterial – of group membership. This is a community eager to provide responses to existential questions by promoting clear norms, values and principles. It is also a community from which individuals expect support in exchange for their loyalty and obedience.

A few decades ago, it was predicted that the influence of religion would fade away under the weight of modern secular society; however, most recently, the decline of some traditional religions in Europe has been contrasted, in particular, with the rise of Islam associated with the establishment of important Muslim communities all over the continent. In the USA, religion remains a powerful force, as the issues and debates in presidential electoral campaigns demonstrate. Similarly, the influence of religion in Africa and Latin America is on the rise and is playing a key role in the reconstruction of national identities there, as it is also in some Eastern European countries. This is a trend that seems likely to spread. In many instances we shall witness a re-appropriation of religion as a mechanism seeking the actualization of tradition; as a body of values and ideas which can be reinterpreted and applied as a 'book of answers' to day-to-day problems. In this context, the surge of Islamic fundamentalism can be read as a response to globalization and a rejection of modernity. It claims to bring back tradition and holds an enormous power as a force capable of addressing the questions faced by contemporary individuals concerning civil and political aspects of societal life.

The return of tradition – or, to be more precise, the selective use of tradition and its reinterpretation to fulfil current demands – emphasizes the value of continuity in a context where constant change and adaptation to new social, political and technological environments is the norm. However, I believe that the concept of nation, as an entity rooted in pre-modern times, and the perception of culture and language as products of the collective life of a community over a long period will retain their strong power to attract individuals. Tradition will continue to be invoked as a legitimizing principle only insofar as it is constantly actualized and reinvented. The new elements brought about by modernity will inexorably be incorporated into and mixed with traditional forms of life.

After a period defined by the conquest of freedom, exemplified by the proliferation of 'liberating social movements' originating in the 1960s, we are now faced with the return of 'authoritarian politics', in some cases reminiscent of the fascisms that emerged in various European countries between 1922 and 1945. Their ascendance is illustrated by the rise of radical right political parties across Europe and the USA. The mounting importance of authoritarianism is an offshoot of the failure to successfully manage modern societies. As such, it responds to the attempt to limit and control some of the key economic, political and social consequences of globalization; however, it remains unclear whether the new radical right would stand up to the challenge if it were to reach political power. For example, one of the main weaknesses of its discourse is the absence of an original theory about how to manage the economy.

The return of authoritarianism is associated with calls for 'order, leadership and a sense of purpose', which partly emerge as a reaction to what many perceive as an unruly world – taken over by the interests of market capitalism. It is a world in which nation-states lose power and become dependent on markets and rating agencies, as individuals witness a retreat of progressive politics, which includes the shrinking of the welfare state and the curtailing of rights. The global economic crisis highlights social inequality, bad financial management accompanied by lack of responsibility and the urgent need to control the power of the markets. It also raises questions about whether emerging economies will be able to maintain and increase growth, and for how long. A further challenge concerns the need to respond to climate change issues by designing an effective global response.

In Europe, the spreading of economic uncertainty – partly emerging as a result of weak political and economic leadership in the European Union, as well as in a number of member states

– generates anxiety and insecurity in everyday life, while the clash of cultures and values within secular, multicultural societies feeds anti-immigrant feelings and mistrust.

The rule of markets – impervious to ethical values and principles other than making maximum profit – is constructing a dislocated society in which the nation-state is losing power and influence vis-à-vis newly created institutions of global governance that many perceive as alien. In this environment, the nation-state struggles to regain the trust of its citizens, which is indispensable if democracy is to survive; however, the outcome of its efforts is not yet clear. We are living through a period where the name 'democracy' remains, but its original content has been impoverished, its original meaning overridden by abusing it.

The widespread assumption that economic hardship is the main factor responsible for the current surge in popularity of the new radical right across Europe ignores the fact that it made notable progress at a time of economic prosperity and also overlooks the structural factors explaining its success. The new radical right attracts individuals dissatisfied with mainstream political parties by combining ethno-politics with political protest. By presenting itself as the defender of otherwise marginalized groups, of a radicalizing of democracy and of the need to sustain social cohesion, new radical right political parties across Europe have managed to obtain significant electoral support, most recently in Greece (2012), France (2012), Switzerland (2011), Denmark (2011) and Sweden (2010).

Belonging to the nation offers a source of pride and it means participating in all its achievements. In so doing, the individual feels important, valuable and proud of being a member of a distinctive community. In these circumstances, the new radical right skilfully portrays the retreat to a national identity, of which citizens can feel proud, as a right, almost a duty.

A significant number of people are able to recognize symbols belonging to various cultures within a multicultural society; however, they are only moved by and feel emotionally attached to those symbols that, for them, have acquired 'sentimental meaning' by means of some kind of emotional identification beyond cognitive definitions and historical explanations of their origin. A shared sentiment of belonging is effected through symbolism and ritual. Symbols are necessary to legitimize, strengthen and also challenge political power. Their somehow open and ambiguous nature makes them well suited to acting as pillars of individual as well as collective forms of identity. The richness and complexity of symbols tolerate a degree of ambiguity in their definition, one that allows for a certain level of emotional creativity on behalf of individuals engaged in the construction of their own sense of identity. In turn, ritual communicates authority and hierarchy, it reinforces sentiments of belonging, but it also underscores dependence from the group or community. In addition, ritual is instrumental in strengthening loyalty and defining the boundaries between members and aliens.

In dealing with the various functions of rituals, I have introduced the distinction between rituals of 'inclusion' and 'exclusion', depending on the aims of ritual in each particular case. I have also established a contrast between 'exclusive' and 'inclusive' groups and associations, to highlight the difference between groups allowing easy access and those restricting their membership by setting up strict rules. The term 'communities of belonging' refers to groups and communities with a distinct identity, structure and hierarchy, within which the individual has a role, is recognized, known and valued as 'one of us'. 'Communities of belonging' stand against the impersonality and anonymity of membership of large complex groups within which the individual has become anonymous.

The binding nature of ritual leads to the distinction between 'loyalty by choice' and 'authoritarian loyalty'. While the former is the product of a free personal decision that contributes to the individual's self-definition, the latter is the result of being compelled to act in a particular manner. Still another concept has to be added, this is 'instrumental loyalty'. It refers to a type of loyalty conditional on provision of expected rewards.

Loyalties provide identity and offer a vantage point from which the individual interprets the world and relates to others; they also foster a powerful sense of belonging connected with the individual's emotional engagement. Shared loyalties yield a solid foundation for the constitution of communities and groups orientated towards the advancement of common aims. They also facilitate communication among individuals and supply an area of agreement for the emergence of cooperation and solidarity.

'Loyalty by choice' involves the emotional commitment and identification with a person, a cause, a community or a group.

At present, one of the most potent triggers of loyalty is a strong sense of belonging to the nation as the 'emotional' community able to muster the highest levels of identification from its members through nationalist mobilization. However, this has not always been the case and, for centuries, religion took precedence and generated the most passionate examples of loyalty, as well as treason, on behalf of a wide range of people across the world.

When applied to the nation, loyalty translates into patriotism. Loyalty to the nation holds a strong emotional engagement, so much so that the individual feels a part of the community and identifies with its aims, rejoices in its achievements and suffers its losses and defeats.

The introduction of loyalty programmes during the Cold War period in the USA initiated a debate about whether or not citizens should be prepared to renounce some civil liberties in order to guarantee that loyalty towards the nation-state would prevail. In that context, the proper standard by which to judge loyalty was spelled out by the 'clear and present danger' doctrine enunciated by Justice Oliver Wendell Holmes.

The relevance of this doctrine came back to the fore after the 9/11 terrorist attacks in New York and Washington. These were the work of Islamic fundamentalists who also became responsible for further attacks in Madrid (2004) and London (2005). These events have caused strong concerns about the loyalty of some citizens who openly display an extremely critical attitude towards Western values and way of life. For instance, in the UK the realization that the perpetrators of the London bombings (2005) were British citizens whose parents or grandparents had come to the country as immigrants horrified the political class as well as fellow-citizens. A wave of Islamophobia followed those events, in turn contributing to widen the gap between mainstream society and Muslim communities now affected by the rise of anti-Islamic feelings.

Modern societies, in their attempt to control certain emotions, have created spaces and conditions for their expression. The quest to 'domesticate' emotions has resulted in the construction of designated settings allowing for their public display according to some limitations: for example, 'healing spaces' to deal with mourning ceremonies.

The neutral nature of technological innovation has resulted in its advancements being used for different, even antagonistic, aims.

Thus, while in the 1960s social movements displayed a predominantly progressive character, today both 'liberating' and 'regressive' social movements coexist and employ similar tools. It is no longer guaranteed – if it ever was – that progress should follow the route towards human emancipation associated with the expansion and deepening of democracy and social justice. In this context, political mobilization remains a potent instrument in the hands of those willing to effect change. Awareness of the power of emotions such as vengeance, *ressentiment*, fear and confidence will shed some light into the various ways in which these can be employed. It will also contribute to our understanding of political mobilization as a complex phenomenon. This book has focused upon the emotional dimension of belonging as a sentiment binding the individual to the group or community. Belonging involves commitment and identification with the group and plays a fundamental role in the construction of individual as well as collective forms of identity. In so doing, it stresses the social dimension of individuals, keen to engage in the construction of all sorts of associations, communities and groups, as a trend that runs against the thesis that individualism is the main defining feature of modern society.

The urge to belong felt by large sections of the population motivates individuals to sacrifice personal interests. It also compels them to renounce substantial degrees of freedom with the purpose of conforming to the rules, norms and values of their community. In return, they enjoy security, protection, solidarity and companionship. At present, the emotional appeal of belonging to the nation, as a political community, stands as the most powerful agent of political mobilization, one able to establish a sharp distinction between those who belong and those who are regarded as enemies and aliens.

Notes

Introduction

1 According to the Business Dictionary, 'a group is defined as a collection of individuals who have regular contact and frequent interaction, mutual influence, common feeling of camaraderie, and who work together to achieve a common set of goals'. In turn, a community is defined as a 'network of people with common agenda, cause, or interest, who collaborate by sharing ideas, information, and other resources' (*http://www.businessdictionary.com/definition/group.html*, accessed 30 January 2013). A further definition of community includes a social, religious, occupational or other group sharing common characteristics or interests and perceived or perceiving itself as distinct in some respect from the larger society within which it exists (*http://dictionary.reference.com/browse/community*, accessed 30 January 2013).

Chapter 1 Identity as a Political Instrument

1 *http://www.bbc.co.uk/religion/religions/islam/beliefs/niqab_1.shtml* (accessed 1 February 2013).
2 Islam is divided into three sects: Sunnis, Shi'ites and Kharejites. The Sunnis are the largest of them.
3 Peter Allen, 'France has first "burqa rage" incident', *The Telegraph*, 18 May 2010 (*http://www.telegraph.co.uk/news/worldnews/europe/*

france/7735607/France-has-first-burka-rage-incident.html, accessed 1 February 2013).

4 Stefan Zweig brilliantly describes the impact of constant religious wars in France upon Michel de Montaigne's views and work in his book *Montaigne* (Paris: Quadrige/PUF, 1982).

5 Frank Tallett and Nicholas Atkin (eds), *Religion, Society, and Politics in France since 1789* (London: The Hambledon Press, 1991).

6 G. J. Holyoake, *The Origin and Nature of Secularism* (London: Watts and Co., 1896), p. 51.

7 Jefferson's Letter to the Danbury Baptists (June 1998) – Library of Congress Information Bulletin (*http://www.loc.gov/loc/lcib/9806/danpre.html*, accessed 1 February 2013).

8 Ernest Gellner, *Postmodernism, Reason and Religion* (London: Routledge, 1992), p. 16.

9 As note 1.

10 Thanassis Cambanis, 'Islamist women redraw Palestinian debate on rights', *Boston Globe*, 21 January 2006.

11 Nira Yuval-Davis, *The Politics of Belonging: Intersectional Constestations* (London: Sage, 2011), pp. 4–5. See also Nira Yuval-Davis, 'Power, Intersectionality and the Politics of Belonging', FREIA-Feminist Research Center in Aalborg, Aalborg University, Denmark, FREIA working paper series, working paper no. 75.

12 Judith Squires, *The New Politics of Gender Equality* (London: Palgrave Macmillan, 2007).

13 Richard Jenkins, *Social Identity* (London: Routledge, 2008 [1996]), p. 150.

14 Ibid., p. 153.

15 Thomas F. Barth, *Ethnic Groups and Boundaries: The Social Organization of Culture Difference* (Oslo: Universitetsforlaget, 1969), p. 167.

16 Roy F. Baumeister, *Identity: Cultural Change and the Struggle for Self* (Oxford University Press, 1986), p. 29.

17 Émile Durkheim, *The Division of Labour in Society* (London: Macmillan, 1984 [1893]), p. 292.

18 Baumeister, *Identity*, p. 59.

19 Erich Fromm, *The Fear of Freedom* (Abingdon: Routledge, 2010 [1942]), p. 84.

20 Alberto Melucci, *Nomads of the Present* (London: Hutchinson Radius, 1989), p. 62.

21 Ibid., p. 88.

22 Jenkins, *Social Identity*, p. 19.

23 Paul Jones and Michał Krzyżanowski, 'Identity, belonging and

migration: beyond constructing "others"', in Gerard Delanty, Ruth Wodak and Paul Jones (eds), *Identity, Belonging and Migration* (Liverpool: Liverpool University Press, 2011 [2008]), p. 46.

24 Erving Goffman, *The Presentation of the Self in Everyday Life* (Garden City, NY: Anchor Books, 1959).

25 See George H. Mead, *Mind, Self, and Society: From the Standpoint of a Social Behaviorist* (Chicago: University of Chicago Press, 1967); Harry Stack Sullivan, *The Interpersonal Theory of Psychiatry* (London: Routledge, 2001 [1955]).

26 Anthony Giddens, *Modernity and Self-Identity* (Cambridge: Polity Press, 1991), p. 80.

27 Liah Greenfeld, *Nationalism and the Mind* (Oxford: Oneworld, 2006), p. 28.

28 Peggy A. Thoits, 'Multiple identities and psychological well-being: a reformulation and test of the social isolation hypothesis', *American Sociological Review* 51 (1983): 259–72.

29 For a comprehensive analysis of the various motivations explaining voting behaviour, see Wouter Van der Brug, Meindert Fennema and Jean Tillie, 'Anti-immigrant parties in Europe: ideological or protest vote?', *European Journal of Political Research* 37 (2000): 77–102; Wouter Van der Brug and Meindert Fennema, 'Protest or mainstream? How the European anti-immigrant parties developed into two separate groups by 1999', *European Journal of Political Research* 42 (2003): 55–76.

30 Holde Coffé, Bruno Heyndels and Jan Vermeir, 'Fertile grounds for extreme right-wing parties: explaining the Vlaams Blok's electoral success', *Electoral Studies* 26 (2007): 142–55 (p. 153).

31 Roger Eatwell, *Fascism: A History* (London: Vintage Books, 2009), p. 53.

32 See Piero Ignazi, *L'estrema destra in Europa* (Bologna: Il Mulino, 2000 [1994]). See also Piero Ignazi, *Extreme Right Parties in Western Europe* (Oxford: Oxford University Press, 2006).

33 Colin Hay, *Why We Hate Politics* (Cambridge: Polity Press, 2007), p. 2.

34 Ibid., pp. 4–5.

Chapter 2 Belonging by Choice

1 Liechtenstein is a principality governed under a constitutional monarchy. It has a form of mixed constitution in which political power is shared by the monarch and a democratically elected parliament. The Prince of Liechtenstein is head of state and exercises

considerable political powers (*http://en.wikipedia.org/wiki/Politics_ of_Liechtenstein*, accessed 7 February 2013).

2   Officially the Grand Duchy of Luxembourg, it has a parliamentary system, and stands as a constitutional monarchy. It is officially headed by a grand duke.

3   Paul Jones and Michał Krzyżanowski, 'Identity, belonging and migration: beyond constructing "others"', in Gerard Delanty, Ruth Wodak and Paul Jones (eds), *Identity, Belonging and Migration* (Liverpool: Liverpool University Press, 2011 [2008]), p. 48.

4   Ulf Hedetoft and Mette Hjort, 'Introduction', in Ulf Hedetoft and Mette Hjort (eds), *The Postnational Self: Belonging and Identity* (Minneapolis: University of Minnesota Press, 2002).

5   Bernard Yack, *Nationalism and the Moral Psychology of Community* (Chicago: University of Chicago Press, 2012), p. 306.

6   Rainer Bauböck, *Transnational Citizenship: Membership and Rights in International Migration* (Aldershot: Edward Elgar, 1994). See also Rainer Bauböck and Virginie Guiraudon (eds) 'Realignments of Citizenship', *Citizenship Studies*, special issue, vol. 13 (October 2009).

7   *http://www.caledonianclub.com/joining-the-club/about-member ship/* (accessed 7 February 2013).

8   *http://en.wikipedia.org/wiki/Orania,_Northern_Cape* (accessed 7 February 2013).

9   *http://hmd.org.uk/genocides/the-holocaust/* (accessed 7 February 2013).

10   Mike Savage, Gaynor Bagnall and Brian Longhurst, *Globalization and Belonging* (London: Sage, 2005), p. 208.

11   Richard Jenkins, *Social Identity* (London: Routledge, 2008 [1996]), p. 105.

12   See Michel Foucault, *Discipline and Punish* (London: Allen Lane/ Penguin, 1977 [1975]).

13   Peter J. Burke and Jan E. Stets, *Identity Theory* (Oxford: Oxford University Press, 2009), p. 124.

14   James R. Bailey and John H. Yost, 'Role theory: foundations, extensions, and applications', in E.F. Borgatta and R.J.V. Montgomery (eds), *Encylopedia of Sociology*, Vol. 4 (New York: Macmillan, 2000).

15   Burke and Stets, *Identity Theory*, p. 140.

16   Anthony Cohen, *The Symbolic Construction of Community* (London: Tavistock Publications, 1985), p. 12.

17   Ibid., p. 74.

18   Ibid., p. 21.

19   A different status and political arrangement applies to Quebec, since

Canada has recognized Quebec as a nation within the Canadian federal state. See Alain-G. Gagnon and Richard Simeon, 'Canada', in Luís Moreno and César Colino (eds), *Diversity and Unity in Federal Countries: A Global Dialogue on Federalism*, Vol. 7 (Montreal: McGill-Queen's University Press, 2010).

20 Charles Jeffery and Daniel Wincott, 'Devolution in the United Kingdom: statehood and citizenship in transition' *Publius* 36, 1 (2006): 3–18. See also Montserrat Guibernau, *Nations without States: Political Communities in the Global Age* (Cambridge: Polity Press, 1999).

21 Ludwig von Bertalanffy, *A Systems View of Man: Collected Essays* (Boulder, CO: Westview Press, 1981).

22 Dan Sperber, *Rethinking Symbolism* (Cambridge: Cambridge University Press, 1988 [1975]), p. 89.

23 F.W. Dillistone, *The Power of Symbols* (London: SCM Press, 1986), p. 213.

24 Émile Durkheim, *The Elementary Forms of the Religious Life* (London: George Allen, London, 1982 [1915]), p. 214.

25 Craig Calhoun, 'Belonging in the cosmopolitan imaginary', *Ethnicities* 3 (2003): 531–68 (p. 535).

26 See David Held, 'Principles of cosmopolitan order', in Gillian Brock and Harry Brighouse (eds), *The Political Philosophy of Cosmopolitanism* (Cambridge: Cambridge University Press, 2005).

27 Émile Durkheim, 'Religion and ritual', in *Selected Writings* (Cambridge: Cambridge University Press, 1987 [1972]), p. 223.

28 Montserrat Guibernau, *Nationalisms* (Cambridge: Polity Press, 1996), p. 47.

29 Durkheim, 'Religion and ritual', p. 231.

30 Durkheim, *The Elementary Forms of the Religious Life*, p. 230.

31 Charles Taylor, 'The politics of recognition', in Amy Gutmann (ed.), *Multiculturalism* (Princeton: Princeton University Press, 1994), p. 25.

32 Montserrat Guibernau, *Catalan Nationalism: Francoism, Transition and Democracy* (London: Routledge, 2004).

33 See Albert Balcells, *Catalan Nationalism* (London: Macmillan, 1996).

34 See Jaume Fabré, Josep Maria Huertas and Antoni Ribas, *Vint anys de resistència catalana (1939–1959)* (Barcelona: La Magrana, 1978); Joan Colomines, *El compromís de viure* (Barcelona: Columna, 1999); Pere Carbonell, *Tres Nadals empresonats* (Barcelona: Publicacions de l'Abadia de Montserrat, 1999); and Hilari Raguer, *Gaudeamus Igitur* (Barcelona: Publicacions de l'Abadia de Montserrat, 1999).

35 Daniel Kryder, 'War and the politics of black militancy in the

twentieth century', paper presented to the annual conference of the American Political Science Association, Washington, DC, August 1997, p. 7.

36 Desmond King, *The Liberty of Strangers: Making the American Nation* (Oxford: Oxford University Press, 2005), p. 85.

37 See Eric Foner, *A Short History of Reconstruction, 1863–1877* (New York: Harper & Row, 1990) and George C. Rable, *But There Was No Peace: The Role of Violence in the Politics of Reconstruction* (Athens: University of Georgia Press, 1984).

38 Jospeh McCormick and Sekou Franklin, 'Expressions of racial consciousness', in Yvette Alex-Assensoh and Lawrence J. Hanks (eds), *Black and Multiracial Politics in America* (New York and London: New York University Press, 2000), p. 339.

39 Harold Cruse, *The Crisis of the Negro Intellectual* (New York: Morrow, 1967).

40 Cruse quoted in Errol A. Henderson, 'War, political cycles, and the pendulum thesis', in Yvette Alex-Assensoh and Lawrence J. Hanks (eds), *Black and Multiracial Politics in America* (London and New York: New York University Press, 2000), p. 339.

Chapter 3 Freedom and Constraint

1 Michael Oakeshott, 'The political economy of freedom', in Paul Kelly (ed.), *British Political Theory in the Twentieth Century* (Oxford: Wiley-Blackwell, 2010), p. 130.

2 Erich Fromm, *The Fear of Freedom* (Abingdon: Routledge, 2010 [1942]), p. ix.

3 Immanuel Kant, *Kants gesammelte Schriften, herausgegeben von der Deutschen* [formerly Königlichen Preussischen] *Akademie der Wissenschaften*, 29 vols (Berlin: Walter de Gruyter, 1902). For clarity, I have used the volume and page of the Akademie edition unless otherwise signalled by use of an endnote.

4 Immanuel Kant, *The Philosophy of Kant: Immanuel Kant's Moral and Political Writings* (New York: Random House, The Modern Library, 1952), p. 192.

5 Immanuel Kant, *The Metaphysics of Morals* (Cambridge: Cambridge University Press, 1996 [1797]), p. 13 (6:214).

6 Kant, *The Philosophy of Kant*, p. 416.

7 Kant, *The Metaphysics of Morals*, p. 92 (6:314).

8 Kant, *The Philosophy of Kant*, p. 423.

9 Ibid., p. 416.

10 Onora O'Neill, 'Enlightenment as autonomy: Kant's vindica-

tion of reason', in Peter Hulme and Ludmilla Jordanova (eds), *The Enlightenment and Its Shadows* (London: Routledge, 1990), p. 194.

11 Isaiah Berlin, *The Sense of Reality* (London: Pimlico, 1996), p. 241.

12 Michel Foucault, *Discipline and Punish* (London: Allen Lane/Penguin, 1977 [1975]), pp. 227–8.

13 Michel Foucault, *Ethics, Subjectivity and Truth: The Essential Works of M. Foucault 1954–1984*, Vol. 1 (New York: New Press, 1997), p. 291.

14 Richard E. Flathman, *Freedom and Its Conditions* (New York and London: Routledge, 2003), p. 14.

15 Foucault, *Ethics, Subjectivity and Truth*, p. 262.

16 Ibid., p. 292.

17 Ibid., p. 292.

18 Ibid., p. 291.

19 Michel Foucault, *Society Must Be Defended: Lectures at the Collège de France* (London: Allen Lane/Penguin, 2003 [1997]), p. 29.

20 Michel Foucault, *The Care of the Self: The History of Sexuality*, Vol. 3 (London: Allen Lane/Penguin, 1986 [1984]), pp. 65–6.

21 Foucault, *Society Must Be Defended*, p. 243.

22 Ibid., p. 252.

23 Ibid., p. 247.

24 Ibid., p. 40.

25 Thomas L. Dumm, *Michel Foucault and the Politics of Freedom* (London: Sage, 1996), p. 4.

26 Erich Fromm, *The Fear of Freedom* (Abingdon: Routledge, 2010 [1942]), p. 91.

27 Ibid., p. 2.

28 Ibid., p. 91.

29 See Quentin Skinner, Isaiah Berlin Lecture 'A third concept of liberty', *Proceedings of the British Academy* 117 (2002): 237–68.

30 Fromm, *The Fear of Freedom*, p. 15.

31 Arthur M. Schlesinger, Jr, *The Politics of Freedom* (Melbourne: William Heinemann Ltd, 1950), p. 47.

32 Søren Kierkegaard, *The Concept of Anxiety* (Princeton: Princeton University Press, 1980 [1844]), p. 61.

33 Jean-Paul Sartre, *Existentialism* (New York: Philosophical Library, 1947), p. 27.

34 See Barry Schwartz, *The Paradox of Choice: Why More Is Less* (New York: Harper Perennial, 2004).

35 José Ortega y Gasset, *The Revolt of the Masses* (New York and

London: W.W. Norton & Company, 1930). See also Salvador Giner, *Mass Society* (New York: Academic Press, 1976).

36 Anthony Giddens, *The Transformation of Intimacy* (Cambridge: Polity Press, 1992), p. 71.

37 Louisa Degenhardt and Wayne Hall, 'Extent of illicit drug use and dependence, and their contribution to the global burden of disease', *The Lancet* 379, 9810 (2012): 55–70.

38 Center on Addiction and Substance Abuse at Columbia University, 'Adolescent Substance Use: America's #1 Public Health Problem', 29 June 2011 (*http://www.casacolumbia.org/upload/2011/20110629 substanceuseslides.pdf*, accessed 13 February 2013).

39 Mario del Libano, Susana Llorens, Marisa Salanova and Wilmar Schaufeli, 'Validity of a brief workaholism scale', *Psicothema* 22(1) (2010): 143–50.

40 Sandra L. Knauer, *Recovering from Sexual Abuse, Addictions, and Compulsive Behaviors: 'Numb' Survivors* (New York: Haworth Press, 2002), p. 183.

41 Roschbeth Ewald, 'Sexual addiction', *AllPsych Journal*, 13 May 2003 (*http://allpsych.com/journal/sexaddiction.html*, accessed 13 February 2013).

42 Kimberley S. Young, 'Internet addiction: The emergence of a clinical disorder', *CyberPsychology and Behaviour* 1, 3 (1998): 237–44. See also Kimberley S. Young, *Caught in the Net: How to Recognize the Signs of Internet Addiction – and a Winning Strategy for Recovery* (New York: John Wiley & Sons, Inc., 1998).

43 Nicola F. Johnson, *The Multiplicities of Internet Addiction: The Misrecognition of Leisure and Learning* (Farnham, Surrey: Ashgate, 2009), p. 127.

Chapter 4 The New Radical Right and the Resurgence of Authoritarian Politics

1 Sigmund Freud, 'The economic problem of masochism', in *The Standard Edition of the Complete Psychological Works of Sigmund Freud*, Vol. 19 (London: Hogarth, 1961 [1924]).

2 Erich Fromm, *The Fear of Freedom* (Abingdon: Routledge, 2010 [1942]), p. 130.

3 Ibid., p. 134.

4 See Sigmund Freud, *Three Essays on the Theory of Sexuality* (New York: Basic Books, 1962 [1905]), p. 50; Jacques Derrida, *The Post Card: From Socrates to Freud and Beyond* (Chicago: University of Chicago Press, 1987 [1980]).

5   Fromm, *The Fear of Freedom*, p. 190.
6   Walter Lacqueur, *Fascism: Past, Present, and Future* (Oxford: Oxford University Press, 1997), chapter 1.
7   Mark Mazower, *Hitler's Empire: Nazi Rule in Occupied Europe* (London: Allen Lane/Penguin, 2008), pp. 204–5.
8   Juan Linz, 'Some notes toward a comparative study of fascism in sociological historical perspective', in Walter Lacquer (ed.), *Fascism: A Reader's Guide* (Cambridge: Scolar Press, 1991 [1976]), p. 15.
9   See Jamie Bartlett and Mark Littler, *Inside the EDL: Populist Politics in a Digital Age* (London: DEMOS, 2011); Jamie Bartlett, Jonathan Birdwell and Mark Littler, *The New Face of Digital Populism* (London: DEMOS, 2011); Matthew Goodwin, 'Right response: understanding and countering populist extremism in Europe', *Chatham House Report* (London, 2012), p. ix; Paul Jackson, 'The EDL: Britain's "new far right" social movement', Radicalism and New Media Research Group, University of Nottingham, 2011; Paul Thomas, *Responding to the Threat of Violent Extremism: Failing to Prevent* (London: Bloomsbury Academic, 2012); and Michael Whine, 'Trans-European trends in right-wing extremism', in Andrea Mammone, Emmanuel Godin and Brian Jenkins (eds), *Mapping the Extreme Right in Contemporary Europe* (London: Routledge, 2012).
10 Hans-Georg Betz, 'The growing threat of the radical right', in Peter H. Merkl and Leonard Weinberg (eds), *Right-Wing Extremism in the Twenty-First Century* (London: Frank Cass, 2003), p. 86. See also Mabel Berezin, *Illiberal Politics in Neoliberal Times* (Cambridge: Cambridge University Press, 2009).
11 Andrej Zaslove, 'Closing the door? The ideology and impact of radical right populism on immigration policy in Austria and Italy', *Journal of Political Ideologies* 9, 1 (2004): 99–118 (p. 106).
12 Pippa Norris, *Radical Right: Voters and Parties in the Electoral Market* (Cambridge: Cambridge University Press, 2005), p. 147. See also Daniel Bell, *The Radical Right* (New Brunswick, NJ: Transaction Publishers, 2008 [2002]).
13 Cas Mudde, *The Populist Radical Right in Europe* (Cambridge: Cambridge University Press, 2005), p. 147. See also Margaret Canovan, *Populism* (New York: Harcourt Brace Jovanovich, 1981); Paul Hainsworth, *The Politics of the Extreme Right* (London: Pinter, 2000); and Michael Mikenberg, *The Radical Right in Europe: An Overview* (Gütersloh: Verlag Bertelsmann Stiftung, 2008).
14 Norris, *Radical Right*, p. 257.
15 Jörg Flecker, Gudrun Hentges and Gabrielle Balazs, 'Potentials of political subjectivity and the various approaches to the extreme

right: findings of the qualitative research', in Jörg Flecker (ed.), *Changing Working Life and the Appeal of the Extreme Right* (Aldershot, Ashgate, 2007), pp. 60–1.

16 Norris, *Radical Right*, p. 18.

17 Ibid., p. 186.

18 For a detailed analysis, see Xavier Casals-Meseguer, *Ultrapatriotas* (Barcelona: Crítica, 2003).

19 *http://nationalsocialism.com* (accessed 19 February 2013).

20 Nora Langenbacher and Britta Schellenberg (eds), *Is Europe on the 'Right' Path?* (Berlin: Forum Berlin, Friedrich-Ebert-Stiftung, 2011), p. 21.

21 *http://www.thelocal.de/national/20101024-30713.html* (accessed 14 February 2013).

22 *http://gatesofvienna.net* (accessed 19 February 2013).

23 *http://www.citiesagainstislamisation.com* (accessed 19 February 2013).

24 Ibid.

25 See Christian Boswell, *European Migration Policies in Flux: Changing Patterns of Inclusion and Exclusion* (Oxford: Oxford University Press, 2002); Sarah Spencer (ed.), *The Politics of Migration: Global Capital, Migrant Labour and the Nation-State* (Aldershot: Ashgate, 2006).

26 See Ash Amin, *Land of Strangers* (Cambridge: Polity Press, 2012); Christian Joppke, *Citizenship and Immigration* (Cambridge: Polity Press, 2010); and Paul Scheffer, *Immigrant Nations* (Cambridge: Polity Press, 2011).

27 Floya Anthias and Nira Yuval-Davis, *Racialized Boundaries: Race, Nation, Gender, Colour and Class and the Anti-Racist Struggle* (London: Routledge, 1992), pp. 86–91; Pierre-André Taguieff, *The Force of Prejudice: On Racism and Its Doubles* (Minneapolis: University of Minnesota Press, 2001).

28 Michael Banton, *The Idea of Race* (London: Tavistock, 1977).

29 Michel Wieviorka, *Le racisme, une introduction* (Paris: La Découverte, 1998); Michel Wieviorka, *Pour la prochaine gauche* (Paris: Éditions Robert Laffont, 2011).

30 Yves Mény and Yves Surel touch upon some of the issues I discuss here: *Par le people, pour le people* (Paris: Fayard, 2000).

31 See Jürgen Habermas, 'Citizenship and national identity: some reflections on the future of Europe', *Praxis International* 12 (1992): 1–19.

32 David Miller, *On Nationality* (Oxford: Oxford University Press, 1995), p. 163.

33 Marine Le Pen, electoral programme 2012, 'La voix du people,

l'esprit de la France', Section 1: 'Autorité de l'État', État fort subsection (*http://www.frontnational.com/le-projet-de-marine-le-pen/*, accessed 15 February 2013).

34 Jörg Haider died in a car accident in October 2008.

35 Mény and Surel, *Par le peuple, pour le people*, p. 211.

36 *http://barenakedislam.com/2012/04/21/austria-freedom-partys-anti-moroccan-* (accessed 15 February 2013).

37 Le Front National, *http://www.frontnational.com/doc-prop-identite* (accessed 17 February 2006; no longer available).

38 Marine Le Pen, electoral programme 2012, 'La voix du people, l'esprit de la France', Immigration (*http://www.frontnational.com/le-projet-de-marine-le-pen/autorite*, accessed 15 February 2013).

39 Le Front National, 'Les Argumentaires: L'Identité' (*http://www.frontnational.com*), p. 3 (accessed 17 February 2006; no longer available).

40 Ibid., p. 4.

41 Pierre-André Taguieff, *Sur la Nouvelle droite: Jalons d'une analyse critique* (Paris: Descartes & Cie, 1994).

42 Alain de Benoist, *Europe, Tiers monde, même combat* (Paris: R. Laffont, 1986); and A. James Gregor, *Mussolini's Intellectuals: Fascist Social and Political Thought* (Princeton: Princeton University Press, 2006).

43 Taguieff, *The Force of Prejudice*.

Chapter 5 The Rituals of Belonging

1 See *http://en.wikipedia.org/wiki/Flag_of_Germany#1989_to_today* (accessed 15 February 2013).

2 See Helen Graham, *The Spanish Civil War: A Very Short Introduction* (Oxford: Oxford University Press, 2005); Jim Jump (ed.), *Looking Back at the Spanish Civil War* (London: Lawrence and Wishart, 2010); Paul Preston, *The Spanish Civil War: Reaction, Revolution and Revenge* (London: W.W. Norton & Co., 2006).

3 David I. Kertzer, *Ritual, Politics and Power* (London and New Haven: Yale University Press, 1988), p. 5.

4 Ibid., p. 158.

5 Lynn Hunt, *Politics, Culture and Class in the French Revolution* (Berkeley: University of California Press, 1984), pp. 56, 61–8.

6 Mary Douglas, *Purity and Danger* (New York: Praeger, 1966), p. 62.

7 Oxford Dictionaries (*http://oxforddictionaries.com/definition/english/ritual*, accessed 15 February 2013).

8 Arnold van Gennep, *The Rites of Passage* (Chicago: University of Chicago Press, 1966 [1960]), p. 1.

9 Émile Durkheim, *The Elementary Forms of the Religious Life* (London: George Allen & Unwin, 1982 [1915]), pp. 418–19.

10 Kertzer, *Ritual, Politics and Power*, p. 38.

11 Durkheim, *The Elementary Forms of the Religious Life*, p. 427.

12 Edward Muir, *Civic Ritual in Renaissance Venice* (Princeton: Princeton University Press, 1981), p. 76.

13 Peter Beaumont, 'Political Islam poised to dominate the new world bequeathed by Arab spring', *Guardian*, 3 December 2011 (*http://www.guardian.co.uk/world/2011/dec/03/political-islam-poised-arab-spring*, accessed 18 February 2013).

14 Emma Bonino, quoted in 'Arab Spring: aid depends on women's rights, Italian FM Terzi', Ansa Med, 16 July 2012 (*http://www.ansa.it/ansamed/en/news/nations/italy/2012/07/16/Arab-Spring-Aid-depends-women-rights-Italian-FM-Terzi_7195341.html*, accessed 18 February 2013).

15 Shirin Ebadi, 'A Warning for women of the Arab Spring', *The Wall Street Journal*, Opinion, 14 March 2012.

16 Stephan Rosiny, *The Arab Spring: Triggers, Dynamics and Prospects* (GIGA Focus, German Institute of Global and Area Studies, no. 1, 2012), p. 5 (*http://www.giga-hamburg.de/dl/download.php?d=/content/publikationen/pdf/gf_international_1201.pdf*, accessed 1 March 2013).

17 Hitler cited by Kertzer, *Rituals, Politics and Power*, p. 165.

18 Shirin M. Rai, *Ceremony and Ritual in Parliament* (London: Routledge, 2011).

19 See Erving Goffman, *Stigma: Notes on the Management of Spoiled Identity* (Englewood Cliffs, NJ: Prentice-Hall, Inc., 1963), p. 1.

20 Paul Preston, *Franco* (London: Fontana Press, 1994), p. 185.

21 Ibid., pp. 185–6.

22 'Speech on opening the seventh term of the Spanish parliament', Madrid, 3 June 1961, in Francisco Franco, *Discursos y mensajes del Jefe del Estado 1960–1963* (Madrid: Dirección General de Información, Publicaciones Españolas, 1964), pp. 217–18.

23 Max Gallo, *Historia de la España franquista* (Paris: Ruedo Ibérico, 1969), p. 80.

24 Hilari Raguer, *La pólvora y el incienso: La Iglesia y la Guerra Civil Española (1936–1939)* (Barcelona: Península, 2001). See also Raguer, *Ser Independentista no és cap Pecat: L'Església i el Nacionalisme Català* (Barcelona: Editorial Claret, 2012).

25 Immanuel Kant, 'What Is Enlightenment?' (1784) (*http://www.colum*

bia.edu/acis/ets/CCREAD/etscc/kant.html, accessed 18 February 2013).

26 Cited in Muir, *Civic Ritual in Renaissance Venice*, pp. 74–5.

27 Durkheim, *The Elementary Forms of the Religious Life*, p. 47.

28 Ibid., p. 416.

29 Ibid., p. 418.

30 See Anthony D. Smith, *Myths and Memories of the Nation* (Oxford: Oxford University Press, 1999).

31 Van Gennep, *The Rites of Passage*, p. 80.

32 Ibid., p. 1.

33 Ibid., p. ix.

34 Jean Evenou, 'Baptism and Christian life' (*http://www.vatican. va/jubilee_2000/magazine/documents/ju_mag_01051997_p-81_ en.html*, accessed 18 February 2013).

35 The account of becoming a gang member is based upon 'Traits of Gang Members', Edmonton Police Service (*http://www. edmontonpolice.ca/CommunityPolicing/OrganizedCrime/Gangs/ TraitsofGangMembers.aspx*, accessed 18 February 2013).

36 Ibid.

37 Ibid.

38 *http://www.gangsorus.com/gangsta_girls.html* (accessed 18 February 2013).

39 Mark Townsend, 'Being raped by a gang is normal – it's about craving to be accepted', *Guardian*, 18 February 2012 (*http://www. guardian.co.uk/society/2012/feb/18/being-raped-by-gang-normal*, accessed 18 February 2013).

40 *http://judaism.about.com/od/lifeevents/a/britmilah.htm* (accessed 18 February 2013).

41 Nadine C. Hoover, 'National Survey: Initiation Rites and Athletics for NCAA Sports Teams', 30 August 1999, Alfred University, USA.

Chapter 6 Loyalty, Citizenship and the Nation

1 For a full account of the origin of the Jehovah's Witnesses position, see *Minersville School District* v. *Gobitis* (1940) (*http://www. pbs.org/wnet/supremecourt/personality/landmark_minersville.html*, accessed 10 March 2013).

2 Ernest Gellner, *Postmodernism, Reason and Religion* (London: Routledge, 1992), p. 5.

3 Ibid., p. 6.

4 Ibid., p. 7.

5 Definition of 'patriotism' in *Collins Concise English Dictionary*, Third Edition (Glasgow: HarperCollins Publishers, 1993).

6 See Benedict Anderson, *Imagined Communities: Reflections on the Origin and Spread of Nationalism* (London: Verso, 1983); Ernest Gellner, *Nations and Nationalism* (Oxford: Basil Blackwell, 1983); E.J. Hobsbawm, *Nations and Nationalism since 1780* (Cambridge: Cambridge University Press, 1999); Miroslav Hroch, *Social Preconditions of National Revival in Europe: A Comparative Analysis of the Social Composition of Patriotic Groups among the Smaller European Nations* (Cambridge: Cambridge University Press, 1985); and Anthony D. Smith, *The Ethnic Origins of Nations* (Oxford: Basil Blackwell, 1990).

7 Montserrat Guibernau, *Nations without States: Political Communities in the Global Age* (Cambridge: Polity Press, 1999), p. 47.

8 Anthony D. Smith, 'History and national destiny: responses and clarifications', in Montserrat Guibernau and John Hutchinson (eds), *History and National Destiny: Ethnosymbolism and Its Critics* (Oxford: Blackwell, 2004), p. 205.

9 Anderson, *Imagined Communities*, pp. 41–9.

10 Montserrat Guibernau, *The Identity of Nations* (Cambridge: Polity Press, 2007). See also *For a Cosmopolitan Catalanism* (Barcelona: Angle Editors, 2009).

11 Samuel P. Huntington, *The Clash of Civilizations and the Remaking of World Order* (London: Free Press, 2002).

12 Paul Preston, *Franco* (London: Fontana Press, 1994), p. 208.

13 John C. Wahlke (ed.), *Loyalty in a Democratic State* (Boston: D.C. Heath and Company, 1952), p. v.

14 In the small city of Terrassa, for example, there were 2,807 political denunciations against people just in the year 1939. The authorities received such a large number of denunciations, many of them invented, that in Barcelona the provincial leadership of the Falange (the Fascist political party defending the dictatorship) had to send an order to its activists warning that anyone who made false accusations would be severely penalized. See Borja de Riquer and Joan B. Culla, *El franquisme i la transició democràtica (1939–1988)*, Pierre Vilar (gen. ed.), *Història de Catalunya*, Vol. VII (Barcelona: Edicions 62, 1989), p. 137.

15 Wahlke (ed.), *Loyalty in a Democratic State*, p. vi.

16 Henry Steele Commager, *Freedom, Loyalty and Dissent* (Oxford: Oxford University Press, 1954), p. 91.

17 Ibid., p. 19.

18 Ibid., p. 93.

19   Quoted in ibid., p. 57.
20   Wahlke (ed.), *Loyalty in a Democratic State*, p. vii.
21   Ibid.
22   Carey McWilliams, *Witch Hunt: The Revival of Heresy* (Boston: Little Brown, 1950), pp. 1–13.
23   Henry Steele Commager (ed.), *Documents of American History*, Ninth Edition (Englewood Cliffs, NJ: Prentice-Hall, 1973), Doc. 579.
24   Leonard A. Nikoloric, 'The government loyalty programme', in Wahlke (ed.), *Loyalty in a Democratic State*, p. 50.
25   After President Truman issued Executive Order No. 9835 (1947) setting up a federal loyalty programme, it became clear that the programme was not strictly employed to identify 'potentially disloyal persons' whose actions might threaten US interests. President Truman acknowledged that and issued the Veto message in 1950. In his own words: 'I cannot approve this legislation, which instead of accomplishing its avowed purpose would actually interfere with our liberties and help the Communists against whom the bill was aimed.' President Harry S. Truman, 'The Internal Security Act: Veto message', quoted in Wahlke (ed.), *Loyalty in a Democratic State*, p. 83.
26   Ibid., p. 61.
27   Wahlke (ed.), *Loyalty in a Democratic State*, p. 8.
28   Commager, *Freedom, Loyalty and Dissent*, p. 15.
29   Wahlke (ed.), *Loyalty in a Democratic State*, pp. 3–4.
30   David Lane, *Soviet Society under Perestroika* (London: Routledge, 1992).
31   Jung Chang and Jon Halliday, *Mao: The Unknown Story* (London: Vintage Books, 2007); Gao Mobo, *The Battle for China's Past: Mao and the Cultural Revolution* (London: Pluto Press, 2008).
32   This section relies on twenty-one in-depth semi-structured interviews carried out in 2011–12 among survivors of the Spanish Civil War (1936–9). The interviews were carried out in Barcelona and Tarragona.
33   Commager, *Freedom, Loyalty and Dissent*, p. 8.
34   Ibid., p. 96.
35   Ibid., p. 95.
36   Iva Toguri was accused of propaganda broadcasts transmitted by Radio Tokyo to Allied soldiers in the South Pacific during World War II. Initially, in 1946, she was released for lack of evidence; however, three years later she was prosecuted and charged with treason. Investigative journalists found that key witnesses claimed they were forced to lie during testimony and subsequently President

Gerald Ford pardoned Toguri in 1977. Tomoya Kawakita was arrested in 1947 and charged with treason after being accused of torturing American POWs. In his defence, Kawakita claimed that he had renounced his US citizenship during his time in Japan. He was sentenced to death; however, President Dwight D. Eisenhower commuted Kawakita's sentence to life imprisonment in 1953 and President John F. Kennedy pardoned him ten years later on the condition that he be deported to Japan for life.

37 Commager, *Freedom, Loyalty and Dissent*, p. 98.
38 Ibid., p. 98.
39 Ibid., p. 20.
40 Ibid., p. 97.
41 Arthur M. Schlesinger, 'What is loyalty? A difficult question', in Wahlke (ed.), *Loyalty in a Democratic State*, p. 14.
42 See, for example, the case of *Erdemovic* at the International Criminal Tribunal for the Former Yugoslavia: Elies Van Sliedregt, 'Defences in international criminal law', paper presented at the Conference 'Convergence of Criminal Justice Systems: Building Bridges Bridging the Gap', The International Society for the Reform of Criminal Law, 17th International Conference, 25 August 2003, p. 20 (*http://www. isrcl.org/Papers/Sliedregt.pdf*, accessed 1 March 2013).
43 John H. Schaar, *Loyalty in America* (Berkeley and Los Angeles: University of California Press, 1957), p. 33.
44 Ibid., p. 33.
45 Ibid., p. 34.
46 Ibid., p. 36.
47 Ibid., p. 49.
48 *http://www.archives.gov/exhibits/charters/declaration.html* (accessed 20 February 2013).
49 Schaar, *Loyalty in America*, p. 59.
50 Ibid., p. 59 fn.

Chapter 7 Emotion and Political Mobilization

1 Ruth Wodak, '"Us" and "them": inclusion and exclusion – discrimination via discourse', in Gerard Delanty, Ruth Wodak and Paul Jones (eds), *Identity, Belonging and Migration* (Liverpool: Liverpool University Press, 2011 [2008]), p. 56.
2 Thomas Scheff, *Emotions, the Social Bond, and Human Reality* (Cambridge: Cambridge University Press, 1997), pp. 10–11.
3 See Talcott Parsons, *The Structure of Social Action* (McGraw Hill: New York, 1968 [1937]), p. 156.

4   Talcott Parsons, *The Social System* (New York: Free Press, 1951), p. 298.
5   J.M. Barbalet, *Emotion, Social Theory and Social Structure* (Cambridge: Cambridge University Press, 1998), p. 24.
6   Ibid., pp. 25–6.
7   Ibid., p. 27.
8   David Hume, *A Treatise of Human Nature: A Critical Edition* (Oxford: Clarendon Press, 2007 [1739–40]), p. 413.
9   Ibid., p. 458.
10 Max Weber, *Economy and Society*, Vol. 1 (Berkeley and Los Angeles: University of California Press, 1978 [1922]), p. 25.
11 William James, 'The sentiment of rationality', in *The Will to Believe and Other Essays in Popular Philosophy* (New York: Dover Publications, 1956 [1897]).
12 Niklas Luhmann, *Trust and Power* (New York: Wiley, 1979), p. 25.
13 Ibid., pp. 10, 25.
14 Georg Simmel, *The Sociology of Georg Simmel* (Glencoe, IL: Free Press, 1950), p. 313.
15 Ibid., p. 84.
16 Max Weber, *From Max Weber: Essays in Sociology* (London: Routledge, 1948), p. 87.
17 Montserrat Guibernau, *Nationalisms* (Cambridge: Polity Press, 1996), p. 47.
18 Ibid.
19 Agnes Heller, *A Theory of Feelings* (Assen, The Netherlands: Van Gorcum, 1979), p. 185.
20 Barbalet, *Emotion, Social Theory and Social Structure*, p. 59.
21 Adam Smith, *The Theory of Moral Sentiments* (London: Penguin Classics, 2010 [1759]).
22 Alexis de Tocqueville, *Democracy in America*, Vol. 2 (London: Fontana Press, 1994 [1840]), part II, chapter 1, p. 506.
23 Heller, *A Theory of Feelings*, p. 209.
24 Montserrat Guibernau, *The Identity of Nations* (Cambridge: Polity Press, 2007), p. 25.
25 Charles Tilly, *Popular Contention in Great Britain, 1758–1834* (Cambridge, MA: Harvard University Press, 1995).
26 Hank Johnston, *States and Social Movements* (Cambridge: Polity Press, 2011), p. 7.
27 J.H. Elliott, *The Revolt of the Catalans: A Study in the Decline of Spain (1598–1640)* (Cambridge: Cambridge University Press, 1963).
28 It is significant that, together with England, Catalonia was one of the first societies to grant itself what amounted to a written feudal constitution. Yet the English Magna Carta (1215) was preceded by

almost one century by the Catalan *Usatges* of 1150, whose very title (the *uses*, i.e. established customs and practices) betrays the fact that the laws the document proclaimed had already been in existence for a very long time. The *Usatges* was an essentially pactist law code.

29 Elliott, *The Revolt of the Catalans*, p. 45. See also Carme Batlle, *L'expansió baixmedieval segles XIII–XV*, Pierre Vilar (gen. ed.), *Història de Catalunya*, Vol. III (Barcelona: Edicions 62, 1987), pp. 217ff.

30 Elliott, *The Revolt of the Catalans*, p. 45.

31 In 1492 America was discovered by Columbus (funded by Queen Isabel of Castile); however, it was not until 1778 – that is, 286 years later – that the Spanish King Carlos III allowed the Catalans to trade with America.

32 Elliott, *The Revolt of the Catalans*, pp. 367–8. Elliott writes: 'From all accounts, the insatiable demands of an increasingly large army were fast completing that alienation of the *Comtats* [Catalan counties] which had already begun with the publication of the royal decrees on trade with France. Troops and inhabitants were involved in constant clashes' (p. 368).

33 Ibid., pp. 485–6.

34 David Heater, *Citizenship: The Civil Ideal in World History, Politics and Education* (London and New York: Longman, 1990).

35 James H. Kettner, *The Development of American Citizenship 1608–1870* (Chapel Hill: University of North Carolina Press, 1978), p. 341.

36 'The Declaration' was adopted on 26 August 1789 by the National Constituent Assembly – although some sources say the 27th because the debate was not officially closed until then.

37 See *http://www.womeninworldhistory.com/TWR-07.html* (accessed 22 February 2013).

38 *Report of the Woman's Rights Convention, Held at Seneca Falls, N.Y., July 19th and 20th, 1848* (Rochester, NY, 1848).

39 Richard Bellamy, *Political Constitutionalism: A Republican Defence of the Constitutionality of Democracy* (Cambridge: Cambridge University Press, 2007), p. 7.

40 Charles Tilly, *Social Movements 1768–2004* (Boulder, CO: Paradigm Publishers, 2004), p. 4.

41 Peter K. Eisinger, 'The conditions of protest behavior in American cities', *American Political Science Review* 67 (1973): 11–28. See also the summary in Johnston, *States and Social Movements*, p. 34.

42 See Barrington Moore, Jr, *Social Origins of Dictatorship and Democracy* (Boston: Beacon Press, 1966), p. 20.

43 Jonathan H. Turner and Jan E. Stets, *The Sociology of Emotions* (Cambridge: Cambridge University Press, 2005), p. 256.

44 Friedrich Nietzsche, *On the Genealogy of Morality* (Cambridge: Cambridge University Press, 2007 [1887]), p. 20.

45 Jean-Paul Sartre, *Being and Nothingness: An Essay on Phenomenological Ontology* (London: Routledge, 2009 [1943]), part 3, chapter 1.

46 Nietzsche, *On the Genealogy of Morality*, p. 21.

47 Ibid., p. 22.

48 T.H. Marshall, *Class, Citizenship and Social Development* (New York: Doubleday & Company, Inc., 1987 [1964]), p. 168.

49 Jonathan Cobb and Richard Sennett, *The Hidden Injuries of Class* (New York: Vintage Books, 1972), p. 135.

50 Theodore Kemper, *A Social Interactional Theory of Emotions* (New York: Wiley, 1978), pp. 55–6.

51 Barbalet, *Emotion, Social Theory and Social Structure*, p. 90.

52 Randall Collins, *Interaction Ritual Chains* (Princeton: Princeton University Press, 2004), p. 108.

53 For an analysis of rational and emotional arguments as employed in Catalan nationalist discourse, see my *Catalan Nationalism: Francoism, Transition and Democracy* (London: Routledge, 2004), pp. 28–32.

Bibliography

Amin, Ash, *Land of Strangers*. Cambridge: Polity Press, 2012.

Anderson, Benedict, *Imagined Communities: Reflections on the Origin and Spread of Nationalism*. London: Verso, 1983.

Anthias, Floya and Nira Yuval-Davis, *Racialized Boundaries: Race, Nation, Gender, Colour and Class and the Anti-Racist Struggle*. London: Routledge, 1992.

Bailey, James R. and John H. Yost, 'Role theory: foundations, extensions, and applications', in E.F. Borgatta and R.J.V. Montgomery (eds), *Encylopedia of Sociology*, Vol. 4. New York: Macmillan, 2000.

Balcells, Albert, *Catalan Nationalism*. London: Macmillan, 1996.

Banton, Michael, *The Idea of Race*. London: Tavistock, 1977.

Barbalet, J.M., *Emotion, Social Theory and Social Structure*. Cambridge: Cambridge University Press, 1998.

Barth, Thomas F., *Ethnic Groups and Boundaries: The Social Organization of Culture Difference*. Oslo: Universitetsforlaget, 1969.

Bartlett, Jamie and Mark Littler, *Inside the EDL: Populist Politics in a Digital Age*. London: DEMOS, 2011.

Bartlett, Jamie, Jonathan Birdwell and Mark Littler, *The New Face of Digital Populism*. London: DEMOS, 2011.

Batlle, Carme, *L'expansió baixmedieval segles XIII–XV*, Pierre Vilar (gen. ed.), *Història de Catalunya*, Vol. III. Barcelona: Edicions 62, 1987.

Bauböck, Rainer, *Transnational Citizenship: Membership and Rights in International Migration*. Aldershot: Edward Elgar, 1994.

Bauböck, Rainer and Virginie Guiraudon (eds), 'Realignments of Citizenship', *Citizenship Studies*, special issue, vol. 13 (October 2009).

Baumeister, Roy F., *Identity: Cultural Change and the Struggle for Self.* Oxford: Oxford University Press, 1986.

Bell, Daniel, *The Radical Right.* New Brunswick, NJ: Transaction Publishers, 2008 [2002].

Bellamy, Richard, *Political Constitutionalism: A Republican Defence of the Constitutionality of Democracy.* Cambridge: Cambridge University Press, 2007.

Benoist, Alain de, *Europe, Tiers monde, même combat.* Paris: R. Laffont, 1986.

Berezin, Mabel, *Illiberal Politics in Neoliberal Times.* Cambridge: Cambridge University Press, 2009.

Berlin, Isaiah, *The Sense of Reality.* London: Pimlico, 1996.

Betz, Hans-Georg, 'The growing threat of the radical right', in Peter H. Merkl and Leonard Weinberg (eds), *Right-Wing Extremism in the Twenty-First Century.* London: Frank Cass, 2003.

Boswell, Christian, *European Migration Policies in Flux: Changing Patterns of Inclusion and Exclusion.* Oxford: Oxford University Press, 2002.

Burke, Peter J. and Jan E. Stets, *Identity Theory.* Oxford: Oxford University Press, 2009.

Calhoun, Craig, 'Belonging in the cosmopolitan imaginary', *Ethnicities* 3 (2003): 531–68.

Canovan, Margaret, *Populism.* New York: Harcourt Brace Jovanovich, 1981.

Carbonell, Pere, *Tres Nadals empresonats.* Barcelona: Publicacions de l'Abadia de Montserrat, 1999.

Casals-Meseguer, Xavier, *Ultrapatriotas.* Barcelona: Crítica, 2003.

Chang, Jung and Jon Halliday, *Mao: The Unknown Story.* London: Vintage Books, 2007.

Cobb, Jonathan and Richard Sennett, *The Hidden Injuries of Class.* New York: Vintage Books, 1972.

Coffé, Holde, Bruno Heyndels and Jan Vermeir, 'Fertile grounds for extreme right-wing parties: explaining the Vlaams Blok's electoral success', *Electoral Studies* 26 (2007):142–55.

Cohen, Anthony, *The Symbolic Construction of Community.* London: Tavistock Publications, 1985.

Collins, Randall, *Interaction Ritual Chains.* Princeton: Princeton University Press, 2004.

Colomines, Joan, *El compromís de viure.* Barcelona: Columna, 1999.

Commager, Henry Steele (ed.), *Documents of American History*, Ninth Edition. Englewood Cliffs, NJ: Prentice-Hall, 1973.

Commager, Henry Steele, *Freedom, Loyalty and Dissent.* Oxford: Oxford University Press, 1954.

Cruse, Harold, *The Crisis of the Negro Intellectual*. New York: Morrow, 1967.

de Riquer, Borja and Joan B. Culla, *El franquisme i la transició democràtica (1939–1988)*, Pierre Vilar (gen. ed.), *Història de Catalunya*, Vol. VII. Barcelona: Edicions 62, 1989.

del Libano, Mario, Susana Llorens, Marisa Salanova and Wilmar Schaufeli, 'Validity of a brief workaholism scale', *Psicothema* 22(1) (2010): 143–50.

Degenhardt, Louisa and Wayne Hall, 'Extent of illicit drug use and dependence, and their contribution to the global burden of disease', *The Lancet* 379, 9810 (2012): 55–70.

Derrida, Jacques, *The Post Card: From Socrates to Freud and Beyond*. Chicago: University of Chicago Press, 1987 [1980].

Dillistone, F.W., *The Power of Symbols*. SCM Press: London, 1986.

Douglas, Mary, *Purity and Danger*. New York: Praeger, 1966.

Dumm, Thomas L., *Michel Foucault and the Politics of Freedom*. London: Sage: 1996.

Durkheim, Émile, *The Division of Labour in Society* (London: Macmillan, 1984 [1893])

Durkheim, Émile, *The Elementary Forms of Religious Life*. London: George Allen, 1982 [1915].

Durkheim, Émile, 'Religion and ritual', in *Selected Writings*. Cambridge: Cambridge University Press, 1987 [1972].

Eatwell, Roger, *Fascism: A History*. London: Vintage Books, 2009.

Eatwell, Roger, 'Ten theories of the extreme right', in Peter H. Merkl and Leonard Weinberg (eds), *Right-Wing Extremism in the Twenty-First Century*. London: Frank Cass, 2003.

Eisinger, Peter K., 'The conditions of protest behavior in American cities', *American Political Science Review* 67 (1973): 11–28.

Elliott, J.H., *The Revolt of the Catalans: A Study in the Decline of Spain (1598–1640)*. Cambridge: Cambridge University Press, 1963.

Ewald, Roschbeth, 'Sexual addiction', *AllPsych Journal*, 13 May 2003: *http://allpsych.com/journal/sexaddiction.html* (accessed 13 February 2013).

Fabré, Jaume, Josep Maria Huertas and Antoni Ribas, *Vint anys de resistència catalana (1939–1959)*. Barcelona: La Magrana, 1978.

Flathman, Richard E., *Freedom and Its Conditions*. New York and London: Routledge, 2003.

Flecker, Jörg, Gudrun Hentges and Gabrielle Balazs, 'Potentials of political subjectivity and the various approaches to the extreme right: findings of the qualitative research', in Jörg Flecker (ed.), *Changing Working Life and the Appeal of the Extreme Right*. Aldershot, Ashgate, 2007.

Foner, Eric, *A Short History of Reconstruction, 1863–1877*. New York: Harper & Row, 1990.

Foucault, Michel, *The Care of the Self: The History of Sexuality*, Vol. 3. London: Allen Lane/Penguin, 1986 [1984].

Foucault, Michel, *Discipline and Punish*. London: Allen Lane/Penguin, 1977 [1975].

Foucault, Michel, *Ethics, Subjectivity and Truth: The Essential Works of M. Foucault 1954–1984*, Vol. 1. New York: New Press.

Foucault, Michel, *Society Must Be Defended: Lectures at the Collège de France*. London: Allen Lane/Penguin, 2003 [1997].

Franco, Francisco, *Discursos y mensajes del Jefe del Estado 1960–1963*. Madrid: Dirección General de Información, Publicaciones Españolas, 1964.

Freud, Sigmund, 'The economic problem of masochism', in *The Standard Edition of the Complete Psychological Works of Sigmund Freud*, Vol. 19. London: Hogarth, 1961 [1924].

Freud, Sigmund, *Three Essays on the Theory of Sexuality*. New York: Basic Books, 1962 [1905].

Fromm, Erich, *The Fear of Freedom*. Abingdon: Routledge, 2010 [1942].

Gagnon, Alain-G. and Richard Simeon, 'Canada', in Luís Moreno and César Colino (eds), *Diversity and Unity in Federal Countries: A Global Dialogue on Federalism*, Vol. 7. Montreal: McGill-Queen's University Press, 2010.

Gallo, Max, *Historia de la España franquista*. Paris: Ruedo Ibérico, 1969.

Gellner, Ernest, *Nations and Nationalism*. Oxford: Basil Blackwell, 1983.

Gellner, Ernest, *Postmodernism, Reason and Religion*. London: Routledge, 1992.

Giddens, Anthony, *Modernity and Self-Identity*. Cambridge: Polity Press, 1991.

Giddens, Anthony, *The Transformation of Intimacy*. Cambridge: Polity Press, 1992.

Giner, Salvador, *Mass Society*. New York: Academic Press, 1976.

Goffman, Erving, *The Presentation of the Self in Everyday Life*. Garden City, NY: Anchor Books, 1959.

Goffman, Erving, *Stigma: Notes on the Management of Spoiled Identity*. Englewood Cliffs, NJ: Prentice-Hall, Inc., 1963.

Goodwin, Matthew, 'Right response: understanding and countering populist extremism in Europe', *Chatham House Report*. London, 2012.

Graham, Helen, *The Spanish Civil War: A Very Short Introduction*. Oxford: Oxford University Press, 2005.

Greenfeld, Liah, *Nationalism and the Mind*. Oxford: Oneworld, 2006.

Gregor, A. James, *Mussolini's Intellectuals: Fascist Social and Political Thought*. Princeton: Princeton University Press, 2006.

Guibernau, Montserrat, *Catalan Nationalism: Francoism, Transition and Democracy*. London: Routledge, 2004.

Guibernau, Montserrat, *For a Cosmopolitan Catalanism*. Barcelona: Angle Editors, 2009.

Guibernau, Montserrat, *The Identity of Nations*. Cambridge: Polity Press, 2007.

Guibernau, Montserrat, *Nationalisms*. Cambridge: Polity Press, 1996.

Guibernau, Montserrat, *Nations without States: Political Communities in the Global Age*. Cambridge: Polity Press, 1999.

Habermas, Jürgen, 'Citizenship and national identity: some reflections on the future of Europe', *Praxis International* 12 (1992): 1–19.

Hainsworth, Paul, *The Politics of the Extreme Right*. London: Pinter, 2000.

Hay, Colin, *Why We Hate Politics*. Cambridge: Polity Press, 2007.

Heater, David, *Citizenship: The Civil Ideal in World History, Politics and Education*. London and New York: Longman, 1990.

Hedetoft, Ulf and Mette Hjort, 'Introduction', in Ulf Hedetoft and Mette Hjort (eds), *The Postnational Self: Belonging and Identity*. Minneapolis: University of Minnesota Press, 2002.

Held, David, 'Principles of cosmopolitan order', in Gillian Brock and Harry Brighouse (eds), *The Political Philosophy of Cosmopolitanism*. Cambridge: Cambridge University Press, 2005.

Heller, Agnes, *A Theory of Feelings*. Assen, The Netherlands: Van Gorcum, 1979.

Henderson, Errol A., 'War, political cycles, and the pendulum thesis', in Yvette M. Alex-Assensoh and Lawrence J. Hanks (eds), *Black and Multiracial Politics in America*. London and New York: New York University Press, 2000.

Hobsbawm, E.J., *Nations and Nationalism since 1780*. Cambridge: Cambridge University Press, 1990.

Holyoake, G.J., *The Origin and Nature of Secularism*. London: Watts and Co., 1896.

Hroch, Miroslav, *Social Preconditions of National Revival in Europe: A Comparative Analysis of the Social Composition of Patriotic Groups among the Smaller European Nations*. Cambridge: Cambridge University Press, 1985.

Hume, David, *A Treatise of Human Nature: A Critical Edition*. Oxford: Clarendon Press, 2007 [1739–40].

Hunt, Lynn, *Politics, Culture and Class in the French Revolution*. Berkeley: University of California Press, 1984.

Huntington, Samuel P., *The Clash of Civilizations and the Remaking of World Order*. London: Free Press, 2002.

Ignazi, Piero, *L'estrema destra in Europa*. Bologna: Il Mulino, 2000 [1994].

Ignazi, Piero, *Extreme Right Parties in Western Europe*. Oxford: Oxford University Press, 2006.

James, William, 'The sentiment of rationality', in *The Will to Believe and Other Essays in Popular Philosophy*. New York: Dover Publications, 1956 [1897].

Jeffery, Charles and Daniel Wincott, 'Devolution in the United Kingdom: statehood and citizenship in transition', *Publius* 36, 1 (2006): 3-18.

Jenkins, Richard, *Social Identity*. London: Routledge, 2008 [1996].

Johnson, Nicola F., *The Multiplicities of Internet Addiction: The Misrecognition of Leisure and Learning*. Farnham, Surrey: Ashgate, 2009.

Johnston, Hank, *States and Social Movements*. Cambridge: Polity Press, 2011.

Jones, Paul and Michał Krzyżanowski, 'Identity, belonging and migration: beyond constructing "others"', in Gerard Delanty, Ruth Wodak and Paul Jones, *Identity, Belonging and Migration*. Liverpool: Liverpool University Press, 2011 [2008].

Joppke, Christian, *Citizenship and Immigration*. Cambridge: Polity Press, 2010.

Jump, Jim (ed.) *Looking Back at the Spanish Civil War*. London: Lawrence and Wishart, 2010.

Kant, Immanuel, *Kants gesammelte Schriften, herausgegeben von der Deutschen* [formerly Königlichen Preussischen] *Akademie der Wissenschaften*, 29 vols. Berlin: Walter de Gruyter, 1902.

Kant, Immanuel, *The Metaphysics of Morals*. Cambridge: Cambridge University Press, 1996 [1797].

Kant, Immanuel, *The Philosophy of Kant: Immanuel Kant's Moral and Political Writings*. New York: Random House, The Modern Library, 1952.

Kant, Immanuel, 'What is Enlightenment?' (1784) (*http://www.columbia.edu/acis/ets/CCREAD/etscc/kant.html*, accessed 18 February 2013).

Kemper, Theodore, *A Social Interactional Theory of Emotions*. New York: Wiley, 1978.

Kertzer, David I., *Ritual, Politics and Power*. London and New Haven: Yale University Press, 1988.

Kettner, James H., *The Development of American Citizenship 1608-1870*. Chapel Hill: University of North Carolina Press, 1978.

Kierkegaard, Søren, *The Concept of Anxiety*. Princeton: Princeton University Press, 1980 [1844].

King, Desmond, *The Liberty of Strangers: Making the American Nation.* Oxford: Oxford University Press, 2005.

Knauer, Sandra L., *Recovering from Sexual Abuse, Addictions, and Compulsive Behaviors: 'Numb' Survivors.* New York: Haworth Press, 2002.

Lacqueur, Walter, *Fascism: Past, Present, and Future.* Oxford: Oxford University Press, 1997.

Lane, David, *Soviet Society under Perestroika.* London: Routledge, 1992.

Langenbacher, Nora and Britta Schellenberg (eds), *Is Europe on the 'Right' Path?* Berlin: Forum Berlin, Friedrich-Ebert-Stiftung, 2011.

Linz, Juan, 'Some notes toward a comparative study of fascism in sociological historical perspective', in Walter Lacqueur (ed.), *Fascism: A Reader's Guide.* Cambridge: Scolar Press, 1991 [1976].

Luhmann, Niklas, *Trust and Power.* New York: Wiley, 1979.

McCormick, Joseph and Sekou Franklin, 'Expressions of racial consciousness', in Yvette Alex-Assensoh and Lawrence J. Hanks (eds), *Black and Multiracial Politics in America.* New York and London: New York University Press, 2000.

McWilliams, Carey, *Witch Hunt: The Revival of Heresy.* Boston: Little Brown, 1950.

Marshall, T.H., *Class, Citizenship and Social Development.* New York: Doubleday & Company, Inc., 1987 [1964].

Mazower, Mark, *Hitler's Empire: Nazi Rule in Occupied Europe.* London: Allen Lane/Penguin, 2008.

Mead, George H., *Mind, Self, and Society: From the Standpoint of a Social Behaviorist.* Chicago: University of Chicago Press, 1967.

Melucci, Alberto, *Nomads of the Present.* London: Hutchinson Radius, 1989.

Mény, Yves and Yves Surel, *Par le peuple, pour le people.* Paris: Fayard, 2000.

Mikenberg, Michael, *The Radical Right in Europe: An Overview.* Gütersloh: Verlag Bertelsmann Stiftung, 2008.

Miller, David, *On Nationality.* Oxford: Oxford University Press, 1995.

Mobo, Gao, *The Battle for China's Past: Mao and the Cultural Revolution.* London: Pluto Press, 2008.

Moore, Barrington, Jr, *Social Origins of Dictatorship and Democracy.* Boston: Beacon Press, 1966.

Mudde, Cas, *The Populist Radical Right in Europe.* Cambridge: Cambridge University Press, 2005.

Muir, Edward, *Civic Ritual in Renaissance Venice.* Princeton: Princeton University Press, 1981.

Nietzsche, Friedrich, *On the Genealogy of Morality.* Cambridge: Cambridge University Press, 2007 [1887].

Nikoloric, Leonard A., 'The government loyalty programme', in John C. Wahlke (ed.), *Loyalty in a Democratic State*. Boston: D.C. Heath and Company, 1952.

Norris, Pippa, *Radical Right: Voters and Parties in the Electoral Market*. Cambridge: Cambridge University Press, 2005.

Oakeshott, Michael,'The political economy of freedom', in Paul Kelly (ed.), *British Political Theory in the Twentieth Century*. Oxford: Wiley-Blackwell, 2010.

O'Neill, Onora, 'Enlightenment as autonomy: Kant's vindication of reason', in Ludmilla Jordanova and Peter Hulme (eds), *The Enlightenment and Its Shadows*. London: Routledge, 1990.

Ortega y Gasset, José, *The Revolt of the Masses*. New York and London: W.W. Norton & Company, 1930.

Parsons, Talcott, *The Social System*. New York: Free Press, 1951.

Parsons, Talcott, *The Structure of Social Action*. New York: McGraw Hill, 1968 [1937].

Preston, Paul, *Franco*. London: Fontana Press, 1994.

Preston, Paul, *The Spanish Civil War: Reaction, Revolution and Revenge*. London: Norton & Co., 2006.

Rable, George C., *But There Was No Peace: The Role of Violence in the Politics of Reconstruction*. Athens: University of Georgia Press, 1984.

Raguer, Hilari, *Gaudeamus Igitur*. Barcelona: Publicacions de l'Abadia de Montserrat, 1999.

Raguer, Hilari, *La pólvora y el incienso: La Iglesia y la Guerra Civil Española (1936–1939)*. Barcelona: Península, 2001.

Raguer, Hilari, *Ser Independentista no és cap Pecat: L'Esglèsia i el Nacionalisme Català*. Barcelona: Editorial Claret, 2012.

Rai, Shirin M., *Ceremony and Ritual in Parliament*. London: Routledge, 2011.

Rosiny, Stephan, *The Arab Spring: Triggers, Dynamics and Prospects*. GIGA Focus, German Institute of Global and Area Studies, no. 1, 2012 (*http://www.giga-hamburg.de/dl/download.php?d=/content/publika tionen/pdf/gf_international_1201.pdf*, accessed 1 March 2013).

Sartre, Jean-Paul, *Being and Nothingness: An Essay on Phenomenological Ontology*. London: Routledge Classics, 2009 [1943].

Sartre, Jean-Paul, *Existentialism*. New York: Philosophical Library, 1974.

Savage, Mike, Gaynor Bagnall and Brian Longhurst, *Globalization and Belonging*. London: Sage, 2005.

Schaar, John H., *Loyalty in America*. Berkeley and Los Angeles: University of California Press, 1957.

Scheff, Thomas, *Emotions, the Social Bond, and Human Reality*. Cambridge: Cambridge University Press, 1997.

Scheffer, Paul, *Immigrant Nations*. Cambridge: Polity Press, 2011.

Schlesinger, Arthur M., Jr, *The Politics of Freedom*. Melbourne: William Heinemann Ltd, 1950.

Schlesinger, Arthur M., Jr, 'What is loyalty? A difficult question', in John C. Wahlke (ed.), *Loyalty in a Democratic State*. Boston: D.C. Heath and Company, 1952.

Schwartz, Barry, *The Paradox of Choice – Why More Is Less*. New York: Harper Perennial, 2004.

Simmel, Georg, *The Sociology of Georg Simmel*. Glencoe, IL: Free Press, 1950.

Skinner, Quentin, Isaiah Berlin Lecture 'A third concept of liberty', *Proceedings of the British Academy* 117 (2002): 237–68.

Smith, Adam, *The Theory of Moral Sentiments*. London: Penguin Classics, 2010 [1759].

Smith, Anthony D., *The Ethnic Origins of Nations*. Oxford: Basil Blackwell, 1986.

Smith, Anthony D., 'History and national destiny: responses and clarifications', in Montserrat Guibernau and John Hutchinson (eds), *History and National Destiny: Ethnosymbolism and Its Critics*. Oxford: Blackwell, 2004.

Smith, Anthony D., *Myths and Memories of the Nation*. Oxford: Oxford University Press, 1999.

Spencer, Sarah (ed.), *The Politics of Migration: Global Capital, Migrant Labour and the Nation-State*. Aldershot: Ashgate, 2006.

Sperber, Dan, *Rethinking Symbolism*. Cambridge: Cambridge University Press, 1988 [1975].

Squires, Judith, *The New Politics of Gender Equality*. London: Palgrave Macmillan, 2007.

Sullivan, Harry Stack, *The Interpersonal Theory of Psychiatry*. London: Routledge, 2001 [1955].

Taguieff, Pierre-André, *The Force of Prejudice: On Racism and Its Doubles*. Minneapolis: University of Minnesota Press.

Taguieff, Pierre-André, *Sur la Nouvelle droite: Jalons d'une analyse critique*. Paris: Descartes & Cie, 1994.

Tallett, Frank and Nicholas Atkin (eds), *Religion, Society, and Politics in France since 1789*. London: The Hambledon Press. 1991.

Taylor, Charles, 'The politics of recognition', in Amy Gutmann (ed.), *Multiculturalism*. Princeton: Princeton University Press.

Thoits, Peggy A., 'Multiple identities and psychological well-being: a reformulation and test of the social isolation hypothesis', *American Sociological Review* 51 (1983): 259–72.

Thomas, Paul, *Responding to the Threat of Violent Extremism: Failing to Prevent*. London: Bloomsbury Academic, 2012.

Tilly, Charles, *Popular Contention in Great Britain, 1758–1834.* Cambridge, MA: Harvard University Press, 1995.

Tilly, Charles, *Social Movements 1768–2004.* Boulder, CO: Paradigm Publishers, 2004.

Tocqueville, Alexis de, *Democracy in America*, Vol. 2. London: Fontana Press, 1994 [1840].

Turner, Jonathan H. and Jan E. Stets, *The Sociology of Emotions.* Cambridge: Cambridge University Press, 2005.

Van der Brug, Wouter and Meindert Fennema, 'Protest or mainstream? How the European anti-immigrant parties developed into two separate groups by 1999', *European Journal of Political Research* 42 (2003): 55–76.

Van der Brug, Wouter, Meindert Fennema and Jean Tillie, 'Anti-immigrant parties in Europe: ideological or protest vote?', *European Journal of Political Research* 37 (2000): 77–102.

van Gennep, Arnold, *The Rites of Passage.* Chicago: University of Chicago Press, 1966 [1960].

von Bertalanffy, Ludwig, *A Systems View of Man: Collected Essays.* Boulder, CO: Westview Press, 1981.

Wahlke, John C. (ed.), *Loyalty in a Democratic State.* Boston: D.C. Heath and Company, 1952.

Weber, Max, *Economy and Society.* Berkeley and Los Angeles: University of California Press, 1978 [1922].

Weber, Max, *From Max Weber: Essays in Sociology.* London: Routledge, 1948.

Whine, Michael, 'Trans-European trends in right-wing extremism', in Andrea Mammone, Emmanuel Godin and Brian Jenkins (eds), *Mapping the Extreme Right in Contemporary Europe.* London: Routledge, 2012.

Wieviorka, Michel, *Pour la prochaine gauche.* Paris: Éditions Robert Laffont, 2011.

Wieviorka, Michel, *Le racisme, une introduction.* Paris: La Découverte, 1998.

Wodak, Ruth, '"Us" and "them": inclusion and exclusion – discrimination via discourse', in Gerard Delanty, Ruth Wodak and Paul Jones (eds), *Identity, Belonging and Migration.* Liverpool: Liverpool University Press, 2008.

Yack, Bernard, *Nationalism and the Moral Psychology of Community.* Chicago: University of Chicago Press, 2012.

Young, Kimberley S., *Caught in the Net: How to Recognize the Signs of Internet Addiction – and a Winning Strategy for Recovery.* New York: John Wiley & Sons, Inc., 1998.

Young, Kimberley S., 'Internet addiction: the emergence of a clinical disorder', *CyberPsychology and Behaviour* 1, 3 (1998): 237–44.

Yuval-Davis, Nira, *The Politics of Belonging: Intersectional Contestations*. London: Sage, 2011.

Yuval-Davis, Nira, 'Power, intersectionality and the politics of belonging'. FREIA-Feminist Research Center in Aalborg. Aalborg University, Denmark. FREIA working paper series, working paper no. 75, 2011.

Zaslove, Andrej, 'Closing the door? The ideology and impact of radical right populism on immigration policy in Austria and Italy', *Journal of Political Ideologies* 9, 1 (2004): 99–118.

Zweig, Stefan, *Montaigne*. Paris: Quadrige/PUF, 1982.

Index